Praise for *Girl in a Band*

"Every subject is handled with careful introspection, detail and real feeling. . . . [*Girl in a Band*] is about survival, both as a person and as an artist. . . . [Kim Gordon] stays cool because she is cool, even in those rare moments when she's not."

—Questlove, *New York Times Book Review*

"Gordon has long been the embodiment of a certain kind of cool—and her book offers an alluring window into a time of life on the cutting edge."

—*Washington Post*

"Gordon approaches her memoirs as she does her music, by defying expectation."

—*USA Today*

"Gordon's emotional honesty about what it's like to rebound from heart-break resonates with anyone who's had to revise their life's script."

—*San Francisco Chronicle*

"A poignant look back and an engaging chronicle of the choppy waters an underground act rides as it bubbles up into the mainstream."

—*Seattle Times*

"Warmly wise and observant. . . . Shapely, thought-provoking, [and] generous."

—*Elle*

"Heartbreaking, raw, articulate, and inspiring."

—*Bust Magazine*

"Full of raw emotion and insight."

—Sofia Coppola

"The best thing one of your heroes can do is make you feel heroic yourself. Kim Gordon has done just that in her memoir; it is full of beauty and power, inspiration, kindness, boldness and hope."

—Carrie Brownstein

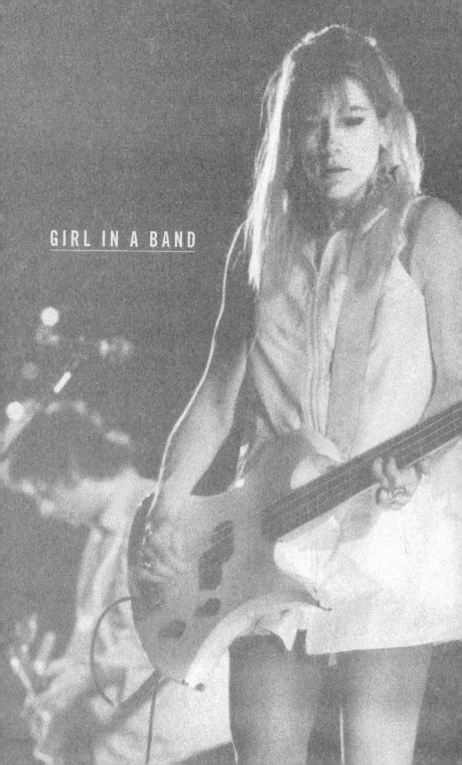

GIRL IN A BAND

GIRL IN A BAND

KIM GORDON

DEY ST.

AN IMPRINT OF
WILLIAM MORROW *PUBLISHERS*

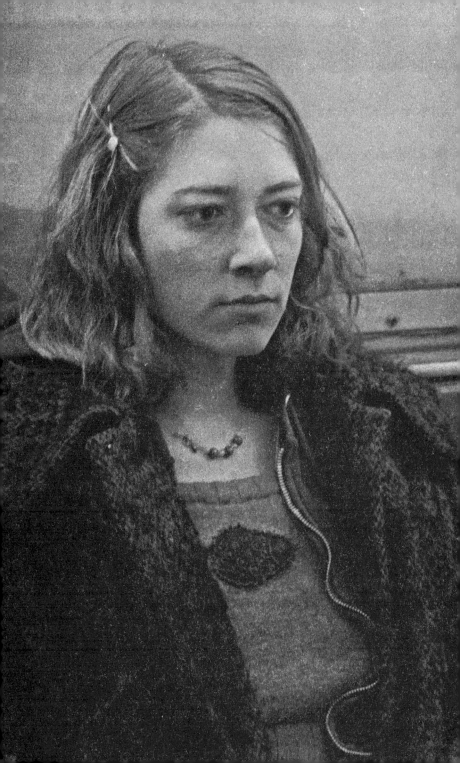

Page 277 serves as a continuation of the copyright page.

HarperCollins books may be purchased for educational, business, or sales pro-
motional use. For information please e-mail the Special Markets Department at
SPsales@harpercollins.com.

A hardcover edition of this book was published in 2015 by Dey Street Books, an
imprint of William Morrow Publishers.

FIRST DEY STREET BOOKS PAPERBACK EDITION PUBLISHED 2015.

Designed by Paula Russell Szafranski

Library of Congress Cataloging-in-Publication Data has been applied for.

ISBN 978-0-06-229590-3

15 16 17 18 19   OV/RRD   10 9 8 7 6 5 4 3 2 1

For Coco, my North Star

Acknowledgments

I'd like to thank:

My editor, Carrie Thornton, for all her patient indulgence and for initiating the project.

Also, Sean Newcott, Carrie's assistant editor.

The rest of the team at HarperCollins and Dey Street Books, including Lynn Grady, Sharyn Rosenblum, Michael Barrs, Kendra Newton, Rachel Meyers, Lorie Pagnozzi, and Paula Szafranski.

The team at Faber in the UK: Lee Brackstone, Dan Papps, Gemma Lovett, and Dave Watkins.

Special thanks to Peter Smith, who was immensely helpful in pulling this book together. I would also like to thank Henry Dunow for getting the process started.

To all the photographers who allowed me to use their images.

All my friends who helped me through the last few years: Elaine Kahn, Luisa Reichenheim, Lili Dwight, Byron Coley, Bill Nace, Julie Cafritz, Marjorie Zweizig, Daisy and Rob von Furth, Rebekah Brooks, Xian Hawkins, Don Fleming, Margaret Bodde, Lizzi Bougatsos, Jutta

Koether, John Kelsey, Isabelle Graw, Tony Oursler, Jon Wurster, Jessica Hutchins, Stephen Malkmus, Chloë Sevigny, Mel Wansbrough, Sofia Coppola, Andrew Kesin, Mathew Higgs, Elissa Schappell, Sheila McCullough, Michele Fleischli, Cameron Jamie, Dave Markey, Emma Reeves, Tamra Davis, Mike D, Adam H, Kathleen, Chris Habib, Mark Ibold, Vicki Farrell, Andrew Kesin, Richard Kern, Carlos Van Hijfte, Tom Caw, Spike Jonze, Keith Nealy, Aimee Mann, Amy P., Carrie Brownstein, Ben Estes, Juan Amaya, Jim O Rourke, J Mascis, Shana Weiss, Hilton Als, Bill Mooney, Barbara Herrington, Patrick Amory, and Jamie Brisick.

Special thanks to Steve Shelley, Lee Ranaldo, and Thurston Moore, without whom there would be no story.

Also, a grateful nod to all the Sonic Youth crew from over the years, Aaron Mullan, Eric Baecht, Nick Close, Suzanne Sasic, Jim Vincent, Jeremy Lemos, Luc Suer, Dan Mapp, Bob Lawton, Peter Van Der Velde, Maurice Menares and all the people at SAM management, Gaby Skolnek, Micheal Meisel, John Cutcliffe, Chris Kelly, John Silva, and Richard Grabel.

To Chris Stone, Nils Bernstein, Patrick Amory, Gerard Cosloy, Chris Lombardi, and the folks at Matador records for putting out the Body/Head double LP.

To Eric Dimenstein for booking us.

To my family: Keller, Kathryn, Eleanor, and Louise Erdman, and Coco Gordon Moore.

To the memory of my exceptional parents: my mother, Althea, and my father, Wayne. Their singular spirit, humor, and intelligence somehow guided me.

And to all the fans, of course, and their support that I never truly believed was there, until I needed it.

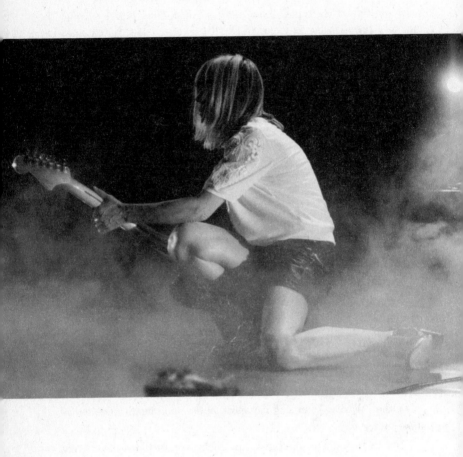

The End

WHEN WE CAME OUT onstage for our last show, the night was all about the boys. Outwardly, everyone looked more or less the same as they had for the last thirty years. Inside was a different story.

Thurston double-slapped our bass guitarist Mark Ibold on the shoulder and loped across the stage, followed by Lee Ranaldo, our guitarist, and then Steve Shelley, our drummer. I found that gesture so phony, so childish, such a fantasy. Thurston has many acquaintances, but with the few male friends he had he never spoke of anything personal, and he's never been the shoulder-slapping type. It was a gesture that called out, *I'm back. I'm free. I'm solo.*

I was the last one to come on, making sure to mark off some distance between Thurston and me. I was exhausted and watchful. Steve took his place behind his drum set like a dad behind a desk. The rest of us armed ourselves with our instruments like a battalion, an army that just wanted the bombardment to end.

It was pouring, slanting sheets of rain. South American rain is like rain anywhere else, and it makes you feel the same too.

They say when a marriage ends that little things you never noticed before practically make your brain split open. All week that had been true for me whenever Thurston was around. Maybe he felt the same, or maybe his head was somewhere else. I didn't really want to know, to be honest. Offstage he was constantly texting and pacing around the rest of us like a manic, guilty kid.

After thirty years, tonight was Sonic Youth's final concert. The SWU Music and Arts Festival was taking place in Itu, just outside São Paulo, Brazil, five thousand miles from our home in New England. It was a three-day-long event, broadcast on Latin American television and streamed online, too, with big corporate sponsors like Coca-Cola and Heineken. The headliners were Faith No More, Kanye West, the Black Eyed Peas, Peter Gabriel, Stone Temple Pilots, Snoop Dogg, Soundgarden, people like that. We were probably the smallest act on the bill. It was a strange place for things to come to an end.

Over the years we had played lots of rock festivals. The band saw them as a necessary evil, although the do-or-die aspect of having no sound check before you played made them sort of thrilling, too. Festivals mean backstage trailers and tents, gear and power cords everywhere, smelly porta-potties, and sometimes running into musicians whom you like personally or professionally but never get to see or meet or talk to. Equipment can break, delays happen, the weather is unpredictable. There are times you can't hear a thing in the monitors but you just go for it and try to get the music across to a sea of people.

Festivals also mean a shorter set. Tonight we would close things out with seventy minutes of adrenaline, just as we'd done the past few days at festivals in Peru, Uruguay, Buenos Aires, and Chile.

What was different from past tours and festivals was that Thurston and I weren't speaking to each other. We had exchanged maybe fifteen words all week. After twenty-seven years of marriage, things had fallen apart between us. In August I'd had to ask him to move out of our house in Massachusetts, and he had. He was renting an apartment a mile away and commuting back and forth to New York.

The couple everyone believed was golden and normal and eternally intact, who gave younger musicians hope they could outlast a crazy rock-and-roll world, was now just another cliché of middle-aged relationship failure—a male midlife crisis, another woman, a double life.

Thurston mimed a mock-startled reaction as a tech passed him his guitar. At fifty-three, he was still the shaggy, skinny kid from Connecticut I first met at a downtown New York club when he was twenty-two and I was twenty-seven. He told me later he liked my flip-up sunglass shades. In his jeans, old-school Pumas, and un-tucked-in white button-down oxford, he looked like a boy frozen in some diorama, a seventeen-year-old who didn't want to be seen in the company of his mother, or any woman for that matter. He had the Mick Jagger lips, and the lanky arms and legs he didn't seem to know what to do with, and the wariness you see in tall men who don't want to overpower other people with their height. His long brown hair camouflaged his face, and he seemed to like it that way.

That week, it was as if he'd wound back time, erased our nearly thirty years together. "Our life" had turned back into "my life" for him. He was an adolescent lost in fantasy again, and the rock star showboating he was doing onstage got under my skin.

Sonic Youth had always been a democracy, but we all had our roles, too. I took my place in the center of the stage. It didn't start out that way and I'm not sure when it changed. It was a choreography that dated back twenty years, to when Sonic Youth first signed with Geffen Records.

It was then that we learned that for high-end music labels, the music matters, but a lot comes down to how the girl looks. The girl anchors the stage, sucks in the male gaze, and, depending on who she is, throws her own gaze back out into the audience.

Since our music can be weird and dissonant, having me center stage also makes it that much easier to sell the band. *Look, it's a girl, she's wearing a dress, and she's with those guys, so things must be okay.* But that's not how we had ever operated as an indie band, so I was always conscious not to be too much out front.

I could barely hold it together during the first song, "Brave Men Run." At one point my voice fell like it was scraping against its own bottom, and then the bottom fell out. It was an old, very early song from our album *Bad Moon Rising*. I wrote the lyrics on Eldridge Street in New York City in a tenement railroad apartment where Thurston and I were living at the time. The song always makes me think of the pioneer women in my mother's family slogging their way out to California through Panama, and my grandmother being a single parent during the Depression with no real income. Lyrically, the song reminded me of how I first brought together my art influences into my music. I took the title from an Ed Ruscha painting that shows a clipper ship angling through waves and whitecaps.

But that was three decades ago. Tonight Thurston and I didn't look at each other once, and when the song was done, I turned my shoulders to the audience so no one in the audience or the band could see my face, though it had little effect. Everything I did and said was broadcast from one of the two forty-foot-high onstage video screens.

For whatever reasons—sympathy, or sadness, or the headlines and articles about Thurston's and my breakup that followed us wherever we went that week in Spanish, Portuguese, and English—we had the passionate support of South American audiences. Tonight's crowd stretched out in front of us and blurred with the dark clouds around the stadium—thousands of rain-soaked kids, wet hair, naked backs, tank tops, raised hands holding cell phones and girls on dark boys' shoulders.

The bad weather had followed us through South America, from Lima to Uruguay to Chile and now to São Paulo—a corny movie-mirror of the strangeness between Thurston and me. The festival stages were like musical versions of awkward domestic tableaux—a living room, or a kitchen, or a dining room, where the husband and the wife pass each other in the morning and make themselves separate cups of coffee with neither one acknowledging the other, or any kind of shared history, in the room.

After tonight, Sonic Youth was done. Our life as a couple, and as a family, was already done. We still had our apartment on Lafayette Street in New York—though not for much longer—and I would keep on living with our daughter, Coco, in our house in western Massachusetts that we'd bought in 1999 from a local school.

"Hello!" Thurston called out genially to the crowd just before the band launched into "Death Valley '69." Two nights earlier in Uruguay, Thurston and I had to duet together on another early song, "Cotton Crown." Its lyrics were about love, and mystery, and chemistry, and dreaming, and staying together. It was basically an ode to New York City. In Uruguay I was too upset to sing it, and Thurston had to finish by himself.

But I would make it through "Death Valley." Lee, Thurston, and I, and then just the two of us, stood there. My about-to-be-ex husband and I faced that mass of bobbing wet Brazilians, our voices together spell-checking the old words, and for me it was a staccato soundtrack of surreal raw energy and anger and pain: *Hit it. Hit it. Hit it.* I don't think I had ever felt so alone in my whole life.

The press release issued a month earlier from our record label, Matador, didn't say much:

> Musicians Kim Gordon and Thurston Moore, married in 1984, are announcing they have separated. Sonic Youth, with both Kim and Thurston involved, will proceed with its South American tour dates in November. Plans beyond that tour are uncertain. The couple has requested respect for their personal privacy and does not wish to issue further comment.

"Brave Men Run," "Death Valley '69," "Sacred Trickster," "Calming the Snake," "Mote," "Cross the Breeze," "Schizophrenia," "Drunken Butterfly," "Starfield Road," "Flower," "Sugar Kane," and closing out with "Teen Age Riot." The São Paulo set list borrowed from when we first started out, lyrics Thurston and I had written apart or together, songs that took Sonic Youth through the eighties and the nineties, and our most recent albums.

The set list may have seemed like a best-of compilation but it was carefully thought through. During rehearsal and all that week, I remember Thurston making a point of telling the band he didn't want to perform this or that Sonic Youth song. It eventually hit me that certain songs he wanted to leave out were about *her*.

We could have canceled the tour, but we'd signed a contract. Performing live is how bands make a living, and we all had families and bills to pay, and in my and Thurston's case, college tuition for Coco to think about. At the same time, I wasn't sure how good it looked to be playing these gigs. I didn't want people to assume that whatever stuff had gone down between Thurston and me, I was playing a supportive, stand-by-your-man role. I wasn't. And outside of our immediate circle no one really knew what had happened.

Before flying to South America, Sonic Youth rehearsed for a week at a studio in New York. Somehow I made it through, with the help of a Xanax, the first time I'd ever taken one during the day. Instead of staying at our apartment, which now felt tainted to me, the others agreed to put me up in a hotel.

True to band form, everyone pretended things were the same. I knew the others were too nervous about how things were between Thurston and me to interact with me much, considering they all knew the circumstances of our breakup, and even knew the woman in question. I didn't want anyone to feel uncomfortable, and after all, I'd agreed to go along with the tour. I knew everyone had his own private judgments and sympathies, but I was surprised at how jovial everyone was acting. Maybe everyone was just too overwhelmed by the unreality. The same went in South America.

Someone later showed me a *Salon* article called "How Could Kim Gordon and Thurston Moore Divorce?" The writer, Elissa Schappell, wrote that we had shown an entire generation how to grow up. She said she cried when she first heard the news.

> Look at them, I thought: They were in love and married and making art. They were cool and hardcore, with a profound seriousness about their art, and they hadn't sold out or gotten soft. In an age of irony, where I'd feign indifference and cover up my insecurity with mockery, they weren't too cool to care . . . What's scarier than a couple deciding—after 30 years of being in a band they created, 27 years of marriage, 17 years spent raising a child—that now they're done with it? As they succeeded, we succeeded.

She closed with the question "Why should they be different than the rest of us?"

Good question, and we weren't, and what had happened was probably the most conventional story ever.

We flew separately to South America. I flew in with the band, and Thurston traveled with Aaron, our front-of-house sound guy.

On tour, after the airplane touches down, vans speed you to your hotel. People scatter, sleep, read, eat, exercise, go for a walk, watch TV, e-mail, text. That week in South America, though, everyone in the band, including the crew and the tech guys, came together for meals. A lot of the crew had worked with us for years and were like family members. Thurston sat at one end of the table, with me at the other end. It was like dining out with the folks, except Mom and Dad were ignoring each other. Everyone ordered up big platters of food and drink, and most of our conversations centered on what we were eating and drinking as a way to avoid talking about what was really going on. What was going on was the silent, unwelcome guest in the room.

Our first show was in Buenos Aires. Sonic Youth hadn't played Argentina in a while, and the audiences were expressive and enthusiastic, and seemed to know every lyric to every song. For the first couple of days, I had my wall up around Thurston, but as the tour went on, I softened a little. With all the history between us, it made me incredibly anxious to hold so much anger toward him. A couple of times he and I found ourselves taking photos outside the hotel, and I made a conscious decision to be friendly, and Thurston did too.

That week, other musicians—people I didn't know, like Chris Cornell, the lead singer of Soundgarden—came up to me to say how sorry they were to hear about our breakup, or to say how much the band meant to them. Bill and Barbara, the married couple who did our merch and T-shirts, and grew their business over the years with us, met us in Buenos Aires as a show of moral support, assuming, as everyone did, that it was the last Sonic Youth show.

What got me through was being onstage, the visceral release of performing. Extreme noise and dissonance can be an incredibly cleansing thing. Usually when we play live, I worry whether or not my amplifier is too loud or distracting, or if the other members of the band are in a bad mood for some reason. But that week I couldn't have cared less how loud I was or whether I accidentally upstaged Thurston. I did what I wanted, and it was freeing and painful. Painful because the end of my marriage was a private thing, and watching Thurston show off his new independence in front of audiences was like someone rubbing grit in a gash, and my friendliness faded away as one city turned into the next, replaced by anger.

It reached a point in São Paulo where I almost said something onstage. But I didn't. Courtney Love happened to be touring South America at the same time. A few nights earlier, she had begun railing against a fan in the audience who was holding up a photo of Kurt Cobain. "I have to live with his shit and his ghost and his kid every day and throwing that up is stupid and rude," she screamed. She left the stage, saying she'd return only if the audience agreed to chant, "Foo Fighters are gay." The clip ended up on YouTube. It was typical Courtney shtick, but I would never want to be seen as the car crash she is. I didn't want our last concert to be distasteful when Sonic Youth meant so much to so many people; I didn't want to use the stage for any kind of personal statement, and what good would it have done anyway?

Someone told me the entire São Paulo concert is online, but I've never seen it and I don't want to.

Throughout that last show, I remember wondering what the audience was picking up on or thinking about this raw, weird pornography of strain and distance. What they saw and what I saw were probably two different things.

During "Sugar Kane," the next-to-last song, an oceanic-blue globe appeared on the screen behind the band. It spun extremely slowly, as if to convey the world's indifference to its own turning and rolling. It all just goes on, the globe said, as ice melts, and streetlights switch colors when no cars are around, and grass pushes through trestles and side-walk cracks, and things are born and then things go away.

When the song ended, Thurston thanked the audience. "I can't wait to see you again," he said.

The band closed with "Teen Age Riot" from our album *Daydream Nation*. I sang, or half sang, the first lines: "*Spirit desire. Face me. Spirit desire. We will fall. Miss me. Don't dismiss me.*"

Marriage is a long conversation, someone once said, and maybe so is a rock band's life. A few minutes later, both were done.

Backstage, as usual, no one made a fuss out of this being our last show, or really about much of anything. All of us—Lee, Steve, Mark, our music techs—lived in different cities and parts of the country any-way. I was too sad and worried I would burst into tears to say good-bye to anyone, though I wanted to. Then everyone went his or her own way, and I flew back home, too.

Thurston had already announced a bunch of solo shows that would start in January. He would fly to Europe and then circle back to the East Coast. Lee Ranaldo was planning on releasing his own solo album. Steve Shelley was playing nonstop with the Chicago-based band Disappears. I would be playing a few gigs with a friend and fellow musician named Bill Nace, and working on artwork for an upcoming show in Berlin, but mostly I'd be home with Coco, helping her through her senior year of high school and the college application process. In the spring, Thurston and I had put our New York apartment on Lafayette Street on the market, and it finally sold six months later. Apart from that, just as the press release said, Sonic Youth had no future plans.

I came to New York in 1980, and over the next thirty years, the city changed as quickly and as slowly as my life did. When did all the Chock Full O' Nuts go, or the Blarney Stone bars with the corned beef and cabbage buffet-table lunch deals? Sonic Youth came together, of course, but before and even after that I worked one part-time job after another—waitressing, house-painting, working at an art gallery, stapling and Xeroxing at a copy shop. I'd switch sublets every couple of months. I lived on grits, egg noodles, onions, potatoes, pizza, and hot dogs. I'd walk home fifty blocks from a bookstore job because I had no money for subway tokens. I'm not sure how I did it. But part of being poor and struggling in New York is making ends meet during the day and doing what you want to do the rest of the time.

All the hours and years since then inside vans, on buses, in airplanes and airports, in recording studios and lousy dressing rooms and motels and hotels were possible only because of the music that sustained that life. Music that could only have come out of New York's bohemian downtown art scene and the people in it—Andy Warhol, the Velvet Underground, Allen Ginsberg, John Cage, Glenn Branca, Patti Smith, Television, Richard Hell, Blondie, the Ramones, Lydia Lunch, Philip Glass, Steve Reich, and the free-jazz loft scene. I remember the thrilling power of loud guitars and finding kindred souls and the man I married, who I believed was my soul mate.

The other night, I walked past our old apartment at 84 Eldridge Street on my way to a Korean karaoke bar where a cross section of people from Chinatown and Koreatown hang out, alongside the usual art-world hipsters. The whole time I was thinking about Dan Graham, the artist who turned me on to a lot of what was happening in the music scene in the late seventies and early eighties, who lived in the apartment above ours and witnessed the early versions of what would someday turn into Sonic Youth.

I joined a friend inside the karaoke bar. There was no stage. People just stood in the middle of the room surrounded by video screens and sang. One of the songs that came on was "Addicted to Love," the old Robert Palmer song I covered in a do-it-yourself recording booth in 1989, which ended up on the Sonic Youth LP *The Whitey Album*. It would have been fun to sing it karaoke-style, but I couldn't decide if I was a courageous person in real life or whether I could only sing onstage. In that way I haven't changed much in thirty years at all.

Now that I no longer live in New York, I don't know if I could ever move back. All that young-girl idealism is someone else's now. That city I know doesn't exist anymore, and it's more alive in my head than it is when I'm there.

After thirty years of playing in a band, it sounds sort of stupid to say, "I'm not a musician." But for most of my life I've never seen myself as one and I never formally trained as one. I sometimes think of myself as a lowercase rock star. Yes, I'm sensitive to sound, I think I have a good ear, and I love the visceral movement and thrill of being onstage. And even as a visual and conceptual artist, there's always been a performance aspect to whatever I do.

For me performing has a lot to do with being fearless. I wrote an article for *Artforum* in the mideighties that had a line in it that the rock critic Greil Marcus quoted a lot: "People pay money to see others believe in themselves." Meaning, the higher the chance you can fall down in public, the more value the culture places on what you do. Unlike, say, a writer or a painter, when you're onstage you can't hide from other people, or from yourself either.

I've spent a lot of time in Berlin, and the Germans have all these great words with multiple meanings inside them. A few visits ago, I came across one of those words, *Maskenfreiheit*. It means "the freedom conferred by masks."

It's always been hard for me to make space for myself emotionally around other people. It's some old childhood thing, a sense of never feeling protected by my parents or from my older brother, Keller, who used to tease me relentlessly when we were growing up—a sense that no one out there was really listening. Maybe for a performer that's what a stage becomes: a space you can fill up with what can't be expressed or gotten anywhere else. Onstage, people have told me, I'm opaque or mysterious or enigmatic or even cold. But more than any of those things, I'm extremely shy and sensitive, as if I can feel all the emotions swirling around a room. And believe me when I say that once you push past my persona, there aren't any defenses there at all.

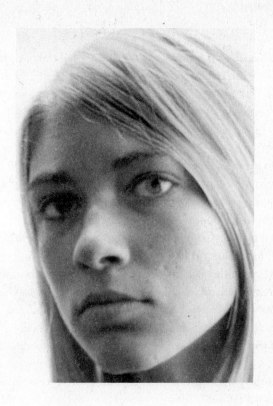

1

IT'S FUNNY WHAT you remember, and why, or whether it even happened in the first place. My first take on Rochester, New York: gray skies, dark, colored leaves, empty rooms, no parents around, no one watching or minding the store. Is it Upstate New York I'm thinking back on, or some scene from an old movie?

Perhaps it is a film my older brother, Keller, and I saw on TV—*The Beast with Five Fingers*. I was around three or four. Peter Lorre plays a man who's been left out of the will of his employer, a famous pianist who's just died. He takes his revenge by cutting off the pianist's hand, and for the rest of the film, the hand won't stop tormenting him. It roams and sneaks around the big house. It plays dark notes and chords on the piano, and hides out in a clothes closet. As the film goes on Peter Lorre gets crazier and sweatier until at the end the hand reaches out and strangles him.

"The hand is under your bed," Keller told me afterward. "It's going to come out in the middle of the night while you're sleeping and it's going to *get* you."

He was my older brother so why wouldn't I believe him? For the next few months, I lived on top of my mattress, balancing there in my bare feet to get dressed in the morning. I fell asleep at night surrounded by an army of stuffed animals, the smallest ones closest to me, a big dog with a red tongue guarding the door, not that any of them could have defended me against the hand.

Keller: one of the most singular people I've ever known, the person who more than anyone else in the world shaped who I was, and who I turned out to be. He was, and still is, brilliant, manipulative, sadistic, arrogant, almost unbearably articulate. He's also mentally ill, a paranoid schizophrenic. And maybe because he was so incessantly verbal from the start, I turned into his opposite, his shadow—shy, sensitive, closed to the point where to overcome my own hypersensitivity, I had no choice but to turn fearless.

An old black-and-white photo of a little house is all I have to prove Rochester was my birthplace. Black-and-white matches that city, with its rivers, aqueducts, manufacturing plants, and endless winters. And when my family headed out west, like any birth canal Rochester was forgotten.

I was five years old when my father was offered a professorship in the UCLA sociology department, and we—my parents, Keller, and I—drove out to Los Angeles in our old station wagon. Once we passed over into the Western states, I remember how excited my mother was to order hash browns at a roadside diner. To her hash browns were a Western thing, a symbol, full of a meaning she couldn't express.

When we pulled into Los Angeles, we stayed at some dive called the Seagull Motel, one of probably a thousand look-alike places with the same name along the California coast. This Seagull Motel was in the shadow of a Mormon temple, a huge monolithic structure on top of a hill, surrounded by acres of trimmed, saturated green grass no one was allowed to walk on. Everywhere were sprinkler systems, little metallic gadgets here and there twisting and chugging away at all hours. Nothing was indigenous—not the grass, not the sprinkler water, not any of the people I met. Until I saw the movie *Chinatown*, I didn't realize L.A. was, underneath everything, a desert, an expanse of endless burlap. That was my first glimpse of L.A. landscaping.

I also had no idea that going to California meant a return to my mom's roots.

In my family, history showed up in casual remarks. I was in my senior year of high school when my aunt told me that my mother's family, the Swalls, was one of California's original families. Pioneers. Settlers. The story went that along with some Japanese business partners, my great-great-grandparents ran a chili pepper farm in Garden Grove, in Orange County. The Swalls even had a ranch in West Hollywood, at Doheny Drive and Santa Monica Boulevard, on land that's today all car washes and strip malls and bad stucco. At some point the railroad laid down tracks, slicing the street into Big and Little Santa Monica Boulevards. The ranches are all gone today, of course, but Swall Drive is still there, swishing north and south, a fossil of ancestral DNA.

I've always felt there's something genetically instilled and inbred in Californians—that California is a place of death, a place people are drawn to because they don't realize deep down they're actually afraid of what they want. It's new, and they're escaping their histories while at the same time moving headlong toward their own extinctions. Desire and death are all mixed up with the thrill and the risk of the unknown. It's a variation of what Freud called the "death instinct." In that respect the Swalls were probably no different from any other early California family, staking out a new place, lured there by the gold rush and hitting an ocean wall.

On the Swall side also was my mother's father, Keller Eno Coplan, a bank clerk. The story goes that at one point he forged a check belonging to his own in-laws and went to jail. My dad always laughed when he talked about my grandfather, saying things like "He wasn't dumb, he just had no sense." Odd, then, and not exactly a blessing, that my parents would name their only son after him. Family tradition, I guess.

With her husband in jail, my grandmother moved with her five kids, including my mother, who was young at the time, up to Northern California, to be closer to the clan in Modesto. During the Depression my grandmother picked up and moved again, to Colorado this time, where her husband's family had roots. When her husband wasn't in jail, he was out roaming the country looking for work. With no money and five kids to feed, she must have put up with a lot.

The only reason I know this is because my aunt figured out that one of his short-term jobs was selling pencils. Turns out only ex-cons got those gigs.

At some point my grandmother and her children ended up making a permanent home in Kansas. This is where my parents met in their early twenties, in a little city called Emporia, where both of them were in college.

My father, Wayne, was a native Kansan, from a big farming family, with four brothers and one sister. He was fragile as a boy, with a middle ear disorder that kept him from enlisting in the military or getting drafted. He was the first child in his family to attend college, his dream being to teach someday at the university level. To help pay his tuition, he taught elementary school in a one-room Emporia schoolhouse, first grade to sixth grade, everything from shapes and colors to spelling, history, and algebra.

My parents were married during college, and after graduating from Washington University in Saint Louis, where Keller was born, it was on to Upstate New York and Rochester, where my dad began writing his Ph.D. Three years later, I came along. The story of how my parents met came out only during cocktail hours, the details always sketchy. My dad was scatterbrained, my mother liked to say, adding that his habit of making popcorn in her house without putting the lid on when they were courting almost made her rethink the idea of marrying him. She always said it with a laugh, though the point she was trying to make, maybe, was that my dad wasn't as down-to-earth and responsible as he appeared.

The names in our family—Keller, Eno, Coplan, Estella, Lola— always make me wonder whether there's some Mediterranean in the mix. There is also the de Forrest side from my mom's mother, who was French and German, but there's an Italian strain, too, flashing eyes and Groucho brows mixed in with all the Kansan flatness. Kansas is where my mother's ninety-two-year-old sister—the source of everything I know about my family history—still lives in a farmhouse at the end of a long dirt road. She's a woman who during her life I never heard utter even one self-pitying word. Her stories are pretty much the only ones I know. My parents told me next to nothing.

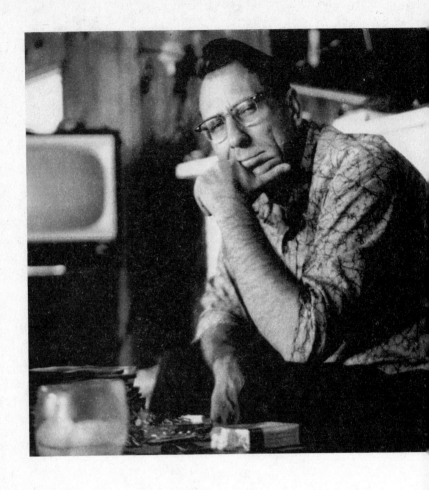

2

ONCE WHEN SONIC YOUTH was on tour in Lawrence, Kansas, opening for R.E.M., Thurston and I paid a visit to William Burroughs. Michael Stipe came along with us. Burroughs lived in a little house with a garage, and the coffee table in his living room was crisscrossed with fantasy knives and daggers—elegant, bejeweled weapons of destruction. That day, all I could think of was how much Burroughs reminded me of my dad. They shared the same folksiness, the same dry sense of humor. They even looked a little alike. Coco, our daughter, was a baby, and at one point when she started crying, Burroughs said, in that Burroughs voice, "*Oohhh*—she *likes* me." My guess is he wasn't somebody who spent much time around kids.

My dad's academic specialty was sociology in education. In Rochester, he'd done his Ph.D. on the social system in American high schools. He was the first person ever to put a name to various school-age groups and archetypes—preps, jocks, geeks, freaks, theater types, and so on—and then UCLA had hired him to create an academic curriculum based on his research.

One of the conditions for my dad taking the UCLA job was that Keller and I were able to attend the UCLA Lab School. That school was an amazing place. The campus was designed by the modernist architect Richard Neutra, with a large, beautiful gully running through it. One side was grass and the other concrete—for hopscotching or Hula-Hooping or whatever. The gully flowed up into an untamed area where a covered wagon and an adobe house sat beneath some trees. As students, we fringed shawls, pounded tortillas, and skinned cowhides out among those trees. Our teacher drove us down to Dana Point, in Orange County, where we tossed our cowhides down on the beach for imaginary incoming boats, copying what the early traders must have done. There were no grades at that school—it was all very learn-by-doing.

My dad was tall and gentle, with a big expressive face and black glasses. He was a gestural guy, physical, emphatic with his arms and his hands, but incredibly warm, too, though the few times I remember his getting angry at Keller or me were frightening. The angry words seemed to start in the soles of his feet and travel up through his entire body. Like a lot of people who live in their heads, he could be absentminded; there was that popcorn story, after all. Once when I was little he put me in the bathtub with my socks on—he hadn't noticed—which of course I begged him to do again and again from that point on.

He'd grown up doing chores beside his mother and sister—cooking and gardening, pretty much anything involving his hands—and the habit stayed with him. During cocktail hour, which my mom and he never missed, he made amazing martinis and Manhattans with a chilled martini shaker kept in the freezer at all times. This was the late fifties and early sixties—people took their cocktail hours seriously. The backyard of our house in L.A. was thick and stringy with the tomato plants he grew. My mom liked to tell me that my dad's skill with his hands was something he'd passed down to me, and I always loved hearing that.

Someone once wrote that in between the lives we lead and the lives we fantasize about living is the place in our heads where most of us actually live. My mom told me once that my father had always wanted to be a poet. It is likely that growing up during the Depression with no money made him want to seek security, pushing him toward a career as a professor instead. But aside from his love of words and the self-deprecating jokes and puns he slung around with his close friends, it was something that until she told me, I never knew about my father, which is striking, especially since my brother later became a poet.

From my childhood I recall days spent home sick from school, trying on my mom's clothes and watching television show after television show. I remember spooning out chocolate or tapioca pudding from the box—*tapioca*, a word no one uses anymore. The smell of the house, damp and distinct. The aroma of old indigenous L.A. houses, even inland ones, comes from the ocean twenty miles away, a hint of mildew, but dry, too, and closed up, perfectly still, like a statue. I can still smell the barest trace of gas from the old 1950s stove, an invisible odor mixed with sunshine streaming in from the windows, and, somewhere, eucalyptus bathed in the haze of ambition.

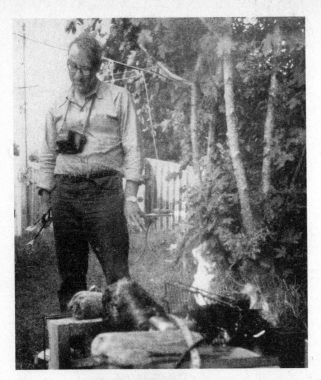

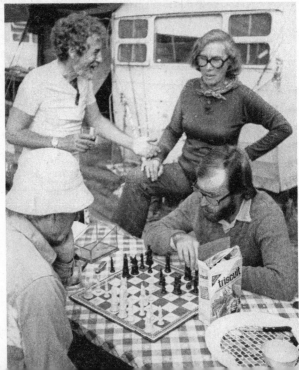

3

UPSTAIRS IN MY HOUSE in western Massachusetts, I have a stack of
DVDs containing old movies of my parents fishing in the Klamath
River, just south of the Oregon border. They're with their best friends,
Connie and Maxie Bentzen, and another couple, Jackie and Bill, all
of them members of the liberal, food-loving UCLA group my parents
belonged to. These were funny, ironic people who also happened to be
passionate fishermen.

Starting in the late sixties, my parents drove up to Klamath every
summer, staying in a rented trailer and spending the next month fishing
with this core group of people, others coming and going. Klamath was

all about fishing and socializing and cooking and eating, and waking up the next day to start over again. My dad made his own smoking devices—homemade baskets he placed in oilcans and submerged in hot coals to smoke fish, chicken wings, or his famous ribs. There were no social rules except that "good times" were to be had. You ate what you caught, and to this day the salmon right out of the smoker that Connie Bentzen made is the best thing I've ever tasted. An actual rule in Klamath: you were only allowed to take home two fish. My mother once smuggled a third fish onto the campsite inside her waders, a story of transgression that turned into an ongoing joke between her and their friends.

The Bentzens were documentary filmmakers, close friends with cinematographers and directors like Haskell Wexler, who worked on films like *One Flew over the Cuckoo's Nest,* and Irvin Kershner, who worked on *Star Wars.* Maxie Bentzen was a funny, lighthearted former grad student of my dad's, the first woman I knew who wore blue jeans day and night. Her husband, Connie, had the same electric-blue eyes as Paul Newman. During the year they lived in Malibu, in a house on stilts, with *Peanuts* cartoons and *New Yorker* magazines on their living room table. If you were spending the night in their guest room, just below the high-tide mark, you could hear the waves fiercely crashing underneath the house, true white noise that sloshed you to sleep. As a kid I remember wanting to be just like the Bentzens, to host dinner parties just like theirs, with my friends' children running around in the backyard, kids who would look back someday and use words like *magical,* because that is what those nights were. I'll always remember the night JFK got elected, the party they threw, the charged sound of adult laughter and chatter.

The Bentzens had first pulled into Klamath in 1953. Over the next few decades the region grew up around them, getting more and more crowded, with lumber companies taking out huge swaths of fir and pine trees, but the Bentzens prided themselves on being discoverers and originators and they pushed back. Klamath got so busy and populated that in the 1980s, to mark off their spot and also keep out the rednecks, Connie erected a big stuffed scarecrow of a UCLA mascot that everyone referred to as "Johnny Bruin."

In the videos, there's my mom, tight-lipped in a button-up blue-black cardigan, and there's my dad, too, with his big glasses. He's holding up a salmon he just caught, cupping the fish under its chin. Friends wander in and out of the frame. *A six-pounder,* I can hear Maxie say. *Look at the size of that thing,* Connie says, and *Take a picture* and *He's getting tired* and *Hard to believe you caught that thing using that little reel of yours, Wayne.* Jackie goes around snapping photos. Then they go for double dry martinis at Steelhead, a lodge nearby where they went to drink at night.

I went along with my parents to Klamath only once when I was a kid, when I was seventeen. When they were gone, Keller and I had the house to ourselves. Fishing was never really my thing, but I loved being there with my parents and their friends. The wilderness could be slow going, and if you weren't out on the river—which could be dangerous and chaotic, like a freeway intersection—there wasn't much else to do but sit and read and eat, do puzzles, and find a quiet spot away from the wind where you could sit alone and relax. The whole scene was tranquil and arresting in its wild American gorgeousness.

At one point in one of the videos—it must be 1986—I show up, and Thurston trails in, though usually he liked to hole up in our camper, reading, until cocktail hour. Keller is there, too, mellow but animated, talking and joking, the usual patch of black stubble covering his chin. Whenever he went up to Klamath, Keller slept in his own private tent, a cave of sorts in the center of my parents' little camp.

Connie is behind the camera, gently firing off questions about what I've been up to. It was around the time of *Evol,* Sonic Youth's third album. "I mean, yeah, we made a *little* money off of that," I say.

"Maybe you'll get to be a millionaire," Connie says. He always had a jokey, gruff, great way of speaking. "Those rock-and-roll people make so much money you can hardly stand it."

"Well, that's a whole different ball game you're talking about than what *we* do," I say.

"And you're not going to get *into* that ball game, Kim?"

"Well, the problem is, we'd have to tailor our music too much. We'd have to start wearing long wigs and eye shadow and glitter pants."

"Okay, okay, well, that's life," Connie says. "Now who wants to *eat*?"

In some ways it was easier not to talk about what I did for a living. New York City and our music were both too hard to translate. And being in Klamath wasn't about what you did out in the world anyway; it was about family and fishing and eating and socializing and making corny jokes, like when I tried to fire some darts into a wall target and someone yelled out, "Kim, that's an *objet d'art!*" Maxie, though, was a great supporter of young people and was always saying, "You guys are so great!" whereas Connie was always saying, "You kids are never going to live up to the older generation," at which everyone would laugh.

My parents were never more relaxed than when they were up at Klamath. The Bentzens were family but even better, a tribe that unlike your real relatives wasn't obligatory and never pressured you. My dad didn't have much contact with his own Kansas relatives. It wasn't snobbery that kept him away, more a culture divide, as most of my dad's family was small-town religious. He did stay in touch with his mother and sister. With Connie, Maxie, their son Mike, Jackie, and Bill, my parents were truly themselves, at ease and off duty.

Today Klamath is unrecognizable, though that's probably true for any place you look back on—it's certainly true about New York. These days you're hardly allowed to fish at Klamath at all, and the tourist industry is pretty much gone. Klamath was always depressed, but it's more low-down now than ever, deserted, creepy, a place that portends abandoned meth labs in the woods.

Jackie still lives in Malibu. Her husband, Bill, is dead. Maxie and her son, Mike, still live in Santa Cruz, but most of the others, including my parents, are gone. In the late 1980s, a short while after my dad stopped working, he was diagnosed with Parkinson's. His basic neurological functions began to leave him, one after another. At some point, my mom really wasn't able to take care of him by herself, and she made it clear he'd be better off—in fact, it was his job and his responsibility to do so, she told him—if he went into a nursing home, which he did. My mom was tough and pragmatic, though in fairness to her, she didn't have the money to pay for the twenty-four-hour nursing staff his condition required.

It wasn't the Parkinson's that killed him. It was the nursing home, where he contracted pneumonia, and then the hospital. A nurse, an old-timer who should have known better, inserted a feeding tube down the wrong pipe. But my family never sued the hospital, as by that point my dad's Parkinson's was so advanced it had taken away most of the person we all remembered anyway. In the year before he died, I remember how he never complained. I'm sure he missed doing things like cooking, and tending to his tomatoes, and playing with his custom-made smokers. I missed the father who'd given me a book of Emily Dickinson poems, sweetly inscribed, for my sixteenth birthday, even though I found Dickinson corny. I missed the man who took me to lunch at the UCLA faculty center, introducing me proudly to the people he worked with, making me so happy in return that he was my dad. During his last year I mostly remember his docility, his sweetness, his acceptance of what was ahead.

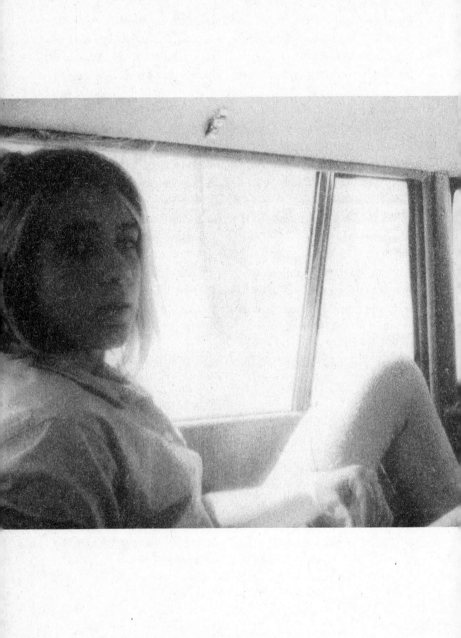

4

AS TEENAGERS, my friends and I used to walk inside one of the giant sewer pipes that led out to the Pacific Ocean. The pipes were huge and echoing, smelling of old age, caked salt, rotten sea grass. There was always the thrilling possibility that a torrent of water would come gushing down with no warning, which is why we had to be ready at any second to scramble up onto a wall ladder. The risk of water thundering down on you and pulling you along, and the prospect of having to think fast, always made that long walk out to the sea worth it. Risk and excitement were in short supply for me in the neighborhood where we lived, so we found it instead on the shifting coastline and farther inland.

As kids, my friends and I used to play on huge dirt mounds, which none of us realized at the time were freeway on-ramps in the making. One time Keller and some of his group went to a nearby ravine and jumped down off the cliff, landing on a squishy, sandy slope below. What's that old parental cliché—*If your friends jumped off a cliff, would you follow them?* The answer in my case was yes. Trying to prove how tough a little sister could be, I landed on my back, the wind rushing out of my body.

I couldn't breathe, to the point where I thought I was going to die. I felt so stupid and embarrassed I didn't even tell my parents. I always hated making mistakes, hated getting into trouble, hated not being in control.

To me the canyons in L.A. held the most glamour. Rustic hillsides filled with twisted oak trees, scruffy and steep, with lighter-than-light California sunshine filtering through the tangles. In the winter, the dripping rain made them look more unkempt than usual. They were also denser, more able to hide the funky, scrabbled array of houses. The canyons were eternally shaded. This was where all the interesting, seemingly non-self-obsessed types were, and where the cool musicians lived—Buffalo Springfield, Neil Young, and so on. In the hills, you could imagine you were anywhere in the world, at least during the day, when the trees and the overgrown landscaping hid the gluey sprawl just below. I listened to Joni Mitchell a lot as a teenager and always thought of her sitting up in a woody, funky, thrown-together canyon house, maybe one with a porch, with trees and vegetation dripping off the roof. She would be melancholy, looking out the window. I was in my room a few miles away, painting, smoking pot, and getting sad listening to her.

The canyons were a big contrast to the banal, flat, middle-class section of L.A. where my family lived. Even when we moved to a nicer, bigger, Spanish-style house in the same neighborhood, it was just the same: freshly mowed green lawns camouflaging dry desert-scape; constant, compulsive watering and pruning; everything orderly but with its own kind of unease, what with the constant pressure to be happy, to be new, to smile. And beneath it all, shadows and cracks and breaks—all Freudian death instinct.

Once I remember my mom pointing to a big undeveloped area of sand, mud, and grass that grew to become Century City. "There's going to be a city there someday," she said, not in a soothsayer way but stating the obvious, that soon every inch of Los Angeles would be overtaken by more cars, more gas stations, more malls, more bodies, and of course she was right.

We were an academic family, as opposed to a showbiz family, a division I picked up on early and one that held a lot of weight in Los Angeles, especially. In high school, I had a good friend who lived with her mom and brothers, and her dad had been a movie director before he died. They lived in an apartment in Beverly Hills, on Beverly Glen. The mother was beautiful and polished, warm and effusive, and more than anything I admired her emotive qualities. One night they came over for dinner, and after they left, my dad immediately said something sharp, and out of character for him, about how she wasn't a "real" person. Being "real" was such a 1960s ideal. He saw, I think, how enamored I was of my friend's mother, how glamorous I found her—the way she called me "darling" and spoke to me about things my mother didn't. He didn't want me to get sucked into all that.

When people ask me what L.A. was like in the sixties, I tell them that there wasn't as much terrible stucco as there is today: no mini malls with their approximation of Spanish two-story buildings, no oversized SUVs bulging out of parking-space lines. What used to say "Spanish-style" is now something diseased looking. Nobody seems to know how to stucco anymore.

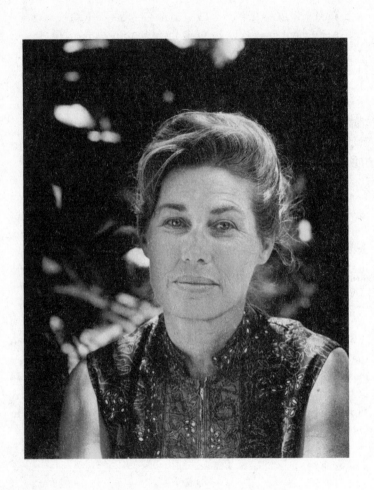

5

WHEN MY DAD was getting his college degrees, he got to be friends with a couple of his students, some hipsters, and later beatniks, who all turned him on to jazz. They lived in Venice in a worn-down house, at a time when it was unheard of to live there. Coltrane, Brubeck, Billie Holiday, Charlie Parker, Dizzy Gillespie, Stan Getz—those were their reigning jazz heroes. John Coltrane was probably the most avant-garde of the bunch, but my dad loved him, too. I'm almost positive my dad's jazz record collection later influenced me, or at least got me used to abstract music—that, and my parents' blues, folk, and classical LPs, as my mom was always coming back from neighborhood garage sales weighed down with box sets of Mozart and Beethoven. But jazz has been a lifelong love and interest of mine. I remember when I was little, my dad and I went to visit one of those Venice beatnik guys, though I mostly remember his glam girlfriend with her long, straight black hair, her red-polished fingernails, and her guitar. She was the first beatnik I ever met. I sat in her lap, thinking, *I wish my mom were as cool as this.*

My mom worked out of our house as a seamstress. She was the go-to person in our neighborhood for tailoring clothes. She made all my clothes growing up, and what she didn't design, cut, and sew, she bought in local thrift shops, a habit that surely came from growing up during the Depression. When I was a teenager, she began making more florid, eccentric stuff—caftans, clothes made out of velvet or chiffon, block-printed by a designer she knew. These were haute hippie-looking outfits that she'd sell alongside the wares of other artistically inclined friends—ceramics, jewelry. Still, I hated that she made my clothes or picked up bargains at secondhand stores. Ironically, during my faux-hippie period in high school, I grew to love vintage stores, and thrifting, a habit that carried into my years in New York—anything but the uptight stocking-and-preppy look that was the current fashion at my school. I would raid my mom's sewing room for funky, exotic caftans and beautiful tie-dyed silk "abas," as she called them.

Basically, I never really knew how to dress during my middle and high school years. I still have a photo of myself in my bedroom at sixteen, sitting on a turquoise bedspread—my favorite color then and now—wearing a pair of baggy, flowered, homemade pants my mom had crafted out of an Indian bedspread, and a wine-colored turtleneck with a zipper up the neck, worn backward. That, or flared hip-hugger cords, or jeans, with a fringed Mexican top. Whenever I told my mom that I wanted to buy some jeans she would let out a theatrical sigh and take me to the army surplus store on Venice Boulevard. It's still there, I think. Along with high-grade military and camping gear, they carried Land-lubber, a popular brand in those days.

Looking back, I'm sure that my mom's creative-but-unconventional fashion sense, coupled with my sense of deprivation, made me covet "new clothes" while also sparking an ambivalence toward conventional fashion, as it was all laid out in the fashion magazines: how a girl or woman is supposed to dress; what expresses her personality; how does she handle wanting to be sexy, or appealing, while still being true to herself? At home I stared for hours at record covers and photos of Marianne Faithfull, Anita Pallenberg, Peggy Lipton, Joni Mitchell, and other cool girls, wanting to be just like them. It was an era of no bras, free-flowing hair, vintage lace, and crushed velvet borrowed from traditional boudoir scenarios of passive female sexuality and placed front and center. Anita Pallenberg's look was wild enough to influence the Rolling Stones. Men wore women's clothes, sheepskin vests, short white pants, lamé scarves, and exotic Moroccan jewelry, while women slipped into pinstripe suits, and boyfriends and girlfriends swapped shirts and pants with no concern, all male-female stereotypes muddled and switched and subverted. The newest, coolest girl around was Françoise Hardy, a French singer who dressed as a tomboy. In Westwood there was a store that sold small, overpriced Jane Birkin–esque French T-shirts, and I think I caved in finally and bought one.

At the same time, from early on my mother feared I was "too" sexy, the result being that I spent a lot of time vacillating between wanting to be seen as attractive, being terrified by too much attention, and wanting to succeed and fit in without anyone's noticing me. In L.A., bodies are always on show, and just walking down the street as a teenager could be scary. Guys in cars would whiz by, slow down, reverse, offer rides to who-knows-where. When I turned fifteen, my mother let me know I was too old to wear short shorts, and Keller, I remember, told her she was a "prude." These days, I find it kind of cool to be slightly old-fashioned.

Still, my mother always knew better than to try to teach me to make my own clothes. A few times I pulled out her sewing machine to take in my jeans, but the technology always overwhelmed me. Plus, I didn't like her telling me what to do, and I still bristle at authority. When Coco was born someone gave her a onesie from the seventies that said

QUESTION AUTHORITY. I could relate. I remember asking my mother once if she thought I would have a good figure when I grew up. "Yes," she said, "you have slim hips and broad shoulders," though when I matured early on, she mostly seemed afraid I would get into trouble, get pregnant, every mother's biggest fear.

If my dad was in his head most of the time, my mom was the practical one, anchored, a little self-absorbed. She ran our house. She was the enforcer, like most stay-at-home moms. She brooded a lot, said little about her own life before her family came along, but still, you would never have mistaken her for an average 1950s housewife. I knew that growing up her older brother was cruel to her, which is why looking back I find her hands-off parenting style so strange when it came to Keller and me. Maybe I became so good at hiding my oversensitivity that she had no idea how much he traumatized me. Maybe she didn't notice. Maybe she noticed but hoped to toughen me up. I was seven or eight years old when my cat was run over, and a few days or weeks later my mom let me know it was time to stop being sad, time to move on. Maybe she was right. As for her, I never saw her cry, except once when I stayed out all night without telling her, and her tears that night had more to do with anger and relief. As I said, until I was in college I knew nothing about her family's early California origins and even when I found out, my mom had nothing to add. Two years before she died, she said in passing to my aunt, "I should have never left California."

I'm still not sure how to take those words, but I remember being disturbed when my aunt told me that. Did my mom mean: *I should never have married your father?* Or, *If I'd never left California to go to Kansas, I would never have ended up as a faculty wife and a mother?* Or, *I would never have been the mother of a paranoid-schizophrenic son?* No one knows what goes on inside anyone else's marriage, especially their parents'. Over the few times they met, my mom and Thurston's mom, Eleanor, who was a decade younger, developed a friendship of sorts. Once my mom confided to Eleanor that she'd considered leaving my dad but was glad she hadn't.

I always got the feeling my mom would rather have been doing something else, that she wanted *more* for herself—more recognition, maybe, as a creative person. Maybe she secretly wanted to be a movie actress, wanted to be recognized less as an academic's wife and more as the person she felt she was inside—I won't ever know. Once, I remember, she made a collage out of *New Yorker* covers that she placed above the stove. It was a grease catcher, she told us, but in truth it was more than that, a piece of clever, unconventional art. Another time she made a series of long, rectangular wall reliefs with shells in colored cement on wood, more art than craft, making me wish she would make more. Maybe, like me, the clothes she cut and designed and stitched were the arena where she felt the freest to show off the things in her life that were blocked or frustrated. When she dressed up to go out at night in the fashion of the 1950s—low-cut dresses, an ample bosom, a cinched-in waist, flared skirts—she laughed and enjoyed herself with an ease I didn't see very often in her everyday life. I couldn't help but feel sometimes that no one ever told her she was beautiful growing up, that she felt like the unattractive one in her family. To me she was gorgeous, like Ingrid Bergman.

My dad was elderly by the time Coco was born in the summer of 1994. The Parkinson's had set in, and he wasn't really able to hold her safely. My mother was nearly the same age as my dad but always did yoga and played golf and walked. My mother really loved Coco—she was her first and only grandchild—but instead of holding her, she spent hours watching her. "She's going to be okay, because you really play and interact with her," my mom once said to me, as if to say this was something she'd never done with me. I was always very independent, she reminded me, but looking back, I missed that closeness with my mother. When I was ten, my family spent a year in Hawaii, and I have a memory from that time of one day wondering, *How come I don't sit in my mother's lap anymore? How come she doesn't hold me or hug me?*

Both my parents were brooders. My dad was preoccupied with academic politics. For years he was an associate dean, and he eventually became dean. My mom was equally absorbed in her own thoughts. In private she worried about a lot of things. Keller would say something to her like "You're so uptight!" and I'd add "Yeah, Mom, why do you look so sad?" and she'd say something like "Because the world is so depressing—the war, for starters."

It wasn't just the sixties. It was family stuff, most having to do with Keller, and the worry and the stress that seemed to follow him. Even after my dad retired from UCLA, he never wanted to travel or take vacations. Instead, he gardened and paced. Sometimes I could hear him out in his jungle of tomato plants in the middle of the night, prowling around, and I felt bad for him. He never talked about what was going on with my brother, but he must have been keeping watch, waiting on the worst, duty-bound to be there in case something went down with Keller, because by then something was always happening with Keller.

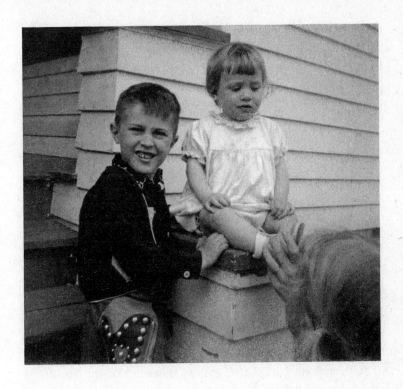

6

KELLER'S WHOLE CHILDHOOD became the stuff of family fables, jokey legends, tributes to his smartness or his independence or both. Here's one: at the exact moment I was being born, Keller, who was three and a half, disappeared down the street with his four-year-old girlfriend to shoplift candy from a neighborhood drugstore. Or this: Keller didn't learn to read until the fourth grade, which seems unlikely if not impossible.

In old photos taken when he was young, Keller's always attired in a cowboy costume, with leather-looking boots and a big hat, smiling a massive, mysterious grin. From a young age he was willful and uncooperative, a troublemaker, and this in our family made him the center of attention, usually the negative kind. He was crazy smart, too, hyperverbal, the torrent of words coming out of his mouth so thick and constant it was as if he were drowning in them. He always had a comeback, a response, a return that cut short any conversation or argument. In many ways he ran over me, erased me, made me feel invisible even to myself.

I worshipped my brother. I wanted to *be* like him. But he was vicious to me throughout our childhood—teasing me nonstop, physically fighting with me—sprinkled with occasional moments of niceness. Looking back, I wonder whether his sadism might have been a symptom of the disease that showed itself later.

His ridiculing and button-pushing went beyond the typical sibling ragging. At dinner, I'd let drop some trendy word or expression and Keller would jump on it, and on me, for my faddishness, my ordinariness, my lack of originality. When a scene in a movie or a Disney special made me laugh or cry, he'd make fun of me for laughing and make fun of me for crying and make fun of me when I didn't say anything at all. He always knew he could get a response from me, which provoked him to do it even more.

At some point I turned off entirely. Knowing I'd get mocked or teased, I would do anything not to cry, or laugh, or show any emotion at all. The biggest challenge as I saw it was to pretend I had some superhuman ability to withstand pain. Add that to the pressure girls feel anyway to please other people, to be good, and well mannered, and orderly—and I backslid even more into a world where nothing could upset or hurt me.

Sometimes my brother's teasing crossed over into physical violence. One night he and I fought so hard on my parents' bed that the TV set smashed to the floor from the vibrations. Another time Keller, who had become something of a neighborhood ringleader, arranged a fight between me and a boy from down the street. He went so far as to place bets among his friends that I could win. I knew I couldn't, but I went along with it anyway because I wanted him to feel proud of me. Whenever I complained to my parents about Keller, or asked them to make him stop tormenting me, they just said, "Oh, go hit him back."

Oh, go hit him back—words that still circle my brain forty, nearly fifty years later. Because no matter how hard I tried, I could never *not* react to Keller, but neither could I depend on my parents to protect me or take my side. If something happened right in front of them, they would step in, but otherwise my dad would say something like "Just knock it off." But there was no justice in that—just eventual retaliation from Keller.

Maybe that's why for me the page, the gallery, and the stage became the only places my emotions could be expressed and acted out comfortably. These were the venues where I could exhibit sexuality, anger, a lack of concern for what people thought. The image a lot of people have of me as detached, impassive, or remote is a persona that comes from years of being teased for every feeling I ever expressed. When I was young, there was never any space for me to get attention of my own that wasn't negative. Art, and the practice of making art, was the only space that was mine alone, where I could be anyone and do anything, where just by using my head and my hands I could cry, or laugh, or get pissed off.

But throughout my teens, my brother was the charismatic one—a nerd with a big, movie-star-sized head and an otherworldly glow, the leader of his small, passionate friend group. Long before *Freaks and Geeks* came out, Keller created a fanzine, which he called *The Fiend Thinker.* It was a celebration of nerd-dom and outsiderness, including definitions of words he'd made up, which he mimeographed and passed out to his followers. In middle school he and his friends even carried out their own sociological study of their eighth-grade class. They interviewed kids from various social groups—surfers, nerds, popular kids, and Spanish-Americans, or SAs as they were known back then. My dad was proud of Keller for this, how he applied his ideas to a contemporary situation, even if the study was a direct appropriation. My brother got a lot of recognition for that study. It was one of his first and last great accomplishments.

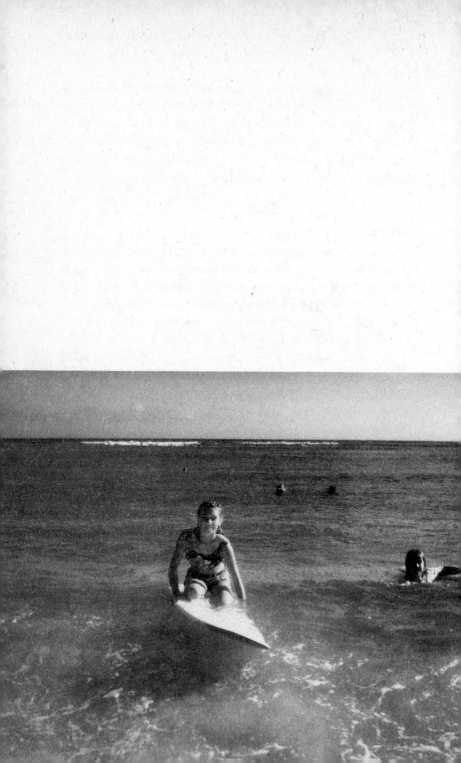

7

IN 1963, the year JFK died and right before the Beatles went on Ed Sullivan, my dad took a yearlong sabbatical at a think tank, and my family went to live in Hawaii. I was incredibly excited to go. When I was little, I loved the musical *South Pacific*, which takes place on an island, Bali Ha'i, and I spent a lot of time reenacting the songs in my room. At ten, I was a restless preadolescent, mature for my age, curious about sex, starting to feel my sensual side, and the encyclopedia entry for Hawaii showed photo after photo of half-naked women with flowers around their necks. On the plane the Pan Am stewardesses were beautiful and served everyone, including me, free champagne. When we arrived, I insisted on getting a two-piece bathing suit with a slightly padded top, which made me feel even more grown-up.

The glamour ended when I began attending a public school, where for the first time I was a minority. In Asian cultures, "Kim" is a male name, and Hawaii's population is mostly Asian, so I was picked on constantly. Still, it wasn't all bad. I remember walking barefoot through the Manoa Valley. The grass was dewy, and the fragrance in the air was an ideal backdrop for my preadolescent sexual feelings. Keller and I had done some surfing out at Latigo Shore Drive just past Malibu, so the beach and the water were familiar to me. I had my new bathing suit and my own surfboard, a small Hobie, and the cute young Hawaiian surf guides in front of the Royal Hawaiian Hotel flirted with me. I always looked older than my actual age—like a classic blonde California girl, in fact. The gap I'd always had between my two front teeth had grown in, and the chicken pox marks on my face, which had always made me feel so self-conscious, blended in with my tan.

Two years later, when I was thirteen, my dad was asked to launch a study-abroad program for UCLA, and our family packed up to spend a year in Hong Kong. Moving away from my friends was the last thing I wanted to do, although having started junior high in the middle of the year and being thrown into the alien public school structure of L.A. after my experiences in the lab school and in Hawaii didn't make me exactly eager to stay. Everything at school had changed. I was tuning out, spending time down at the gully that ran through the school, courting a little bit of trouble. In Hawaii, I'd been something of a wild child, going to school barefoot, and in L.A. I was thrust into the public junior high school, where the other girls wore pleated skirts and little sweaters. I hated it. Still, I made it clear to my parents I had no desire to go to Hong Kong. There was even talk of my going to live in New Jersey with old friends of my parents, a family who had lived next door to us in Rochester, who had two boys around my age. Or that Keller and I could even go to a Swiss boarding school, which, in retrospect, sounds ridiculous.

In the end, we did none of those things, and I still love to say that my dad inaugurated a study project in China for UCLA.

The four of us arrived in Hong Kong during the tail end of a typhoon. At the airport, staffers handed out umbrellas that blew away instantly. Hong Kong was like nothing I had ever experienced before. The air was so hot and humid it was like stepping inside a kiln, and you had to gasp to catch your breath. The smells and sounds were overpowering. My first night there, I remember knocking into people on the street, and crying, which fogged and blurred the city's yellow lights even more. I felt so overwhelmed by Hong Kong's heat, chaos, clamor, and odors that I was convinced I would never—never—survive there a year.

That first month we lived in downtown Kowloon in a hotel. Chinese girls in fifties-style chiffon layered skirts played Beatles songs in the downstairs hotel bar. Walking along Hong Kong's streets was like moving inside a slow riot. At night, you could hear the palmed dice and quiet slap of mah-jongg games. Then as now, the city's prevailing backdrop seemed to be the exchange of money for goods, at all hours. Merchandise was cheap, too. Morning would dawn, and with it the familiar onrush of wet heat, and the aggressive, sleazy shop owners would take up position in their doorways, beckoning to me and to any other girl passing by. In those days Hong Kong was an English colony and a major port, and now I wonder how my parents allowed me to wander around by myself. Sailors from all over the world roamed the sidewalks, calling out suggestive things, one even lightly jabbing me in the stomach with a "Hey, girl, what are you doing?" I walked by him fast, mortified, but thrilled too that in a strange new world I felt visible and noticed.

Because we were living in a hotel, Keller and I had to share a room, and one night, he tried to climb into my bed. He was naked. When I pushed him and told him to get away, he called me a slut, a word I found hard to shake, though I knew he was not in his right mind. Still, I was afraid to ask my parents if they would pay for a separate room. They would ask why, and as usual, no matter how scared and upset I felt, I didn't want Keller to get into any trouble. I still idealized him, convinced myself he was better than he was, wanted to protect him, and I always hated hearing my dad yell at him. Back then Keller was eccentric, but no one, especially me, recognized the signs of his eventual schizophrenia. Instead, I let myself feel guilty, as if I were somehow responsible for everything he did wrong.

Our Hong Kong school, named after King George V, was about two decades behind the schools we had known in America. Along with swats, caning, and mandatory uniforms (which I kind of liked, in a romantic movie–like way), there were punishments that included writing the same sentence over and over hundreds of times—"I must not talk during class"—among other wonderfully useful skills. The most feared and ruthless teacher on the faculty was the school's religious instructor. He scrutinized the class for the slightest hints of bad behavior and wore such stiffly starched white colonial shorts you could see up them whenever he took a seat.

English schools began a year earlier than U.S. schools, which meant that everyone in my class was a year younger than I was. The boys came up to my chest. As the semester went on, I met an older English boy, a fifteen-year-old drummer who became my first boyfriend. Our relationship was extremely ceremonial. The two of us would go to his house and make out in his bedroom, followed by a silent formal lunch in the old-fashioned dining room with his parents, the meal served by the family's amah—a domestic servant. In Hong Kong, it seemed, everyone had at least one amah, but his family had two.

I was very aware of Hong Kong's legendary red-light district, Wan Chai—it was well-known, even to tourists—as I was becoming curious about sex. I went there once with a friend, and in the daytime its brothels and massage parlors and girlie bars looked ordinary, uninteresting. In an attempt to brush up on my limited sexual knowledge, I read *The World of Suzie Wong*, but in that respect it was disappointing. I also read all of Ian Fleming's books, at the time a step up from Nancy Drew. My mother gave me, or let me read, *Lolita* and *Candy*, Terry Southern's popular sex farce, which I read with eyes wide open, taking in every word. As my growing sexuality seemed to upset and worry my mom, she must have thought these books would show me how *not* to be. Around that time I also remember her telling me that boys might like girls because of the way they looked, but the quality of a girl's brain was the ticket to a more satisfying relationship. It was advice that caused me all kinds of neuroses. It also proved to be wrong.

Hong Kong is divided up into three parts, and after a month in Kowloon, we moved into a hilltop apartment in the New Territories section of the city. It was mountainous and peaceful, about an hour's car drive from downtown, with a veranda that looked out across a shimmering, placid sea usually dotted with one or a pair of distant Chinese junks. If you hopped a train, you would eventually arrive at the Great Wall of China, but I wouldn't see the wall until Sonic Youth played there many years later.

Keller and I had an American friend named Barry Finnerty, who lived down at the bottom of the hill beside the train tracks. A pimply-faced adolescent two years older than me who was just learning how to play Beatles songs on his electric guitar, and whose mother was always getting complaints from the neighbors about the noise, Barry had managed to get himself kicked out of King George V on the second day of school for making up swear-word lyrics to the hymns during the morning assembly. He liked to go around exclaiming loudly that he was a "retired Jew and an agnostic atheist." Freight cars would stop in front of Barry's apartment building, some of them carrying pigs for slaughter, their snouts poking through the endless train bars. Wrapped in his American revulsion for all things earthy, carnal, and exotic, Barry would run out into the station and take photos of those hundreds of snouts, one of his favorite things to do.

Barry later became a respected jazz guitarist, at one point playing with Miles Davis, and he and I stayed friends for a long time. When my family moved back to L.A., I used to fly up to San Francisco, where Barry lived with his mother. In those days, the last flight on PSA Airlines was at ten or eleven P.M. Friday night, and the ticket cost $10. At fifteen, I might have been too young to hang out on the Sunset Strip—there was a ten P.M. curfew if you were under the age of eighteen—but in San Francisco I was free to roam around and see bands at the Fillmore and the Avalon Ballroom. I loved San Francisco and told myself I would someday go to art school there.

In the meantime, we took full advantage of how cheap Hong Kong was, the tailors especially. Keller ordered button-down shirts in various colors with a big surfer "Competition Stripe" across the middle, custom-made to fit him. Me, I spent all my allowance money on a bikini, though when I finally tried it on, it didn't match the way girls and bikinis looked in women's magazines. My idea of heaven was frequenting a Hong Kong store that sold English mod-style clothes: red corduroy hip-hugger bell-bottoms, dusty-pink pants that laced up in the front, crop tops. I'd spend my days wandering through racks of clothes I couldn't afford, thinking of all the places I would wear them. As usual, Keller grabbed all the attention when one night he and some friends snuck off to the island of Macau, the dark, nefarious port where gambling was legal. My parents had told him repeatedly he couldn't go there and were furious when they found out he'd done it anyway. This was the beginning of Keller's rebellious teen years, a time when he also made friends with a boy named Mitch, whose parents were visiting missionaries. A year later Mitch would play a cameo role in Keller's unraveling.

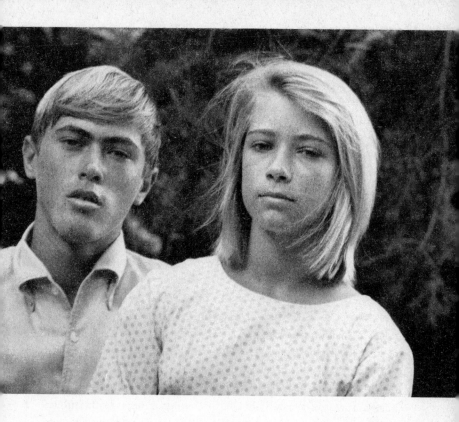

8

BACK IN L.A., going on fourteen, I was again faced with the prospect of public junior high school. I didn't fit in with the "nice middle-class girls." I didn't really understand the idea of grades or of dressing up conventionally. Instead I hung out with the white-trash kids and tried to avoid the attention of the Mexican girls who would beat you up if you dared look at them the wrong way. I was much happier a few years later in high school when the late sixties were in full bloom, the dress code became more chaotic, and I could find more natural peers.

Keller was now in high school and no longer a nerd. Becoming a surfer had brought out his good looks, and he began going out with a series of beautiful girlfriends. His Hong Kong buddy, Mitch, had moved in with us, as his parents wanted him to finish up high school in the States. In retrospect, this wasn't the best decision by any means, as Mitch and Keller spent most of their time in their room, smoking dope and dropping LSD, the walls plastered with black-light posters and the space glowing with light boxes.

After high school, Keller started attending college and became interested in Shakespeare and Chaucer, though he would later drop out. He wrote sonnets that sounded eerily Bard-like, and went around publicly reciting these and ancient works. "You want to hear my new poem?" he would ask. Not waiting for me to answer, he would begin intoning lines or whole stanzas. Even then it didn't occur to me that Keller's behavior was extreme, compulsive, or all that strange. Everyone smoked pot and dropped acid. The atmospherics of the era were all about breaking boundaries, flipping conventions, and acting "far out," and at the time I didn't consider it to be tied up with mental illness. Keller was a player in an era that made it possible for anyone's behavior to slip from charmingly eccentric to worrisomely antisocial to schizophrenic without anyone's raising even a small flag. On the contrary, it fit perfectly with the whole hippie take on the Elizabethan lifestyle embodied back then by Renaissance fairs.

By now my brother and I had become friends, allies, and conspirators against our parents. He was at the pinnacle of his coolness, an evolution that began in Hawaii and intensified in Hong Kong. Inside our house, serious talk was happening—what if Keller got drafted to go fight in Vietnam? After all, he had attended college for a while but quit going, and during my last year of high school, he lived in a trailer in my parents' driveway. Even if you weren't in college someone his age could still get drafted. But inside the trailer, all conflicts were smoothed and blurred in hash smoke and audio recordings of *Hamlet*, *Macbeth*, and *Twelfth Night*. Keller turned me on to Nietzsche, Sartre, Balzac, Flaubert, Baudelaire, and all the other French thinkers, writers, and poets my high school felt it unnecessary to teach. We listened to avant-garde jazz—Ornette Coleman, Coltrane, Albert Ayler, Don Cherry, and Archie Shepp. Our lack of any musical training didn't keep us from impromptu jam sessions in my parents' living room with an African drum, a Chinese gong, a recorder, and our own junky upright piano. It was just something Keller and I did together, wild, disorganized improv music, with me by far the more self-conscious, inhibited one.

But my brother was going downhill in very slow motion. He moved his trailer out to Malibu. No one saw how nonsocialized and solitary he was becoming, how he was pushing away one old friend after another. He broke up with his beautiful girlfriend abruptly, without giving her any reason, and his reclusiveness made me concerned. Most of the time he was alone, writing sonnets to a world that didn't care about sonnets. A year after high school, I had for all intents and purposes moved in with my boyfriend, and one night, Keller came over to the boy's house. He couldn't stop crying. He was depressed all the time, he said, and didn't know what to do. I became alarmed and told my parents I thought he should see a psychiatrist, but they dismissed the idea.

It was a strange role reversal. Suddenly Keller was looking to me, his little sister, for help. I'd become a symbolic older sibling, a protector, which is the role I still play for Keller today. He had never played that role for me.

There wasn't a name back then for what was happening to him. My parents were from a generation where you tended to your own problems, one where psychotherapy was an indulgence. They both came from families where you kept your problems to yourself and got on with life. If Keller was starting to act a little out of the ordinary, wasn't everybody trying to quote-unquote *find themselves* in Southern California in the early seventies? Not to mention that psychiatry had a cuckoo's-nest edge of paranoia about it. Articles appeared in the papers constantly about frustrated parents committing their iconoclastic kids to psych hospitals, which led to a law being passed in California that hospitals couldn't legally hold patients against their will for longer than forty-eight hours. My parents were educated but they weren't psychologically minded, and therapy and psych meds were for the truly mad, not for the idiosyncratic, and certainly not for their own idiosyncratic son. Even though they finally relented and found Keller a psychiatrist, it was too little too late. We would all get to know the forty-eight-hour law well over the next few years.

At some point, while living in Malibu, my brother started dressing entirely in white. He grew a long beard and carried a Bible, not for any religious reason, he'd say if anyone asked, but more for its literary excellence. He began making up words, his own private alphabet and language. He began referring to himself as Oedipus, intended to be a funny reference to Sophocles. Still, this didn't seem all that extraordinary, as back then there were *lots* of eccentric bearded guys dressed in white roaming around L.A. Charlie Manson was starting to make appearances around the beaches and canyons of Malibu. Keller used to crash sometimes at a house at the foot of Topanga Canyon, where one night he met another Manson Family member, Bobby Beausoleil. Bobby would say repeatedly, "You should come up to the ranch sometime." Fortunately, Keller never did. In high school, one of my brother's ex-girlfriends, Marina Habe, was allegedly killed by the Manson Family. Marina was seventeen, and beautiful, and drove a red slinky sports car. She was home in L.A. for Christmas break from the University of Hawaii when someone shoved her inside a car and abducted her. Her body was later found off Mulholland Drive. She'd been stabbed over and over again.

Keller and I used to hitchhike up to Malibu, just as Manson had done. In fact, I was constantly meeting people who had picked Manson up and given him a ride or dropped him off by the side of the road. "I met this strange guy who was talking about the end of the world and 'Revolution 9' and the desert," they would say. After the Sharon Tate murders in 1969, I kept telling myself that things were going to be okay, that I lived in a middle-class neighborhood where nothing like that could ever happen in a million years.

Keller eventually got his bachelor's degree at the University of California in Irvine and went on to Berkeley, where he got his master's degree in classics. My brother's educational path was lengthy and stop-start, and it was probably for that reason that neither my parents nor I was there the day he graduated from Berkeley. That was the day he had his first full-blown psychotic episode. In the grip of a Shakespeare-inspired delusion about the women around him being "maidens," he lunged at a girl in the cafeteria, and the campus cops ended up dragging him off to the psych ward.

When he was released, he came back home and moved in with my parents. Over the next few years, it became harder and harder for them to control him. He would move into a halfway house, pledge to start taking his meds again, and then break his word and end up on the streets, or turn up at my parents' house, aggressive, threatening, and paranoid. They would return him to the psych ward at UCLA, and forty-eight hours later, he'd be rereleased and the cycle would start all over again. Eventually he ended up in the jail system.

This is just the way it is was my parents' response—a tragedy, organic, inexplicable. How much my mom read or knew about Keller's condition I don't know. At one point she reached out for help, as I remember her telling me once that schizophrenia support groups for families were "depressing." She always held out the hope that Keller would get better, turn a corner, restart his life. It didn't happen. Eventually a place in Santa Monica that offered something called Step Up on Second helped my parents figure out the best way to navigate the system.

Despite its large homeless population, California is low down on the list of states that offer decent social services or mental health programs, and Reagan went out of his way to shutter mental institutions across the U.S. In those days almost no programs existed to help families dealing with mentally ill relatives who were over eighteen, unless you could prove they planned on harming themselves or someone else. There were only halfway houses, some better than others, but most were sad, dangerous places.

In the end, my parents had no choice but to make Keller a ward of the state. It meant they were no longer legally responsible for his well-being, no longer the go-to people whose phone rang at two in the morning whenever some crisis happened. In the end they found him a place out by CalArts, a rehab facility filled with a mixed population of drug addicts, alcoholics, and people like Keller. Later he moved to something like a nursing home in the San Fernando Valley, where he lived for many years until recently.

Every year, sometimes twice a year, I fly out to California to visit him. I've been making this same trip for the past few decades. The home where he currently lives is in a lower-middle-class Latino neighborhood, and it's run by a group of Christian African-American women. Only two other patients live there. The rooms are bright, the food is good, and there's a backyard of struggling grass. I bring him cigarettes, potato chips, and Coca-Cola. He's completely happy. There are no computers or e-mail, and he and I don't speak on the phone during the year as I know he'll inevitably end the conversation with "Where are you?" and "When are you coming out to see me?" and I don't want to get his hopes up or disappoint him.

Keller is in his midsixties now and seems better than he has in a long time. His brain is still the same, skittering from reality to fantasy and back again, though the medication he's taking has made him nicer, warmer. It's hard sometimes to recall the aggressive, paranoid, on-the-cusp-of-violence person that his disease turned him into. One minute he'll be discussing the Nobel Peace Prize he was just awarded in Oslo, and the next minute he'll bring up some scarily precise detail about an actual person or place I'd forgotten about myself. Last year, he recited a poem he told me he had written in German, a language he doesn't speak, though from his flowery German accent you could have sworn he was a native Berliner.

He's still my brother, the only connection I have left to my family of origin, and to a place and a time. I still struggle with the idea that I let him make me feel bad about myself. The modern-day self-help notion is that "only you can make yourself a victim." I wonder what or who I would have been without him as my brother.

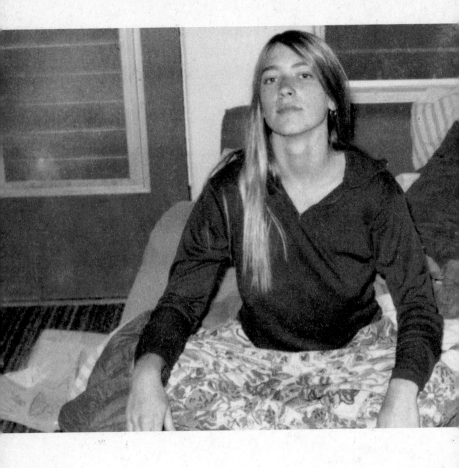

9

L.A. IN THE LATE SIXTIES had a desolation about it, a disquiet. More than anything, that had to do with a feeling, one that you still find in parts of the San Fernando Valley. There was a sense of apocalyptic expanse, of sidewalks and houses centipeding over mountains and going on forever, combined with a shrugging kind of anchorlessness. Growing up I was always aware of L.A.'s diffuseness, its lack of an attachment to anything other than its own good reflection in the mirror.

My mom wouldn't allow me to hang out with the other kids on the Sunset Strip. To her, the Strip was evil territory, flashy, fast, destructive. One of my closest elementary school friends had a nanny, and I remember the day she complained to me that my friend was hanging out on the Sunset Strip, plastering on way too much makeup. The nanny asked why my friend couldn't be more like me. I found this humorous. The thing is, I really wanted to go to the Strip, except I would have needed a phony ID, and my mother and I argued a lot about that, since I took it as my responsibility and duty to question authority. Then and now, under the palm trees and sand and daily light, L.A. is a police state with strict curfew laws. Spelled out, "It is unlawful for any minor under the age of eighteen (18) years to be present or upon any public street, avenue, highway, road, curb area, alley, park, playground or other public ground, public space or public building, place of amusement or eating place, vacant lot, or unsupervised place between the hours of 10:00 pm on any day and sunrise of the immediately following day." In 1967 a low-budget movie, *Riot on Sunset Strip,* was released into theaters, its plot revolving around the on-off riots that took place on the Strip between 1966 and 1970. It depicted what was going on there accurately, and who wouldn't have wanted to be a part of that?

High school was a dark period for me—I never felt like I fit in, and the other kids seemed alien to me, because, in fact, they were—but I got through. In those days people threw around the words *identity crisis* about teenagers, and some still do. A bizarre phrase, and one I used to spend hours thinking about. I thought that the older generation was framing the idea of growing up in such a fearful way. That term instills so much anxiety and dread around becoming who you actually are and who you'll be someday. Why is *Who am I?* considered a crisis? I had no crisis. My identity was straightforward: I had made art since I was five years old, and aside from dance, art was the only thing that interested me. If that didn't fit into the conventions of the day, who cared?

In the late sixties Alan Watts and other thinkers were introducing America to ideas from Eastern philosophy and Buddhism. The idea of banishing the ego was in play, in contrast to Western thought, which was all about the three-act Hollywood structure of beginning, middle, end. I was much more interested in the nontraditional narrative flow, the kind embodied by French New Wave cinema. That, combined with taking acid and smoking pot, set me off in a new direction of thinking. From that point on, I would never feel sure, or comfortable, about making conclusions or bold, definite statements about anything. Questioning things fit in with "becoming," which in turn brought me closer to living in the present and farther away from the idea that you're done, ready, formed, or cooked at some preset age like your early twenties. Maybe that's why the HBO series *Girls* resonates with so many people. It shows that stage in life when older people assume that just because you've graduated college you know who you are, or what you're doing, and in fact most people don't. I did know this much: I couldn't find out who I really was until I'd left L.A. and my family. Until that day arrived, I was just waiting, suspended. Families are like little villages. You know where everything is, you know how everything works, your identity is fixed, and you can't really leave, or *connect* with anything or anybody outside, until you're physically no longer there.

Boys helped kill the time. They had always liked me, though I was never sure if I liked any of them back. In their approach they all used the California clichés of the moment. "You're so *negative,* Kim," one would say, followed by an invitation to go out with him. "You have to be more *open,*" another said, while another was into positive thinking, and still another wanted me to chant with him. One boy wrote me a dream-drenched poem about how I'd be happiest dancing around freely, alone, in a jungle. I was seventeen years old, a little wild and rebellious, though not a fraction as bad as Keller, and it was the late sixties in Southern California. Hypervigilance was my mode.

In junior high school I dated a Mexican boy a couple of years my senior. *Be careful,* my mother used to say. *Where are you guys going?* She was afraid the two of us would get harassed on account of the fact we were a "mixed couple." At the time my mother worked for the ACLU, which always made me roll my eyes. There were other boyfriends in between, none of them serious. Then I met Danny Elfman.

Today Danny is a musician and film composer known for a lot of things—being the lead singer and songwriter for Oingo Boingo, scoring most of Tim Burton's movies, even writing the theme song for *The Simpsons*—but in those days he was more into film and surrealism than anything else. Danny seemed to materialize one day at our high school. He was a grade ahead of me, charismatic and politically attuned, a boy who at least gave the impression he had a road map going forward. It was the fall of 1969 and a volatile time in the culture, to say the least. Our school was a microcosm of the world. There were demonstrations and teachers' strikes. Lorna Luft, one of Judy Garland's two daughters, was a student there, at one point bringing in Sid Caesar to direct a play. Later some people came to believe an actual cult had infiltrated the school, even though by then it was hard to tell the difference.

I was undergoing my own mini-mutiny, cutting school, wanting to be anywhere but in a classroom. Danny took it upon himself to launch a demonstration, leading the students in a march around the school to show our solidarity with the teachers. Around that time he and I started officially going out. It was the first time I felt like I'd met a peer, and Danny was the first boy I felt I could really talk to, who shared my viewpoints as well as the itch to go against the grain.

Danny and I went camping a lot. We spent time in Sequoia and Yosemite, sleeping in sleeping bags without a tent over us, and Danny shot a short film filled with aching teenage significance: My hand was framed against a patch of snow, with blood in it, which Danny added afterward by painting the film cells red—but that's love, maybe, when you're in high school.

For the next few years Danny and I were on again, off again—but we couldn't seem to stay out of each other's lives. We broke up when Danny graduated and went to Africa with a friend. Or so I thought. While Danny was overseas, he and I didn't communicate—there seemed to be an unspoken competition over which one of us, him or me, cared less about our relationship—so I went on with my life.

My bedroom at home had a door that opened up into the backyard. One night, another boy was over when Danny—whom I hadn't seen since he took off for Africa—knocked at the door. I had to come out and tell him I had a guest. Danny was very upset. Later he told me with great seriousness that this incident had humiliated him, and was responsible for turning him into, in his words, a complete "asshole." Of course things between us weren't over, and when we briefly got back together later on, it was Danny's turn to leave me. Still, Danny opened up to me in a way he hadn't to anyone before—one of the benefits, maybe, to meeting people before they're fully formed—and he always encouraged me in my art.

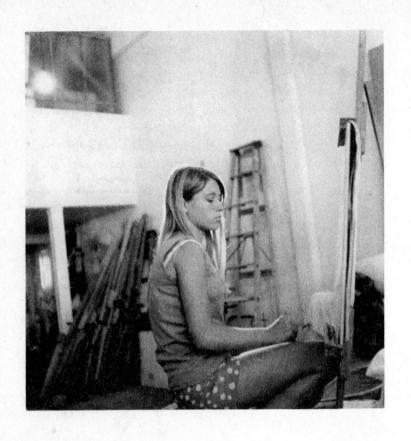

10

MICHAEL BYRON, an aspiring musician I had dated before Danny, lived close to school, and during senior year my friends and I would sneak out and climb over the tall wire fencing to get to his house, where we would get stoned, listen to Miles Davis's *Bitches Brew,* and make out. I had another good friend, Willie Winant, whose older brother later created the TV show *My So-Called Life,* which was coincidentally filmed at my high school. Willie was a drummer, and none of the other girls in our class wanted much to do with him—he was bighearted but not especially attuned to his body. I used to choreograph dance pieces in our free-form modern dance class, with Willie always at the center of the piece. To me it was a challenge to show the other girls, and my teacher, who knew nothing about dance, that body type didn't matter.

Outside of school I took classes at a Martha Graham studio from an eccentric French woman, but my mother didn't want me to pursue dance—it was too showbiz for her. The dance teacher at my high school also taught gym, and to me those classes were the only truly creative classes I had. What was the most outrageous thing you could do and still call it a "dance" while not getting kicked out of school? I remember choreographing one performance to Frank Zappa's song "Dog Breath, in the Year of the Plague" from the album *Uncle Meat*. Willie mimed going to the bathroom, while my fellow dancers and I were the toilet mechanisms, tossing toilet paper out into the audience. A year later, Matthew Bright, who went on to direct the infamous Reese Witherspoon film *Freeway*, bragged that during his own dance performance he'd tossed chicken livers out into the audience.

My best friend at the time was a girl named Marge. Marge and I would sneak out at night and meet each other halfway between our two houses. One night, a few of us stole some big ice blocks out of the school ice machine and snuck onto the Bel Air golf course at two A.M. We laid towels over the ice and slid down the dark slopes. Another time we drove to Beverly Hills and swiped flowers from people's front lawns. It was a harmless thrill, we reasoned, because after all, Beverly Hills was too perfect in the first place.

Marge also liked to drag me to peace demonstrations and love-ins. As the oldest of three kids, and a take-charge person, she was far tougher and more grown-up than I was. On the surreal, shocking night Bobby Kennedy was shot, Marge had gone to the Ambassador Hotel to see him speak. One moment she was talking about going over there, and two hours later RFK was dead—in L.A., too, that safe and beautiful place of movie-lot landscaping, shiny new cars, and tanned good-looking people, a city where thanks to the curfew laws no one was allowed to so much as loiter.

I graduated high school as a midterm grad. I was glad it was over, and as a "young" high school grad who had just turned seventeen, I decided to take a year off before starting Santa Monica College. My parents wouldn't pay for me to go to CalArts, but I was bullheaded and had no interest in going anyplace else. Eventually I got bored waitressing and doing other menial jobs, and I moved in with a friend, Kathy Walters, a Santa Monica College student. If memory serves, the tuition at Santa Monica College was $30 a semester. Of course this was before Ronald Reagan wrecked the entire California school system, from the community colleges up to the state university level, with his brilliant ideas about freezing property taxes, thereby leaving no money for education. Next he would go after the whole country.

The fall after high school, I was going out with a quiet, introverted, gentle guy named Rick, who was in his early twenties. Rick lived in Westwood Village, which during the early seventies was the only place that had any kind of a scene, a hive for creativity. Rick introduced me to another resident of Westwood Village, his friend Larry Gagosian.

Larry was hanging out in Westwood, dealing art books in the street. Entrepreneurs always exhibit signs early on of who they'll become, I guess. Larry had rented an outdoor space, which he subleased to other vendors, in order to create a sort of mini-plaza. There he sold schlocky, mass-produced prints of works by contemporary artists—the kind that appeal to teenage girls or women in their twenties who think of themselves as dreamy romantics—in cheap, ugly metal frames. Marge and I were looking to make money—I was trying to be as financially independent as possible, having watched Keller rely on my parents for years, and being unemployed, and stressing them out, which I didn't want to add to—so we started working for him.

Frame after frame—I must have assembled thousands of those things, and the dimensions twenty-four by thirty-six inches are still carved in my brain. It would have been straight-ahead, decent grunt work if Larry had been a good boss, but he wasn't. He was mean, yelling at us all the time for messing up, being too slow, just plain *being*. He was erratic, and the last person on the planet I would have ever thought would later become the world's most powerful art dealer. Larry had a bull terrier named Muffin that he was always trying to get rid of, and he once told me that whenever a woman slept over at his place, Muffin would get jealous, and go under the bed and tear up the woman's clothes with her fangs.

Eventually I quit working for Larry—I just couldn't take it any longer—but our paths would keep mixing up again and again.

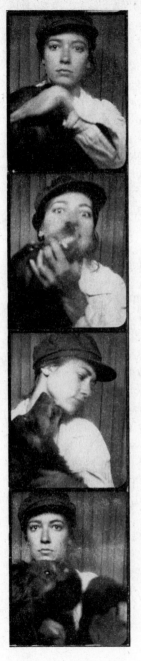

11

SOMETIMES I THINK we know on some level the person we're going to be in our life, that if we pay attention, we can piece out that information. I find it strange when people *don't* know what they want to do in life. Because even when I was a young kid pushing around clay objects at the UCLA Lab School, I knew I wanted to be an artist. Nothing else mattered. I cringe when I recall Andrea Fraser, the performance artist and one of the most fearless artists I know, using that line in one of her performances to critique art institutions and artist myths: "The exact words are, 'I wanted to be an artist since I was five.'" Because that was my line.

My mother always thought I'd become a graphic artist someday, even though I never showed any interest in graphic design (I was a painter/sculptor—all sloppy work, no graphics in sight). Then again she sometimes also told her friends that I'd end up as an interpreter for the United Nations—"She's so good with people," she would tell them, though it still confuses me why she'd say something like that about someone so obviously shy and uncommunicative. Eventually both my parents, especially my dad, supported the idea of my pursuing a creative life. Keller's breakdown might have eroded their expectations, setting the bar that much lower: *Kim can do anything she wants as long as she doesn't go crazy.*

I remember a friend's older brother interrogating me when I was a teenager: *An artist? How are you going to be an artist? What are you going to do if you don't make it as an artist? What if you fail? Do you have a backup plan?* It never occurred to me I would fail. "Your art is very personal," Danny said to me once. "So it'll be popular." *Personal* is something I still equate with Sunday painters. I still carry around with me a battle between working conceptually—art based on some overriding idea—and my pure carnal sensory love of materials.

In 1972, I started attending Santa Monica College. By this point, Rick, my then boyfriend, had started suffering from seizures. At eighteen I felt too young to be living with the constant fear of someone having a seizure and me sitting there helplessly, not knowing what to do. That, and my leaving for college, contributed to our breakup.

I became involved, again, with Danny and I moved to Venice with a couple of friends. Postmodern architecture was the thing then, and parts of Venice were all funky wood construction, with oddball angles and unexpected windows of wood and corrugated sheet metal intertwined alongside the little indigenous cottages intended for weekend use by Hollywood actors and drifters. In the midseventies Venice was also a rough, scary place. One street would be fine but a block away was a potential drug war zone. I lived on one of the rotten streets. On the day we were unpacking stuff from my '68 VW Bug, a deranged-looking guy approached us holding a long butcher knife. His movements were so slow and balletic he could only have been high, and we circled around him before tearing into the house and locking the door. Another night when I wasn't home, someone drove down the street firing gunshots into all the houses on our side of the street.

Guillermo, my landlord, was an Argentinian who was also a roadie for Crosby, Stills, Nash & Young. He lived next door, which meant there was always a party atmosphere. At the time I was friends with a guy named Richie O'Connell and Richie's good friend Bruce Berry, who was somehow related to Jan Berry of the sixties rock duo Jan and Dean. Whenever Guillermo and Bruce came home from touring, a bunch of us would go carousing until dawn. One night, we went to Jan's house high in the hills, a cheesy contemporary glass box on a tacky hilltop in a would-be neighborhood, surrounded by nothing. Cocaine was prevalent, heroin more under-the-table, but I wasn't into that stuff. I do remember being there one morning at around eight A.M. watching a topless girl float through the living room playing a violin.

Later Bruce started working just for David Crosby. When he told everybody he knew that someone had jacked David's car and stolen his Stratocaster, we all knew it was Bruce and that he had sold David's guitar to get heroin. In the early nineties, when Sonic Youth went on tour with Neil Young, I realized that Neil's song "Tonight's the Night," about a roadie who had overdosed, was written for that same Bruce Berry. He had died in 1973.

That would all come later. When I lived in Venice, Richard, Bruce, and I would stay up all night driving around the Hollywood Hills, dropping in at the houses of unlikely people, like Hal Blaine, the famous studio drummer who'd worked with Elvis, the Beach Boys, and Steely Dan. Another night a bunch of friends and I went up to Arthur Janov's house. Janov was the creator of the primal scream, a therapy technique that was supposed to return you to your birth trauma experience and release you by encouraging screaming and other vocal disinhibitions. The Janovs lived in one of those houses way up high on Mulholland

Drive. The place wasn't as creepy as the famous *Body Double* house but it was close—a coldly beautiful, empty, modern house with a huge wraparound-window view of downtown L.A. I didn't know their daughter, Ellen, well; she was a friend of a friend. She was deeply troubled, and also a junkie, though I wasn't aware of that at the time. Rumor had it she hung out with the Rolling Stones, who were friends of her parents. As the night went on, all my friends vanished into one or another of the cold rooms, and I remember waiting there by myself until the next morning, until they were all ready to leave. A few months later, Ellen died in a house fire.

It is said that Joni Mitchell's guitar playing on *Song to a Seagull* made Jimmy Page cry. I wonder if like so many of those English musicians who grew up in the fog and the bleakness, Jimmy Page was in love with California and the idea of the canyons, if not the canyons themselves. Even if I had to leave L.A. to become myself, I loved the mystique of the canyons, too, and all they represented. By the mid-1970s the California aesthetic was definitely being exported, and I would have to take it with me.

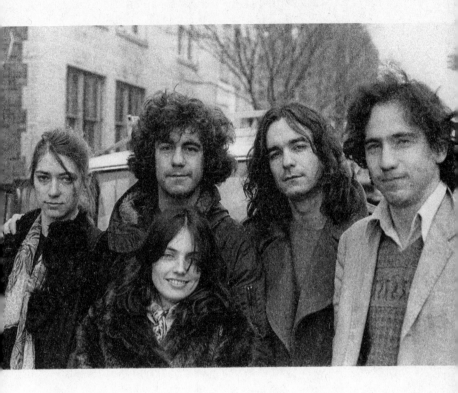

12

AFTER TWO YEARS at Santa Monica College, I transferred to York University in Toronto. Willie Winant, my friend from high school and dance class, was planning to study percussion there and told me about the place. York had an interdisciplinary program, and I fantasized I could study dance there as well as visual art. Money was a big factor, too. I learned that Canadian colleges cost next to nothing, so that made York much more appealing, as I was still trying to rely as little as possible on my parents, even though they footed the bill.

We drove together in tandem, me following Willie cross-country in my VW Bug. When we got to Saint Louis, suddenly the world turned

brown. The landscape became ugly, hard to face, the buildings miniature and lopped off, like pieces in some sad board game. I wasn't used to
brown, or shadows even—Southern California light transformed even
the scraggly parts and ruined colors of the city into toothy, opal grays—
and I began to feel that I'd made a giant mistake leaving California.

Toronto was starkly different from Los Angeles too—a shiny, gleaming
downtown area, mixed with row-house architecture that felt ordinary and
cheerless. I moved into a big good-looking Victorian house with the sister
of a high school friend and two of her friends, all of them younger, all of
them dancers. You'd think it would have been a match, but they were all
freshmen, and hard to relate to, and I didn't like being in a roommate
situation where I was obliged to contribute money to the collective food
budget or take my turn going to the supermarket, especially if I wasn't
planning on being there most of the time. Neither was the York arts program as interdisciplinary as I thought it would be, which meant I was
pretty much on my own, doing art in a small room. Willie and I soon
became friends with the other American grad students at York, as well as
with two Chilean boys who were cousins. It wasn't until recently when I
reconnected with one of them that I realized the boys were at some point
members of a seventies Chilean cult prog-rock band called the Blops,
who'd emigrated to the U.S. to escape Chile's dictatorship.

My media class at York was taught by the Fluxus filmmaker George
Manupelli. George was by far the most interesting teacher in the college, a heavy drinker with a much younger girlfriend who was a former
student. Fluxus explored art as a process, using the viewer, or the audience, to complete the work. It asked, *What can art be?*

For a project, a group of my friends and I decided to start a band. We
called it Below the Belt, and the lineup was me, a Canadian girl named
Rae, Willie on regular drums (though he was a percussionist, Willie
wasn't used to a conventional drum set and would just end a song when
he got tired), and the two Chilean boys, Felipe on guitar and Juan Pablo
on bass. Rae, a raven-haired beauty, and I sang and played tambourine.
In their tight, satin green trousers, the two Chilean boys were much

more Rolling Stones–like in their appearance and approach than the rest of us, who were far more casual about the whole thing.

Our second gig was at the Ann Arbor Film Festival. Before the show, we all got drunk. That night Willie wore a dress and a hat, and before the show started, he blew fire across the stage, a style and a trick he'd developed during his short stint with the Mystic Knights of the Oingo Boingo with Danny Elfman. Willie liked shocking people, and he summoned us onstage by asking "the spics and cunts to come on out and play." We were, I remember, an explosive mess, pure mayhem and caterwauling. We danced, tossed our tambourines onto the ground, and let everything fall apart into a garage noise jam. It didn't take management long to pull the plug. We played only two or three times, mostly for fun, but I knew this band wasn't going anywhere. Years later, my lifelong friend, the artist Mike Kelley—who always derived immense pleasure from the unacceptable—told me he was in the audience that night, and that our performance had inspired him to go home and start a "noise garage band." In retrospect, I realize that the band Mike started became Destroy All Monsters and grew to include ex-members of the Stooges. Until Mike told me this, I had no idea what genre Below the Belt even was, if any. But I did know one thing: I liked performing.

York University had just rolled out a brand-new music department—there were always small concerts going on, including performances of works by the resident composers. I saw lots of great contemporary music while I was there, from the Art Ensemble of Chicago to the premiere of John Cage and David Tudor's bicentennial *Rainforest* piece, though mostly I was bored, making minimalist, gooey, unstretched paintings, with no instructor. Rather than write a paper for my film class, I decided to make a silent surrealist film about Patty Hearst, who'd just been let go by the Symbionese Liberation Army. With her shoulder-length black hair, my fellow bandmate Rae made a picture-perfect Patty. Felipe, who was also a filmmaker, shot and helped me edit the movie. George Manupelli lent me a sixteen-millimeter camera and film. I was immersed in art, but unformed and trying anything and everything.

But I was homesick, too, less and less happy as the bleak Toronto winter moved in. Without the benefit of California sunshine, my hair grew darker and darker, and I had no idea how to dress for the cold. When the school year ended, I drove home to California, and instead of making plans to return to York, I began attending Otis Art Institute in downtown L.A. At $600 a semester, Otis was undistinguished but cheap. I lived here and there: Culver City, Silver Lake, Venice again. To pay my bills, I found work in a little Indian restaurant called Dhaba, which served home-cooked, endlessly simmered Indian food. My parents weren't all that happy—they wanted me to finish what I'd started at York—but Otis changed my life.

For one thing, I became very close to John Knight, a conceptual artist with an architectural background who'd come to Otis as an artist in residence and taught a seminar. I was twenty-four, he was thirty-one. John was captivating, the first real mentor I'd ever had. I'd never met anyone like him, and the landscape of L.A. was our playground for any kind of mutual intellectual discussion. John was born and raised in L.A., and his art practice centered on whatever political and social forces were inherent in the design, architecture, history, and function of the visible world, while simultaneously taking in a viewer's relation to the art or the spectacle in question. His career has recently become more visible and influential.

Then, though, he was an intellectual light, and a minor renegade, having been kicked out of Otis in his day for cutting the school's hedges as part of a sculpture. He and I spent hours driving around L.A., looking at assorted local oddities and suburban inventions, drive-throughs and outlying tract-house developments with their small deadening model homes. He showed me neighborhoods on the Eastside I'd never seen before. As usual, everywhere and everything in L.A. was either a blunt, bizarre juxtaposition—an old quaint one-story ranch house squeezed in beside a mammoth McMansion—or a potential picnic destination, whether it was the Huntington gardens or a green grass patch fronting some new development. No matter where I go in my life, visually L.A. will always be my favorite place on earth.

John Knight taught me that anything—a car, a house, a lawn—could be seen and talked about in aesthetic terms. He introduced me to conceptual art, showed me how all art derives from an idea. Every week, his class met at a different place, typically one of his students' houses or apartments. We would discuss in detail whatever came up or whatever happened to be around—what kind of font a typewriter used, for example. Was it Helvetica, or Futura, or a less predictable, flouncier typeface? This may sound trivial, but it taught us that detail mattered—in John's own work, as in most conceptual art, detail practically *becomes* the work—but big things mattered too. It was John, after all, who told me I had enough credits to petition my way out of Otis, which turned out to be surprisingly easy to do. But before that happened, Dan Graham came along.

13

IN 2009, THURSTON and I were asked to appear at SculptureCenter in Long Island City, which was honoring Dan Graham as part of their annual fund-raising gala. Knowing how obsessed Dan is with astrology, I asked a friend who does charts professionally to interpret his chart for us. He did, and we incorporated snippets in our introduction—Capricorn rising, Aries sun, ruled by Mars in Gemini conjunct Jupiter in the Sixth House, and so on—before Dan finally came onstage. We also played his favorite song by the Fall, "Repetition," lead singer Mark E. Smith being one of Dan's longstanding Marxist punk heroes.

Dan was a peer of John Knight's, though slightly older. John had spoken a lot about Dan's work in class, enough for me to know that Dan was a hero underdog of the contemporary art world. When Dan spoke at CalArts that spring, I followed John's advice and went to see him, not knowing all the roles he would play in the next part of my life.

Dan was an original. In 1964, he'd launched the first conceptual art show in New York in the John Daniels Gallery, an exhibition space he opened with a few friends. At the time he spoke at CalArts, his best-known work was *Homes for America,* a series of photos of New Jersey tract housing that *Arts* magazine published in 1966. The development, where Dan had moved when he was three, was one of America's first-ever tract housing developments. Critics referred to Dan's work as the first-ever "minimalist photos." Those little houses were sad and similar, bland, box-cut, and haunting. They reminded me of a family of low-to-the-ground arrowheads. Dan later described *Homes for America* as a "fake think-piece."

Dan was, and still is, a volatile, wild thinker and communicator, a self-educated social anthropologist who spent his teenage years poring through the works of Margaret Mead, Jean-Paul Sartre, and Wilhelm Reich. Reading an essay Dan once wrote for *Fusion* magazine about Dean Martin, where he compared Dean Martin with his cigarette and cocktail glass to Brecht and Godard, and called Martin's persona both a "myth" and a "scaffold," made me realize anyone and anything could be made interesting.

Dan got a huge kick out of astrology's dime-store, lowbrow, circus-show vibe, a six-thousand-year-old art and science of observation doomed to end up in the twenty-first century on the slippery back pages of women's magazines. Astrology wasn't remotely intellectual, and though Dan never studied the planets in depth, he got pleasure out of placing a great trashed knowledge into a formal dialogue. Peppering his conversation with zodiacal references was Dan's way of being a brat, a punk. It gave him shortcuts to understanding people, helped him elbow up close to them. Some of Dan's later work, which explored the relationship of the artist to the audience as a mirror, matched uncannily what he told me was his own astrological makeup, how he absorbed the qualities of whoever he was talking to at the time.

I was in the audience when Dan showed up to lecture at CalArts. I found him unforgettable. With his head cocked to one side, his fingers winding around sickles of his own hair, Dan spoke quickly and haltingly, lobbing random, curvy perceptions into the audience left and right. My dad's sociology background probably made Dan's work all the more appealing to me, but I also knew I'd never been in the presence of someone so brilliant.

Among the subjects Dan talked about during this lecture were the origins of punk rock. Who started it? Was it Malcolm McLaren or someone else? Mike Kelley, who was also there that night, flipped up his hand and began arguing the point. As a Detroit native, Mike believed that Iggy Pop and the Stooges were the first-ever punk rockers, and that Detroit was ground zero for punk music. Dan acknowledged that point, and also talked about how McLaren had gone to New York and witnessed Richard Hell and Television at CBGB with their torn attire and safety pins and took it back to England, mixing it with Situationism. Mike and Dan were essentially in agreement but nitpicking over details. Their back-and-forth grew more intense, Dan's voice getting higher and louder, and Mike's growing agitated. It's a conversation I've witnessed since many times. What was most clear about that day and that exchange was how passionate Dan and Mike both were about music and how, if given the choice, they'd both much rather talk about rock and roll than about art.

When the lecture ended, I introduced myself to Dan, and also to Mike. A few months later, Mike and I became friends and then briefly romantically involved. Dan came back out to L.A., and I remember taking him to a community music event in a park in Orange County. Every weekend the park hosted a different music theme. That week's theme was punk, and specifically Black Flag. Families dotted the hyper-green grass, spread out on blankets and plastic chairs with their kids.

At the time, the lead singer for Black Flag was a guy named Keith

Morris. I liked Keith. Unlike other punks of that era, he avoided dressing in stylized punk fashion. In his ratty camo jacket, he looked more like a dream-haunted military vet. When Black Flag started playing, a few of the little kids in the audience started throwing bottles at the stage. The emcee finally came onstage to warn the audience that if it didn't simmer down, he'd end the show right there. In response, everyone began applauding. Before Orange County became known as the cooler-sounding O.C., it was just known as conservative.

For years afterward, Dan talked about that Black Flag concert. Southern California was a never-ending source of amusement for him: its pockets of sun-struck conservatism; the bizarre good manners and politeness, as if everyday life had been reduced to a series of curves, blunted, similar, unchanging.

It was the beginning of two of the most important relationships in my life. Mike's influence on me, if there is one, was subtle, as he and I were more like peers. I got a lot of pleasure out of seeing another artist making work that looked nothing at all like conceptual art, that was unconventional, that mixed together high and low. Through Mike I also met some important people in my life, like Tony Oursler, the multimedia and video installation artist, who is both a generous person and an imaginative genius, and who always supported whatever I was doing. Tony later helped me shoot and edit a mini-documentary I wanted to make about the club Danceteria and also shot an incredible video for the Sonic Youth song "Tunic." I also collaborated with Tony and the film director Phil Morrison on a project called *Perfect Partner,* a multimedia extravaganza I concocted and performed more than a half dozen times in Europe and once in the U.S. I had written a script based on car ad copy that was intended to be a takeoff on Nouvelle Vague. Michael Pitt acted in it. My improv quartet performed a live, roughly scripted soundtrack between two screens, one displaying backgrounds that Tony had filmed, and the other, front and center and semitransparent, showing the action and the actors that Phil had shot. The effect was like a giant 3-D Tony Oursler piece. Tony and I still collaborate on projects and remain friends.

Dan's influence was stranger, harder to define. In a concrete way, Dan turned me on to any and all No Wave bands that were playing in downtown New York on any given night, and I also loved the poppy-but-deep way he wrote about or dramatized psychological or sociological issues, like the idea of viewing art as a kind of voyeurism. Dan's passion for music was as strong as his interest in art, and rock and roll often found its way into his subject matter. Once Dan told me he wished he could make art that was like a Kinks song. (A lot of artists listen to music while they work, and many think, *Why can't I make art that looks as intense as the sounds I'm hearing?* I don't have an answer.)

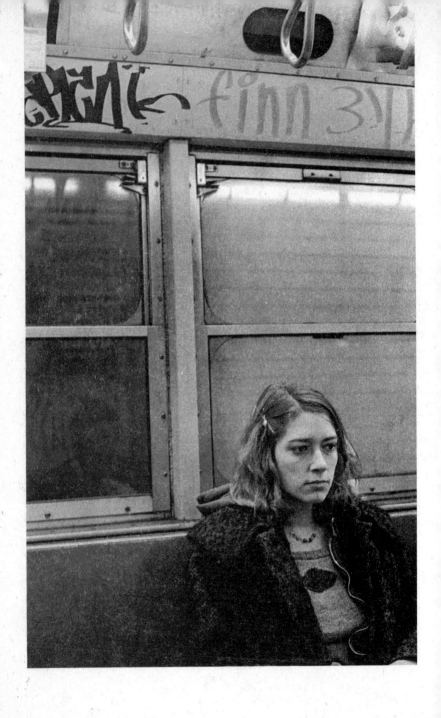

14

DRIVING DOWN the West Side Highway, I still get the same thrill I did when I first drove over the bridge into Manhattan in 1980. I don't think I'll ever lose that feeling. Today the Henry Hudson Parkway is buffed, a tarred straightaway for little low-slung cars and Range Rovers with Connecticut and Westchester plates. Across the river, New Jersey construction stabs up above the river, shoulder blades pressing back hard against the Palisades. When I first drove down the Hudson Parkway it was bumpy and nerve-wracking, as if your car were being shot from a pinball machine down a slope into some rough forest. It was all unknown and possibility.

In 1980 New York was near bankruptcy, with garbage strikes every month, it seemed, and a crumbling, weedy infrastructure. These days, it gleams and towers in ways most people I know hate and can't understand. Hugging the parkway in the West Sixties and Seventies is an ugly sheet of Trump buildings, a monument to urban corruption, soft money, and natives who should have taken to the streets saying nothing. Farther down the island, joggers, baby strollers, and blue and red bikes flow alongside a fluted, flower-filled river walkway alongside once-scary, now-forgotten docks, where gay men once met up in the dark for dates, hookups, and hookers in mink coats and high boots worked the nights until sunrise and breakfast.

The Westway, the old strip club on Clarkson Street, is still there, but today it's owned by a hipster restaurant entrepreneur who caters to the ironic cultural lifestylers, more fashion world than art, people who are "cool" because they live in New York. The little park with the basketball court is still on the corner of Spring and Thompson, an old slate-gray bookmark from an era otherwise written over by branded shops and shoppers from West Broadway down to Tribeca. Any place I depended on once to be deserted now teems with bodies and long black cars and faraway accents all day, all night.

When I first came to New York, the gallery building at 420 West Broadway housing both Leo Castelli and Mary Boone was pretty much all there was for big, established downtown galleries. The Dia Art Foundation stood across the street, and farther down you could find extremely raw but formal spaces that once housed "eternally" minimalist art like Walter De Maria's "The Broken Kilometer." Today Soho has been taken over by one echo-effect mall-friendly chain store after another: American Apparel, the Gap, Forever 21, H&M. No one else can afford the rents, I guess. Dave's Luncheonette, the twenty-four-hour joint on Broadway and Canal, one stop after the Mudd Club, is long gone. Canal Jean, whose $5 bins fronting the sidewalk once dressed everyone I knew in bright-colored jeans and black tops, is another institution worn down and chased out. The Italian part of Little Italy is another seedy ghost. Its men's clubs, empty except for espresso machines and ambiguous back-room goings-on, have disappeared. Maybe the methadone clinic on Spring Street where Sid Vicious used to go is still there. Otherwise, nothing's left but the big Catholic church on Church Street, though today it's being squeezed hard by boutiques and little specialty restaurants.

Overtaking Little Italy and the once mostly Jewish Lower East Side is Chinatown, forever edging outward, a mini-universe of fashionable, carefully dressed Asian women and storefronts resembling canal-side art installations. At night no one, me included, ever felt safe walking between Grand and Houston Streets anywhere east of the Bowery. For that matter, in Alphabet City no block east of Second Avenue to the river was safe—too many drug dealers. Today it's all students, a melee of cheekbones and stubble and tight jeans. The scary park between Forsyth and Chrystie Streets has been reclaimed to the point where today kids actually play games there.

These days, when I'm in New York, I wonder, *What's this place all about, really?* The answer is consumption and moneymaking. Wall Street drives the whole country, with the fashion industry as the icing. Everything people call *fabulous* or *amazing* lasts for about ten minutes before the culture moves on to the next thing. Creative ideas and personal ambition are no longer mutually exclusive. A friend recently described the work of an artist we both know as "corporate," and it wasn't a compliment. The Museum of Modern Art is like a giant midtown gift store.

New York City today is a city on steroids. It now feels more like a cartoon than anything real. But New York has never been ideal, and people have always complained sourly about the changing face of the city, the loss of authenticity.

When you study contemporary art in Los Angeles, New York is continuously touted as the only possible place to live and do art. It was always in my frame of vision as a possibility. I was still interested in dance, even taking ballet while I was in art school. I recall reading about the loose collection of New York City–based dancers who collaborated with filmmakers and composers to perform avant-garde pieces at the Judson

Memorial Church in Greenwich Village. I was especially taken by the idea of Yvonne Rainer's "No Manifesto." Yvonne rebuffed all technique, all glamour, all theater in her dance. She focused instead on the amazing, beautiful ordinariness of bodies in movement. The idea that a film could be dance blew my mind.

Everything seemed to be happening in New York, and I set my sights there once I was deemed a graduate of Otis. It wouldn't be my first trip there. A few months earlier I'd taken the bus east on a reconnaissance mission, partly to check out the city, partly to escape a relationship with an older artist that I knew was bad for me. I knew that if I stayed in that relationship no one would ever take me seriously or treat me as anything other than an older guy's bright young female protégée. I spent six months in New York before taking the bus back to L.A. to save up money to fund a possible future there.

Before I could leave I was involved in a car accident. It happened the same day Keller had his first psychotic episode after his graduation from Berkeley. I was sitting in a driveway in heavy Southern California traffic in my old VW Bug, waiting to turn onto Robertson Boulevard in Culver City, when a car driving down the street bashed into a second car. *I'm the witness,* I told myself, and just then that same car swerved up onto the sidewalk, hitting my VW and folding it up against a wall. My injuries weren't serious—my back was sprained, I got a few stitches, and the incident was turned over to the insurance companies—but a year later the money I got from that accident would make life in New York possible.

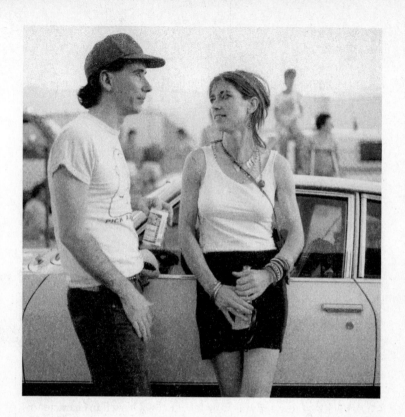

15

WRITING ABOUT NEW YORK is hard. Not because memories intersect and overlap, because of course they do. Not because incidents and times mix with others, because that happens too. Not because I didn't fall in love with New York, because even though I was lonely and poor, no place had ever made me feel more at home. It is because knowing what I know now, it's hard to write about a love story with a broken heart.

I drove east with Mike Kelley. Mike had decided to accompany me cross-country, and maybe peel off and visit some friends. Late at night, exhausted and borderline delirious, we detoured into New Orleans, a city that held out so many mythical, clichéd promises of good times that Mike kept describing it to me as a haven for pleasure.

Every single hotel in New Orleans was booked, which is how Mike and I ended up staying in some flophouse in a sleazy business area, about as far from the thrill and romance of the French Quarter as anyone can get. We woke up the next morning to images of the New Orleans city sidewalk snaking and swirling around the walls of our crappy room. Upside-down secretaries and businesspeople flared around us like an alphabet on fire. It seemed someone had painted over the room window with black paint, leaving only a tiny dot in the center, turning the entire room into an oversized pinhole camera—to my mind, a near-perfect art installation. Mike and I may have been captive in a dank room in a rundown hotel, but the images on all four walls were crisp, fresh, almost like a revelation. It was a moment whose weird sorcery was impossible to explain to anyone, but Mike and I lay there for a long time, staring and giggling at it.

A few days later, we arrived in New York. We stayed at Cindy Sherman's place down on Fulton Street. It was the first time I'd ever seen Cindy's work—those early eight-by-ten photos of herself in character on her wall. Mike then drove back home to L.A., and I was officially on my own. I had no money to speak of, which meant I couldn't even begin looking for a long-term living situation, so for the first few months I stayed with assorted friends and loose acquaintances. I spent two weeks on Fulton Street with a good friend's younger sister, Elena, who graciously let me stay in her big, beautiful space with its wraparound windows and big loft bed. Elena, who worked in fabric restoration at the Metropolitan Museum, was a sweet, extremely quiet girl who'd somehow managed to maintain her bohemian Mexican-influenced Southern California style of shawls and moccasins even in the harsh wind tunnels of downtown.

New York was in crumbling shape in late 1979 and 1980. During the day, Wall Street bustled with secretaries and other business types, but at night it turned into a postapocalyptic hell, with rats, wrappers, and cans interspersed every few feet with piles of stinking trash, thanks to what felt like a continuous garbage strike. Wherever I walked I kept a good distance from the sides of buildings, fearing rats might come out and attack me. Mysterious graffiti had taken over the doors, garages, and buildings of Soho, with a single word, *SAMO*, in big block letters everywhere you looked. It turned out later that *SAMO* was the pseudonym of two graffiti artists, Jean-Michel Basquiat and his friend Al Diaz. Jean-Michel was working at the time for the Unique Clothing Warehouse at 718 Broadway. When he and Diaz had a falling-out in the late seventies, Basquiat left his last entry, SAMO IS DEAD, scrawled here and there across the city landscape.

It was all incredibly stimulating. Since I'd lived in Hong Kong, downtown New York, and especially Chinatown, felt familiar. I used to wander through Chinatown with a pork bun in one hand, the smell and the uproar of the city wafting around me, everything new to my senses but familiar, too.

Tabloid newspapers screamed from every city corner—the *New York Post*, the *Daily News*, both foreign press to a girl from Southern California. Sid Vicious and his girlfriend Nancy Spungen were still dominating the headlines. Nancy had been found stabbed in the bathroom of the Chelsea Hotel on Twenty-Third Street. Sid claimed he didn't know what happened but was arrested anyway, and later released on bail. Four months later he OD'd. The story was dramatic and pulpy, with new tidbits squeezed out every morning and blood-lit from the siren covers of those rags. And then it was over, gone, the newest, latest things taking its place—MOB BOSS HIT, MONEY LAUNDERING SCHEME EXPOSED, WOMAN PUSHED ONTO TRAIN TRACKS, CAR CRASH KILLS BEAUTIFUL VIOLINIST.

In contrast to always-new L.A., where everything had its place, New York was a jumble, all colors, shapes, angles, altitudes. The city seemed to care less about money, at least the showing-it-off side, than L.A., where the symbols of wealth surrounded you at all times: a BMW to your right, a Porsche hanging a left, a tall driveway gate, shrubbery concealing someone's estate. Of course this was before Soho and the art scene exploded, and New York itself turned into a kind of moated kingdom.

After leaving Elena's on Fulton Street, every couple of months I'd find a different short-term living situation. January, I'd be staying in some Chinatown walk-up with fragmenting plaster walls. February, I'd drag my stuff uptown to apartment-sit for a friend of a friend who was traveling. I crashed with Michael Byron, my old high school boyfriend, and later sublet from Peter Nadin, a friend of a friend, who lived on Chambers Street in a combination gallery and living area. Peter's space was incredibly dusty, and people who stayed there had to make their way around whatever exhibit was going on that month. The gallery had an overriding concept: every new artist who entered was asked to add something to the artwork on display. Daniel Buren wall stripes topped with someone else's. A sequence of peepholes placed into a built-in secret passage around the walls. The gallery was almost never visited, making it a kind of silent installation, unseen by anyone except Peter and whoever happened to be passing through. At the time Peter was going out with the conceptual artist Jenny Holzer, who later sublet me a corner of her loft.

It was at Jenny's that I met Mary Lemley, a party girl who owned a guitar that her boyfriend had given her. When Mary and her boyfriend broke up, inexplicably Mary passed that guitar on to me. It was nothing much—a funky, beat-up instrument with the brand name the Drifter on the neck. Still, wherever I went from that point on, the Drifter came with me. When Thurston visited my apartment on Eldridge Street for the first time, he caught sight of the Drifter leaning against the wall. "I *know* that guitar," he said.

At the time we barely knew each other. Thurston had been living in New York for four years, since 1976. He'd moved there from the suburbs of Connecticut when he was nineteen and was in a band called the Coachmen, made up of guys from the Rhode Island School of Design. "How can you possibly know that guitar?" I said.

"I know it, and I've also *played* it," Thurston said. It turned out that he too had crossed paths with Mary Lemley. Later, he would jam drumsticks inside the Drifter during the Sonic Youth song "Eric's Trip."

It was a weird, instantaneous connection between us, not that we needed another.

Though I'd never made it to the Sunset Strip as a teenager, I always had a feel for the seediness and sadness there—underneath anything, for that matter, that's new, flashy, and fresh. I had always loved Andy Warhol, the Strip-like aesthetic that showed up in his movies and in the spray-painted Factory in New York—the use of tacky, impure elements like metallic material and glitter, the lo-fi glamour of it all. Taking a tree branch, covering it over with black glitter, and painting over it to make it crusty and brittle has always reminded me of L.A. architecture. One day I caught a glimpse of Warhol himself crossing West Broadway—the blond-white wig matching the white of his face, the black-framed glasses. It amazed me how in New York celebrities felt free to roam around the city with no one ever hassling them, in contrast to L.A., where famous people hid out in hidden gated hilltop communities. New York felt so much more real. Later when people would ask Thurston or me why Sonic Youth's music was so dissonant, the answer was always the same: our music was realistic, and dynamic, because life was that way, filled with extremes. The first time we played with Richard Edson, our first drummer, Thurston cut his finger on a piece of unsheathed metal sticking out of his guitar, where the knob had fallen off. Blood began spurting all over the place, but Thurston didn't seem to mind or even notice. Richard stopped playing. "God, what are you doing?" he said. "This isn't civilized." Thurston heard him and just laughed.

In 1980s New York, there were no Starbucks, no Pret A Mangers, no Duane Reades, but every few blocks you'd run into a Chock Full O' Nuts, a chain of countertop diners that sold doughnuts, muffins, bagels, and coffee that tasted like hot black water but kept you awake and alert. One of the few things I could afford to eat was Chock Full O' Nuts corn muffins, grilled and buttered. They didn't have corn muffins on the West Coast, and the concept of a "regular" coffee, meaning one with milk, was alien to me.

With no money, I had to find some way to make a living. My first job was in a bookstore, the Marlboro, on Fifty-Seventh Street, near the old Horn & Hardart Automat. Over the years Horn & Hardart would morph into Shelly's New York steakhouse, the Motown Café, and the New York Deli, and today it's been taken over by the Hilton hotel chain. I was living downtown at a friend's, and I remember walking the fifty blocks uptown and back to eat, since I didn't want to spend what little money I had on subway tokens. I also worked as a bus girl at Elephant & Castle, a Greenwich Village restaurant that is one of the few remaining from those days, as well as the graveyard shift at an all-night restaurant on the corner of Twenty-Third and Tenth in Chelsea.

The overnight gig was by far the worst job. In 1980 Chelsea was a dead zone, empty and desolate at night and hardly better during the day. Weirdly enough, I had company at the diner: my old friend and crush from Venice Richie O'Connell—the one who had introduced me to Bruce, the CSNY roadie. Richie was a busboy at the diner and we pulled the overnights together. Richie's was the first familiar face I saw in New York but not the last.

Even after Sonic Youth's first two albums came out in the mid-1980s, I kept my day job, working at Todd's Copy Shop on Mott Street in Little Italy, an area now known as Nolita. Even with a band and a record deal, I still needed a regular source of income. Todd, the owner of the place, was an unofficial Friend to Artists, and his store was a hub for all the local creative types. If you went there, or worked there, you knew which grant everyone was applying for or what art they were making. Jim Jarmusch's girlfriend, also a filmmaker, worked there with me and would make copies of his scripts for free, and Thurston would come in and make copies of his zine, *Killer*.

It was thanks to Larry Gagosian, of all people, that I got my first job in the art world, as an assistant in an office Larry shared with Annina Nosei, inside a loft on West Broadway in Soho. Needless to say

I couldn't type, or, for that matter, do much of anything, except Larry knew I was interested in art. Annina was Italian, extremely flamboyant, and had once been married to the art dealer John Weber. Dan Graham always told me it was Annina who discovered John Chamberlain, one of my favorite artists. She was also Jean-Michel Basquiat's first dealer, infamous for having Basquiat make paintings in her Prince Street gallery basement, which some people found exploitative.

It was kind of Larry to help me out, but it also meant I had to deal with him. He would show up at the loft and try to hug me and I would kick him in the shins. "You fucking asshole," I would say, and he would just laugh. I just couldn't take Larry seriously, ever. Over the years I gave him the hardest possible time about exploiting the art world and about his complete absence of credibility as an art dealer. I never, ever dated him, but Larry has made it a point over the years to go around telling people I used to be his girlfriend, which was and is a complete untruth. I'm totally surprised by what Larry became, and just as surprised that he would go around telling people we were involved.

A couple of years ago I ran into Larry at a dinner honoring the artist Richard Prince in Los Angeles. As usual Larry's hug was unnecessarily long and hard. "You're the best employee I ever had," he said, adding, weirdly, "I've gotten *so* much out of you," and then laughed. His gallery director came up to him then and said, "Oh—you should have her play at your wedding, Larry." "Oh, are you getting married?" I asked him, and Larry said, "No."

The Annina Nosei Gallery was a small apartment loft within a West Broadway co-op, across the street from the Leo Castelli and Mary Boone galleries. For most of the downtown art world, West Broadway was New York's Boardwalk and Park Place. Annina was the public face of the new gallery, with Larry working behind the scenes as her silent partner. Since the gallery was located in a co-op building, by law it couldn't be used as a commercial space, which is why interested buyers had to make an appointment before they were buzzed up.

I was probably the least qualified person ever to hold down a part-time assistant job, but Annina herself was a portrait of inconsistency as to when, and until what time, she and Larry needed me to be there. I was a disorganized person pretending to be an organized one. I couldn't type or file. I'd deliberately never learned in order to eliminate the awful possibility of ever toiling nine to five as some guy's secretary or gal Friday. I could barely get it together enough to answer the phone. The first show at the Annina Nosei Gallery was an exhibition by the artist David Salle. It was Salle's debut as a picture maker, and it caused a sensation. Salle's paintings were reminiscent of Picabia, single-color fields with outlines of women appropriated as line drawings, taken from pages of sex magazines, and they sold out almost immediately. One day I picked up the phone to hear a middle-aged female voice asking if there were "any green Salles" left; she wanted to match Salle's art to the color scheme of her living room furniture. *It's all such a joke,* I remember thinking, *the cliché of it all.*

Years afterward, a friend of mine who sat next to David Salle at a formal dinner party reported that Salle told her I was the worst assistant he'd ever met in his life. I was so surprised he even remembered me with my Swedish clear glasses, bad clothes, and short blond-brown hair—the East Coast weather had sucked away most of the blond. I couldn't help laughing.

It was a strange time in the New York art world, the beginning of what would eventually become a commercial feeding frenzy, with the artists themselves becoming overwhelmed by their own exaggerated early success. If the 1970s art scene was about politics and justice, the 1980s had brought back painting. They had also created an investor's market. Galleries, not museums, were the go-to destinations and overnight, art buying became an investment, linked to fashion, money, and the good life. Money was in the air, but so were AIDS and the controversy of politicians quarreling over National Endowment for the Arts funding. No collector wanted to be left behind or left out. Graffiti taggers were suddenly seen as both cool and collectible, and art gallery owners were becoming almost as well-known as the artists they exhibited. Mary Boone started trolling for the hottest young downtown stars. Launched by two employees from the Castelli Gallery and Artists Space, Metro Pictures opened up a big gallery in Soho, and their first exhibition included Cindy Sherman, Robert Longo, and Richard Prince. Later, when the galleries got priced out of Soho, Metro Pictures would be the first gallery to move to Chelsea.

Women artists were making waves, too. The feminist artist Barbara Kruger, who had a background in design, layered images and texts centered around what the commercial world was telling everyone about power, sex, consumerism, and identity. By combining black-and-white magazine photos with stark white words pressed against red—*Your Body Is a Battleground* or *I Shop Therefore I Am*—Barbara faced down the viewer, and it could be uncomfortable, too, which appealed to me. Her art was all about blowtorching clichés, and so was the work of Jenny Holzer, an artist who started with posters as a format, and then later projected LEDs against giant buildings and billboards, with fiats like *You Are My Own*, or just *My Skin*. There was also Louise Lawler, who took on what was happening in the art world—the commerce, the fact that some in-demand artists now had waiting lists, the phenomenon of beauty becoming the object of a supply-and-demand market—and turned it into photographs of artwork on museum walls or inside the homes of rich collectors, and others of spectators shuffling past sculptures or installations in galleries and museums.

At some point Annina started asking my advice and opinions on art, and whether she should take on this or that new young artist. I began visiting the studios of artists I met through the gallery, people like Michael Zwack and Jim Welling. A couple of years ago, a painting by the abstract painter Brice Marden was auctioned at Sotheby's for nearly eleven million dollars, but in 1980 Larry would ask me to walk one of Marden's fragile paintings, completely unwrapped, across the street to 420 Broadway. I began to entertain the fantasy of someday becoming a legitimate gallery curator, especially when Annina told me she would let me curate my own show once she moved to her new commercial gallery space on Prince Street.

One day, a young artist named Richard Prince came into the gallery with a portfolio of rephotographed watch ads. Aesthetically the pieces were way too conceptual to be a good fit with the gallery, and what stuck out immediately were the familiar generic metal frames enclosing them. I joked with Richard, giving him a hard time for using Larry's signature awful frames, and the two of us began hanging out.

The hot artists' hangout at the time was a place called Mickey's, at One University Place, started by the same Mickey who owned Max's Kansas City. Mickey's vibe was utilitarian chic—low-key tables and chairs, nothing fancy, but at the same time intimidating to me as an art-world outsider. At Mickey's I would see the conceptual artist Lawrence Weiner, friendly, charming, and always fun to talk to, and his wife, Alice, an eternally refreshing contrast to the art world's general free-floating pretension and angst. Before his career took off, Julian Schnabel worked at Mickey's as a cook—Schnabel later became the very symbol of the gathering, spinning tornado of artistic commercialization. One night Richard and I found ourselves at Mickey's with an up-and-coming artist named Jeff Koons. With the exception of Richard, pretty much no one liked Jeff. In an era of appropriation without consequences, Koons had a show at the Mary Boone Gallery made up of standing vacuum cleaners behind plastic, and a lot of people hated it. The artist Sherrie Levine would eventually get sued when she re-represented Walker Evans photos in her work, whereas Jeff, it seemed, got away with serving up Duchamp.

Richard Prince was a figure of mystery to most, an art-world outsider who traveled without a coterie of art-world colleagues or peers. He also played the guitar and was a member of a band that supposedly had a record deal, though he was always secretive about his musical life. He and I were never more than friends but we bonded as outsiders. We are friends to this day.

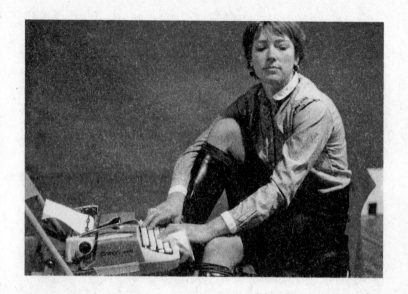

16

COMPARED TO THE PEOPLE I saw every day in New York, I was a mess—my wardrobe a hodgepodge of thrift-shop styles, boho symbols mixed with conventional ones. A few years earlier, in conjunction with getting my driver's license, I'd also gotten my first pair of glasses, and to make them look less conventional and dreary, I bought a pair of flip-up sunglass lenses. Myopia could at least look good, plus I couldn't afford to buy contact lenses.

One night I accompanied a friend to Veselka, an all-night Polish restaurant on the corner of Saint Mark's and Second Avenue. Somehow my friend was personally acquainted with the Senders, a popular 1970s

New York band best known for their "rock-and-roll" style and Frankie Avalon greaser appearance. Johnny Thunders, who was a member of the New York Dolls, was hanging out with the Senders that night, which meant that by default I was hanging out with Johnny Thunders.

You would think it would have been the coolest night of my life, but it wasn't. To me, a white, middle-class Southern California girl, Johnny Thunders was just a tired junkie. My friend and I were sitting in a booth in between the Senders and Johnny Thunders when Johnny started tossing sugar across the table at his friends. Pissed off, I yelled at him for getting sugar in my eggs. Johnny fixed with me an entitled, druggie, rock-and-roll look and called me "Four Eyes." It was funny in some respects, but also a night that reinforced my feeling that I could never attain any degree of coolness or style in New York. Johnny Thunders and people like him were breaking all the rules and the rest of us were condemned to watch.

I'd remained friends with Dan Graham, and whenever Dan went to Europe, he let me stay in his railroad tenement apartment at 84 Eldridge Street on the Lower East Side. The apartment was a long, arrow-shaped space crammed foot-to-ceiling with books and LPs, the walls covered with artworks, including two Jo Baer paintings, a Robert Mangold, and one of Gerhard Richter's beautiful "gray paintings" that looked like the texture of an old wall. Gerhard was the fiancé of a German artist named Isa Genzken, and somewhere along the line Dan introduced the three of us.

It was a typical Dan intro: "Kim's a Taurus, Isa, and you're a Sagittarius, and you're not supposed to get along, but her moon is in Libra so you might find that . . . ," or words to that effect. Back then, Isa was doing a residency in New York. One of her "things" was photographing people's ears and turning them into large-scale photos, so naturally she took a picture of mine. Ten minutes later she and I were taking photos of each other. Isa, always deliberate, went first. Perched before a typewriter in the dark blue gallery, I wore a light-blue button-down shirt with a white collar, a black dance skirt, tights, and black rubber riding boots. Isa and I both assumed the same pose—a profile with the blue wall behind us. Isa was statuesque and way more photogenic than I felt in my plain clothes.

Gerhard and Isa Genzken were married by the time Sonic Youth toured Germany a few years later. Thurston and I paid them a visit in Köln. In Gerhard's studio there, I remember looking at all his candle paintings. They were lovely, especially their scale, tiny, as if you could palm one, slide it into a large purse, and vanish into the night. Gerhard was always extremely polite, but his English was awkward and he was skeptical of anything—any trend, any movement—that aligned with popular culture, specifically the newer, less conceptual generation of painters like Jörg Immendorff and Julian Schnabel. By the late eighties, the art world had blown up into a huge financial enterprise, with many jostling at the top. Immendorff once asked us to play at his birthday party, and I remember Isa's being all for it and Gerhard's being strongly against.

If it weren't for Isa and Dan, I'm sure Gerhard would never have let us use one of his candle paintings for the cover of *Daydream Nation*. We were still thinking in vinyl terms back then, and the painting was the perfect scale for a record cover, a Duchamp ready-made, almost, to enter the mainstream.

Later during her marriage, things began falling apart for Isa. A few years after we met, Isa began creating tiny architectural sculptures with the goal of placing one on top of the Philip Johnson–designed AT&T building. It was a great but of course unrealistic idea. Having read that Philip Johnson ate lunch regularly at the Four Seasons, Isa called me one day to ask if I would go with her there and wait for Johnson outside, which I did; I had no idea what else to do or how else to help her. She was clearly going through a manic phase and was feeling vulnerable and lonely. Naturally, the management didn't let us in, and Johnson wasn't even there that day. The last time I saw Isa, Sonic Youth was in the middle of a sound check at CBGB. She showed up out of the blue and began yelling—really yelling—at us. I never saw her again.

From the moment I arrived in New York, Dan was my shepherd, my emcee and guide to the downtown New York City art and rock-and-roll scene. Through Dan, I discovered Tier 3, the No Wave club at the corner of West Broadway and White Street in Tribeca, and Franklin Furnace, the arts organization then and now devoted to anything avant-garde. Dan was friends with Jeffrey Lohn and Glenn Branca, members of one of the original No Wave bands, Theoretical Girls, who released precisely one single, "You Got Me." At night, Dan would go to No Wave shows and record the bands with a huge stereo cassette player, all the while tossing in comments and narrations that trickled up through the final live mix.

Dan also introduced me to his best friend, Dara Birnbaum, the video and installation artist. Dara was smart, verbal, and slightly intimidating, a living symbol of the new fast-talking New York style I was just getting used to, and that made me, a California girl, feel slurred in comparison. Never mind, because I was eager to learn, and I did, too, just from being around Dara and some of Dan's other artist friends.

A lot of CalArts and Rhode Island School of Design grads came to New York around this time. Art was happening in the city, and being surrounded by peers made these artists feel less like outsiders. Dan was always telling me and Vicki Alexander (a transplanted Canadian artist friend), "You guys should have a group." Initially, Vicki and I were going to do it together, but I decided to do it by myself and started De-sign Office. For me, Design Office was a means to do things without having a gallery. The idea was to conduct a sort of intervention in a private space, such as someone's home, that reflected something about that person. Dan was a willing guinea pig in letting me alter his apart-ment. Eventually I did a show at White Columns, the nonprofit public and independently founded art space, which at the time was located on the far western end of Spring Street, near Varick, across from the Ear Inn—today it's moved to the West Village. For the show I brought chairs in from different people's homes and made the office look less like a community-oriented space and more like a dining room. The show was called *Furniture Arranged for the Home or Office.*

In the meantime, I was going out a lot at night. One of the biggest appeals of seeing and hearing No Wave bands in downtown New York was how purposefully abandoned and abstract the music sounded. In a way it was the purest, most free thing I'd ever heard—much different than the punk rock of the seventies and the free jazz of the sixties, more expressionistic, and beyond, well, anything. In contrast, punk rock felt tongue-in-cheek, in air quotes screaming, "We're playing at destroying corporate rock." No Wave music was, and is, more like "*No*, we're *really* destroying rock." Its sheer freedom and blazing-ness made me think, *I can do that.*

As a term coined by people tired of the media's habit of defining any scene or genre in some cheap, easy shorthand, *No Wave* took in everything from film to video art to underground music. But that also made it undefinable. Basically it was *anti*-Wave, which is why strictly speaking No Wave can't even properly be called a movement at all and shouldn't even have a name. It was also a direct response to the "New Wave" trend in music, e.g. more commercial, melodic, dance-able punk—Blondie, the Police, Talking Heads—which was seen by a lot of people as a lame sellout. A lot of the members of the No Wave scene were artists by training who had come to New York and fallen into music as a side project. Glenn Branca of Theoretical Girls, for example, came out of the theater, and guitar theorist and composer Rhys Chatham had studied music with La Monte Young and Philip Glass. Even though Sonic Youth is associated with it, it would be wrong to call us No Wave. We didn't sound No Wave. We just built something out of it.

I was a 1960s teenager, too young to be a hippie but brushed by whatever rebellion and amped-up freedom there was in the air. Art had always given me direction, a way forward, even when I sometimes felt I was floating. But when I saw and heard No Wave bands, some equation in my head and body pieced together instantly. A phantom *thing* had been missing from my life and here it was, finally, unconventional, personal but at the same time not, and confrontational. What's more, every

No Wave gig felt precarious, a rush, a cheek-burn, since you knew the band onstage could break up at any moment.

More than once Dan Graham had told me it wasn't enough to be an artist in a studio, because the next obvious step was a gallery, and then what? No, he said, artists have a responsibility to contribute to a bigger, more daring cultural dialogue. "Kim, you should write something," Dan suggested, adding that if I wasn't preparing for or exhibiting a show, then writing was the next-best way to get my brain out into the larger New York art community. At the time Dan himself was writing articles about girl groups, like the Slits, and going around making authoritative declarations about feminism. Like most guys, he was just a big fan of female sexuality. "You're going out to see things," he added, "and you're obviously getting something out of it—so you have to give something back."

I'd never written a word, but I took Dan's advice. I decided to write about men, and how they interact onstage with one another and bond by playing music.

I remember staring endlessly at the books lining the walls of my dad's study as a little girl. I didn't know what a sociologist did, but the books had titles like *Men and Their Work*. What did that even mean? Obviously, men—and boys—spent time, most of it in fact, engaged in an activity known as *work*. Keller, for example, had his rock collection, Erector set, and assorted other boy-passions. Whereas whatever I made up or imagined in my own head lacked that builder's significance or invention, and the train set I presumed would someday magically appear must have died on the tracks on its way to me. Looking back, I was clearly devaluing what women did. How had that happened? Was it just that my parents placed higher expectations on Keller as the firstborn? Did I ask for, and in return get back, a little smile rather than any attention?

Guys playing music. I *loved* music. I wanted to push up close to whatever it was men felt when they were together onstage—to try to ink in that invisible thing. It wasn't sexual, but it wasn't unsexual either. Distance mattered in male friendships. One on one, men often had little to say to one another. They found some closeness by focusing on a third thing that wasn't them: music, video games, golf, women. Male friendships were triangular in shape, and that allowed two men some version of intimacy. In retrospect, that's why I joined a band, so I could be inside that male dynamic, not staring in through a closed window but looking out.

The piece I wrote, "Trash Drugs and Male Bonding," was published in the first issue of a new magazine called *Real Life*. It was a good issue to be in, and I got a lot of positive feedback and felt suddenly as though I had an identity in the downtown community. That essay topic unlocked the next thirty years of my life. By writing about men locking into one another onstage, I indirectly pushed myself inside the triangle, and whatever doubts I had about pursuing a career in art commingled to create a forward wave of momentum, noise, and motion. It was also my way of rebelling—writing about men when it would be more natural to write about women. It was a conscious faux-intellectual premise I could indulge in, and a nod to the work that Dan, my mentor, was doing. The next, clear-cut step was to actually begin playing music.

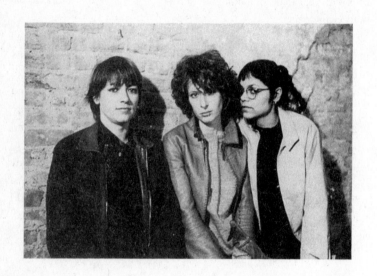

17

GROWING UP I'D never sung, much less sung along to music, choosing instead to smoke a little pot, make art, and listen to Bob Dylan, Buffalo Springfield, Tim Buckley, the Beatles, Archie Shepp, and the Art Ensemble of Chicago. I liked the same music my brother liked, with the exception of Joni Mitchell and Billie Holiday.

After my piece was published, Dan asked if I was interested in putting together an all-girl band to restage one of his best-known performance pieces, *Performer/Audience/Mirror*, which examines, and flips inside out, the relationship between a performer and a crowd. Whenever Dan did the piece, he stood before audiences with a huge mirrored wall behind him. He described the audience before him in a staccato monologue, the meaning of every detail of their every movement. Then he overturned it by describing himself to the mirror in relation to what the audience saw.

When I tentatively agreed, Dan introduced me to bass player Miranda Stanton and Christine Hahn from the group The Static. The three of us began rehearsing. We decided we'd call our band Introjection, with Christine on drums, me on guitar, and Miranda on bass. Introjection performed *Performer/Audience/Mirror* at the Massachusetts College of Art and Design, with the visual artist and composer Christian Marclay curating the evening.

We took the stage with the tall lakelike mirror behind us. Dan's plan was for Christine, Miranda, and me to take turns interacting with the audience in between songs, but nothing happened as scripted. I played guitar, my song lyrics appropriated from ad copy I'd torn from women's magazines. One song, "Soft Polished Separates," described how to mix and match tops and bottoms. Another, "Cosmopolitan Girl," was a word-by-word lift from an oversized *Cosmopolitan* ad telling the world what it was like to live the life of a *Cosmopolitan* girl.

It was an intense evening. All three of us were nervous, and Christine got so rattled during her turn that she left the stage and disappeared into the bathroom. We were supposed to play a song, and then one of us would interact with the audience in some way, in effect stepping through the unseen, unspoken line between audience and performer. Followed by another song, another interaction. At the same time I felt as if something new was lodging in my brain. Mixed in with the nerves was another sensation, as if I were a kid on a high-altitude ride I'd never had a ticket to go on before. I woke up the next day, and even though Introjection had performed precisely one show, I told myself we were now officially on tour. This was surely what the Stones or the Yardbirds felt like the first time they played, I thought, but it wasn't to be.

Dan was disappointed with our performance and told us as much.

Introjection hadn't done what we were supposed to. The problem was we'd all been so nervous we weren't thinking about what Dan expected from us. Then again, it *was* a loaded situation: a male artist using women to interact with an audience, in the process turning himself into a voyeur. As far as I was concerned it wasn't a failure, and whatever happened was a part of the performance, even if it didn't formally fulfill Dan's expectations. The fact that we *didn't* do what Dan wanted created another interesting moment in which music and art intersected in a climate of punk rock and rebellion.

Introjection didn't last long. Christine departed the band to join the ultra-cool German all-girl group Malaria!. Miranda pulled in a few guys for us to rehearse with, but nothing gelled, and Introjection never played another note or show.

I was apartment-sitting for Annina, at her rangy apartment on Riverside Drive. One of my responsibilities was to take care of Annina's big desert turtle, who was allowed to roam free, which meant I had to watch where I walked. It was during this time that I had an amazing shot of luck: my car-accident money came through in the form of a $10,000 check. It was the first real money I'd ever seen, an amount that made staying on in New York possible. I could pay a landlord both the first and last month's rent and secure my own place. What's more, the apartment right underneath Dan's happened to be open and available, and the rent was cheap, too, $150 a month. I would stay on in that apartment at 84 Eldridge Street for the next decade, with Thurston moving in with me soon after.

In 1980, the block between Hester and Grand on Eldridge Street in lower Manhattan was half-Chinese to the south, the other half made up of Jewish wholesale fabric owners. My landlord was Belgian, and rent control caused him to go around referring to himself as a "captive landlord." He claimed to make no money on any of the apartments. Dan kept insisting to the landlord that I was a California hippie, which annoyed me to no end. Later, when Sonic Youth first went out on tour,

I had to be extremely discreet about subletting out my place so the landlord wouldn't think a bunch of long-haired hippie degenerates were crashing his building.

Like most of the apartments at 84 Eldridge, my new space was a railroad flat. There was a bathtub in the kitchen and bars on the windows by the fire escape. The bed, a mattress on the floor, sat in the middle, at a slant, as railroad apartments were known to buckle slightly down the middle. Cockroaches were a problem, too, and to me the people who invented Combat, the little black roach-trapping contraption, are urban folk heroes.

There was one benefit of Introjection, though. Before Miranda took leave of my life, she wanted to introduce me to Thurston Moore.

"He plays in a band called the Coachmen," Miranda said. "In fact, they're playing tonight, it's their last gig." She went on to say she thought there was something special about Thurston.

Later that night, Miranda and I showed up at a venue on Fifteenth Street called Plugg, run by a guy named Giorgio, who had some vague association with Led Zeppelin or the Stones. Plugg, of course, isn't there anymore. But it *was* the Coachmen's final show, and the rhythm guitarist *was* special.

He was very tall and skinny, six foot six, he told me later, charismatic and confident seeming, with pillowy lips. Height never came up for the Coachmen, since the others were even taller than Thurston, except the seated drummer. Afterward, Miranda made the introduction. I was surprised by how excited I was to meet this guy. About our first meeting, Thurston would later tell people that he was very taken by my dark flip-up glasses. There was no Internet back then, no e-mail, no texting, so at some point he and I must have exchanged phone numbers.

All my life up to then I'd been involved with older guys, and I remember thinking, *Oh, Thurston is five years younger than I am.* I decided to be open to this. He had a glow about him I liked, and he also seemed extremely sure about what he wanted and how to get it, though it was more a quiet self-confidence than anything brash.

A couple of weeks later, Thurston and I met up at Danceteria, but our first "formal" date was at A Space, a small alternative art space that featured performances and shows, and afterward Thurston came back to my apartment. I remember feeling so excited he was there, surrounded by my few belongings. We were talking about this and that when he laid eyes on the Drifter tilted against the wall. It sealed the deal, in a way.

18

EARLY ON, THURSTON told me about an incident where someone at an art opening made some disparaging comment about his coat. It was a short black trench. I found that comment incredibly endearing. He was genuinely hurt by the remark, and telling me about it revealed his vulnerability. His feelings matched up perfectly with the fatigue and intimidation I felt around the gallery scene and about the fact that art-as-money was now the prevailing atmosphere.

I could also tell that Thurston was skeptical about the art world, and he was right to be, though he knew little of it. Today the traditional art discourse of creating a show around an idea has almost completely deteriorated into setting up a room with objects for sale. Even then the tide was turning in that direction.

There was something wild, but not *too* wild, about Thurston. His guitar-playing may have been free and untamed, but we came from similar middle-class academic backgrounds. One night not long after he and I started going out, Thurston filled in for the Hungarian actress Eszter Balint—who would later go on to appear in Jim Jarmusch's film *Stranger Than Paradise*—by deejaying at the Squat Theatre. Nico played that night, as did the Heartbreakers, a band led by Johnny Thunders. It was a depressing evening. Nico cried, and though they meant a lot to Thurston, Thunders's band was only interesting for its heritage. Onstage they were a bunch of rock-and-roll burnouts.

We were slowly getting to know each other. When Thurston was eighteen, his dad had died very suddenly from a benign brain tumor—he hemorrhaged following a brain operation. Thurston attended college for half a semester and then dropped out. Later he told people he moved to New York with the fantasy of starting a band with Sid Vicious. Thurston and his good high school friend Harold used to come into the city from Connecticut, soaking up the scene. Years later, when we saw the film *The Ice Storm,* Thurston likened himself to the main character, the kid in the train seat heading into the big city. He told me story after story about going to CBGB in the seventies to see Tom Verlaine, Television, the Ramones, Richard Hell, and Patti Smith—all the music and the people I'd missed out on.

When Thurston and I met, I was still recovering from the end of the relationship I'd had with the older male artist in California. The man and I had been incredibly close, our relationship intense but in retrospect maybe slightly off-kilter. With him I felt I'd found something great, maybe even lasting. He and I talked endlessly about ideas and art, about anything visual in fact. In the end he betrayed me, and it was traumatic. When I met Thurston I was still feeling shaky.

They say you always learn *something* from relationships, even bad ones, and that what your last one lacked, or you missed out on, is what you're primed to find in the next—unless, that is, you insist on repeating the same pattern over and over again.

The codependent woman, the narcissistic man: stale words lifted from therapy that I nonetheless think about a lot these days. It's a dynamic I have with men that began, probably, with Keller. Growing up I needed to believe he was bigger than life, a distorted genius, declaiming and wild in white. I did all I could to shield him from disapproval, anger, trouble. I defended him when he dropped out of college, lost sleep over the fear he'd be drafted to go fight in Vietnam, but during that reverent period, he foxed me into squatting in a small room off his larger one, smothering every attempt I ever made to figure out my own place in the world.

Thurston wasn't a larger-than-life character in the way Keller was, not, at least, in those days. He could be shy. He was good at concealing what he didn't know and pretended sometimes, for example, to be more knowledgeable about the downtown New York art scene than he actually was. At the same time he exuded a confidence, a certainty about who he was and where he was going. From the start I knew that our relationship wouldn't center on mutually shared ideas about art. But that excited me, too. Our relationship felt more like an intersection of two separate lines. By coming together the two of us could maybe make something new and bigger. Because he was younger, and I was used to going out with older men, I convinced myself I was breaking an old pattern. As for Thurston, he'd recently ended a relationship with a married woman who had a young son. We were starting out on equal emotional footing, and we wouldn't do to each other what had been done to us in our other relationships—or so I believed at that moment. Early in our relationship, I remember the two of us walking down Eighth Street together, holding hands, on our way to a movie—it could have been *The Rocky Horror Picture Show*. That night I felt so happy, and so close to him, as if in this dirty, scrappy, adopted place he and I were the only two people who existed within a perfect moment. Soon after that, I started playing music with him.

One day, in our first months together, Thurston told me we were going to visit his mother in Connecticut. He didn't ask me—he just proclaimed it, and though I was upset that he hadn't conferred with me first, that was Thurston's style. It was hard for me to imagine leaving New York for any reason, even for a place as close as Connecticut, but I went along, being, at the time, more of a follower. It was Anne DeMarinis, in fact, the woman Thurston was playing music with at the time, who read my mind, Anne who told Thurston how inconsiderate and self-centered it was of him to assume I was ready to meet his mother, not to mention the rest of his family.

That same unpredictability made Thurston fun and even thrilling to be around, that and his gregarious manner. Outwardly, Thurston was friendly, good-natured, funny, extremely likable. When I finally met his mom, she told me that when Thurston was little, everyone in the neighborhood and the town knew him. "They would say to me, 'Oh—are *you* Thurston's mother?'" Clearly, with his height and long hair, he was the golden child, and as the youngest of three kids he was used to being doted upon. "Is he as easygoing as he seems?" John Knight asked me the first time the two of them met. The truth was that no, Thurston was not that easygoing. Among other things he had a temper, which flared up whenever he put together an issue of his zine, *Killer,* and he would become incredibly stressed out. Once, when his stapler wasn't working, he picked it up and threw it through a window, shattering the glass. It scared me.

Today, when I think back on the early days and months of Thurston's and my relationship, I wonder whether you can truly love, or be loved back, by someone who hides who they are. It's made me question my whole life and all my other relationships. Why did I trust him, or assume I knew anything at all about him? Maybe I imposed on Thurston a dream, a fantasy. When I look back at old photos of us, I have to believe we were happy, at least as happy as any two creative people who are stressed out with commitments and fears about the future and what's next, and about their own ideas and inner demons, ever can be.

A friend once told me that he thought Thurston and I were a great match, as both of us were so independent, which he speculated must contribute to the success and longevity of our marriage. Thurston would do his thing, including assorted side projects, and I had side projects of my own. No marriage can maintain the thrilling-ness of the early days, and over time, in spite of what my friend said, and as creative as our relationship was, our marriage got progressively lonely, too. Maybe it became too professional. Maybe I was a person—like a stapler—who just didn't work for him anymore.

But at the time, the rumpled shirts Thurston wore with the too-short sleeves and the elbows worn out, the cat he owned named Sweetface, the tortoiseshell guitar that was the same color as Sweetface's fur, the subtle charisma and sensitivity, the fact that he'd lost his dad at eighteen and didn't seem to want to talk about it—all those things made me fall for him.

At the time, as I mentioned, Thurston was playing music with a girl named Anne DeMarinis. Anne was the girlfriend of the artist Vito Acconci, and the two of them lived together in a big loft in Brooklyn. A musical prodigy of some kind, Anne was young and beautiful, though she wore scruffy sweaters with holes in them as if to eradicate her good looks, and she rarely washed her hair. She was grunge before grunge existed. I remember taking the subway to Brooklyn to play music with the two of them; I remember, too, that Dan and Vito had been friends once, members of the New York City poetry scene, but for whatever reasons had become competitors.

Their rivalry made it odd for me to go from Eldridge Street, where Dan lived above me, to playing music in Vito's loft in the middle of what's now Dumbo. Anne played the keyboards. The band, for lack of a better word, had a bunch of different names—the Arcadians, Male Bonding—and also featured a few different drummers. We were playing at Vito's the night John Lennon was shot. Such an unbelievable thing to have happen—New York, the place where everything seemed possible, filled at the same time with so much darkness and violence.

Of the two of us, Thurston lived on the far worse block, Thirteenth Street in Alphabet City. Eldridge Street between Hester and Grand wasn't a block anyone with sense wanted to walk on at night—it was shadowy, scary, and druggy—but it wasn't nearly as bad as Thirteenth Street between Avenues A and B. Drug dealers were everywhere, selling, with users hunched over on stoops and slung in doorways. The first time I went over to his apartment, it was empty except for a few books, some records, a guitar, and a huge pile of shirts in a mountainous heap, all of them specked and gouged with holes, like some blowout sale at a discount retailer's. I remember being impressed by the sight of all those shirts; if nothing else, a bunch of stacked shirts was, you have to admit, kind of interesting.

It didn't take long for Thurston to move into 84 Eldridge. It saved on rent, and we didn't want to be apart anyway. Sweetface, whom Thurston had gotten from a health food store on Prince Street, joined us. The two of us had Sweetface until 1996. She moved with us to our apartment on Lafayette Street in the late eighties and died when Coco was two. When Coco was old enough to talk, she told me how sad she was at losing Sweetface, which surprised me, because who ever knows if a baby remembers anything at all.

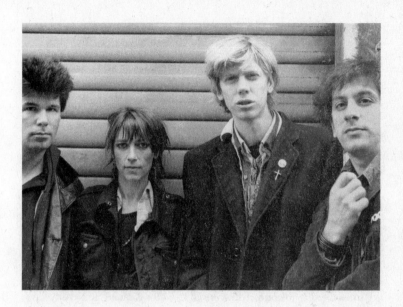

19

ONE SUNDAY AFTERNOON, before I met Thurston, I went to a place I'd been hearing about a lot, the Mudd Club. The Mudd Club was owned by Ross Bleckner, a successful artist who was a member of the Mary Boone stable. It was on White Street, a couple of blocks below Canal, and named after the doctor who treated John Wilkes Booth after he shot Abe Lincoln. The Mudd Club had no sign or awning, bore no indication whatsoever that it was more than just another doorway, but inside was another universe, one that hosted No Wave, New Wave, experimental music, poetry readings, and even catwalk shows. There was a column placed before the stage and a bar that sat in the center of the room like a dry island. I got there early and hardly anyone was there. An hour later, people started showing up. A fashion show was happening, with a young girl strutting onstage to the sounds of a barely visible band. It all seemed so decadent, especially as it was taking place on a sunlit Sunday afternoon in New York.

The Mudd Club was technically illegal, in that it skirted New York's cabaret license laws—but in those days no one cared so long as the proper authorities were being paid off. I also found out that nothing at the Mudd Club ever started when it was supposed to. That was just the way it worked there. If a show was scheduled to begin at three P.M., you knew it wouldn't get under way until five P.M., with the crowd assembling at around four forty-five. In the ragged, pre-gentrification, pre-art-boom landscapes of downtown New York, the Mudd Club had an anything-can-happen-and-no-one-would-care air, mixed with a touch of glamorous ennui. Sometimes the place would be jammed and other times dead, with only a few upright bodies dancing in syrupy slow motion or in a hyperactive frenzy, depending on what drugs they were taking or the music playing overhead.

As it got better known, the door policy got stricter. Unless you knew the guy at the door, you might have to stand out in the cold for a long time. The only club that rivaled the Mudd in terms of great music was Tier 3, where English bands would play along with their bigger-venue gigs at Hurrah's or the Ritz. Joy Division was scheduled to play at Tier 3, but Ian Curtis killed himself a week before the gig. Tier 3 is where I saw 8 Eyed Spy—the band Lydia Lunch formed after Teenage Jesus—as well as DNA, Malaria!, Young Marble Giants, and a whole bunch of other No Wave acts. And these days the Mudd Club is just a throwaway line in an old Talking Heads song.

But by the time I got to New York in 1980, No Wave was almost gone, and New Wave acts like Blondie and the Talking Heads had already hit it big. I'd missed out on Lydia Lunch and Teenage Jesus. One of the original No Wave bands, DNA, was still performing, as was Mars, and they were a big influence on me, too. I was especially drawn to the way that Tim Wright played bass. He would appear in his socks, walking the stage in balletic motion like an insect folding backward, cutting and jabbing the air with his instrument, etching out space as he went, as if every single second had been choreographed. I never saw anyone play that way before or since.

What killed No Wave? Probably a famous show at Artists Space that Michael Zwack organized put the final nail in the coffin. Brian Eno had been invited to come, and he decided to produce a No Wave compilation. Since only some bands could be included on the compilation and not all, a rift was created in the scene. By the time Sonic Youth started in 1981, No Wave was essentially over. Maybe it was time to start something new.

In the early eighties, there weren't a lot of restaurants in Soho, outside of Fanelli's, the bar on Prince Street. On the corner of Prince and Wooster Streets was Food, a cooperative restaurant that the artist Gordon Matta-Clark began as an ongoing art happening that later evolved into an actual restaurant. Gordon was best known for his "building cuts," in which he would lop off sections of floor and ceiling within abandoned buildings. From my perspective, there was nothing better than this—nothing.

For a while in the early eighties Thurston worked at Food as a dishwasher and brought back giant slices of cake to Eldridge Street. Between the two of us, we had so little money that those slices felt absurd in our hands and obscene in our mouths. Food served everything from borscht to rabbit stew and also holds the honor of being the first New York restaurant to serve sushi and sashimi.

Back then, almost every building in Soho was caked over with band posters. Thurston and I used to go out at night and plaster over other bands' posters with ours, unless it was a band or a musician one of us knew and liked. The poster war was a battle to stand out, though the enemy, if we'd ever thought about it, was the union guys whose job it was to publicize more mainstream entertainment. In the early eighties, you could land an actual *gig* putting up posters at the Kitchen on Broome Street, where a lot of No Wave and new music performances took place. But you had to be fast, you had to know what you were doing, and you had to have mastered one of two tools. The first was Elmer's Glue, which was hasty and easy to conceal under your shirt. The other involved wheat paste in an oversized bucket, which could be messy, especially in the winter, when the paste froze on your hands and fingers.

Despite the number of bands playing around the city, clubs were closing down left and right. Hurrah, a club on West Sixty-Second Street that was one of the first big New York City dance clubs ever to showcase punk and industrial music, shut its doors in 1980. The owner, thinking he owed the world an elegy, said, "Oh, there aren't any good bands anymore anyway. They all sound like noise."

Back then, *noise* was an insult, a derogatory word, the most scornful word you could throw at music. But it was from Hurrah's owner that Thurston got the name for the nine-day-long festival he launched in June of 1981 at White Columns. Thurston said he wanted to reclaim the word *noise,* even though nobody really knew what a "noise band" was or was supposed to sound like.

Basically, the Noise Fest came about because there was nowhere else for downtown bands to go onstage and play. I organized an exhibition of visual art by some of the musicians playing the festival. Over a nine-day period, three to five bands performed nightly, one of which was Sonic Youth. Later, a cassette was put out, documenting the performance.

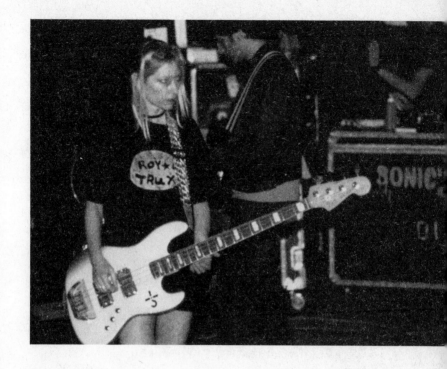

20

THERE WERE SO many moments of formation for Sonic Youth; it's hard to pinpoint one. In the beginning, the band was just Thurston, Lee Ranaldo, and me, with different drummers entering and exiting like pedestrians stopping to stare briefly at a shop window. We had many different names before deciding on Sonic Youth: Male Bonding, Red Milk, and the Arcadians. These were phrases taken from current passions, names that vanished as fast as moods. But as soon as Thurston came up with the name Sonic Youth, we simultaneously knew how we wanted the music to sound.

Lee had played with David Linton at the Noise Fest. We had seen him before, playing around the city, and asked him to join us. We lined up a couple of gigs as Sonic Youth. The first practices were us sitting in a loose circle playing with no drummer at all. It wasn't exactly what you'd call "playing," to be honest. We strummed and made droning sounds on our guitars. That's when Thurston came up with the idea of playing his guitar percussively, with a drumstick. We didn't have a drummer, and there was no other way to keep a beat.

We were a baby band and, as such, had no idea what we were doing. Thurston, as I said, was a longtime student of CBGB. CBGB was his chapel, his temple, and so, with concrete logic, Thurston said he would go ask the owner, Hilly Kristal, for a gig. Just by showing up at CBGB so often, Thurston felt he'd established a relationship with Hilly, or that at the very least Hilly would recognize him as the tall, lanky kid who said hi to him almost every night. Thurston was successful, and Sonic Youth got a slot at CBGB as the first of four bands on a bill. There is no worse positioning for a band. But we approached what we were doing as the first in a series of stepping stones, one of which included recording our first album.

It was an EP, recorded in 1981. Five songs total. You could listen to the whole thing in less than half an hour. *Sonic Youth,* the EP—I'm not sure what it was to be honest. We recorded it for Glenn Branca's label. Josh Baer, the director of White Columns, had asked Glenn to create a record label. Glenn said yes, the label was christened Neutral Records, and Sonic Youth was its very first artist.

To put it mildly, we didn't have a lot of money for recording. Finally we scored a deal at a place called Plaza Sound, a big, old, spectacular room in Rockefeller Center where Blondie, the Ramones, and entire symphony orchestras had recorded, as rumor had it the place was owned by Columbia Records. We were allotted two eight-hour sessions. Our then drummer, Richard Edson, had a big hand in helping structure our music before we got started. Richard also played in a band called Konk, which was considered "cool" in the downtown scene but was stylistically very different from us. Konk was rhythmic and minimal, and

Sonic Youth was dissonant and wild, but first records succeed now and again because you don't quite know what you're doing but you go ahead and do it anyway.

First we recorded all the basics, coming back later to do the vocals and mix. We had no specific tunings—they were either regular ones or else we detuned. From start to finish, the entire process took about two days. It was the first time I saw how our big loud sound was transformed in the end into something relatively contained. It was a complaint we would hear from many over the years—that Sonic Youth's sound wasn't nearly as intense recorded as it was live.

A lot of the first songs we all wrote and recorded were droning, with vague middles and even vaguer endings. "*I dreamed, I dream . . .*" was originally done as an instrumental. The lyrics were random. All of us, I remember, wrote down lines on a piece of paper, and when it came time to overdub the vocal, I randomly cherry-picked from the list. It's a way of working I sometimes still use. We told the sound engineer we wanted a big bass sound, like Johnny Rotten's post–Sex Pistols band, Public Image Ltd. I whispered my vocals and Lee Ranaldo added his own vocal accompaniment.

"*The days we spend go on and on.*" Those lyrics somehow became a foreshadowing of all the events, all the music, to come. Sonic Youth would go on for three decades, and our first record was reissued twenty-five years after its initial release. Critics would point out how meaningful the lyrics were, not realizing how randomly they came about in the first place.

When Thurston and I finally left the Rockefeller Center studio, it was four A.M. A blizzard was coming in, the sidewalks and streets piling up with snow. It was New York at its most muted and beautiful. We had our big amps with us, but we couldn't find a taxi. Back then New York still had its fleet of checker cabs, big boxy things, tailor-made for moving equipment, and we eventually flagged one and shoved our lo-fi gear into the trunk and backseat and squeezed ourselves in. There we were, two transplanted downtowners, immigrants amid the hard bones of those tall, unlit skyscrapers, as the heavy snow padded down. For a few moments, I felt like I belonged to some grown-up uptown showbiz world, and then the cab prowled home through the snow back down to Eldridge Street.

That studio worked like a good-luck charm for us. When the master came in, Glenn was pleasantly surprised by how good we sounded. The EP's cover was taken from a self-portrait the artist Jeff Wall made where he basically created a doppelgänger of himself in an enlarged print light box. We copied the idea, adding our picture twice over, so we came across as a band of eight instead of just four. Later, when Sonic Youth played Ann Arbor, Michigan, for the first time, and I met Niagara, the lead singer of Mike Kelley's Destroy All Monsters, she said to me, "I can't believe you let yourself be photographed without lipstick."

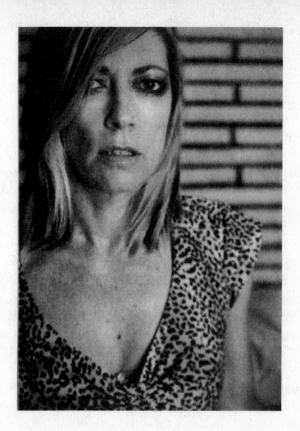

21

WHEN I FIRST began playing onstage, I was pretty self-conscious. I was just trying to hold my own with the bass guitar, hoping the strings wouldn't snap, that the audience would have a good experience. I wasn't conscious of being a woman, and over the years I can honestly say I almost never think of "girliness" unless I'm wearing high heels, and then I'm more likely to feel like a transvestite. When I'm at my most focused onstage, I feel a sense of space with edges around it, a glow of self-confident, joyful sexiness. It feels bodiless, too, all weightless grace with no effort required. The need to be a woman out in front never entered my mind at all until we signed with Geffen.

But in the beginning, I was just trying to make it through. No one in the band ever thought about being on a major record label. None of us were thinking that far ahead. Thurston was the one who often came up with what to do next.

What do bands do after making a record? They go on tour. It seemed like the right thing to do, and somehow we got ourselves a gig at the Walker Art Center, a progressive museum in Minneapolis. We also got to tour in England for the first time. For the kind of music we were making, it was frankly easier to find an audience in Europe. Bands are treated better over there, which I chalk up to the socialist governments and the way clubs double as cultural centers that governments partially fund.

In the early eighties, the music scene in England was large for an island, chaotic and cutthroat. Musicians literally paid to get onto a bill. Via a friend, we landed a gig opening up for an industrial band, with another girl named Danielle Dax opening for us. Before the show, Danielle cornered me in the bathroom. "Look," she said, "there are a lot of important people coming here tonight to see *me*."

Her meanness and competitiveness were almost shocking—it was like junior high all over again. Like a lot of English acts, Danielle had a specific look about her, a mask, an almost freakish persona. For the English, rock and roll has a lot to do with climbing over that country's class structure, kicking out the bars of their birth. They saw us, four New Yorkers, as a bunch of middle-class brats who probably lived in lofts right above art galleries, who were putting on an act that wasn't real, wasn't authentic, wasn't *earned*. This is made all the more ironic by the fact that many British bands, including the Beatles, came right out of art school.

Our first London show was a semi-disaster, with one of my bass strings breaking midway through. Thurston ended up hurling his guitar into the audience, and then the metal grille that separated bands from the audience slowly lowered down and the show ended. Some people thought Sonic Youth was the best thing on the bill, while others thought we were pretentious and arty. It wasn't a perfect introduction to England.

I also felt limited as a singer. When the band first started, I went for a vocal approach that was rhythmic and spoken, but sometimes unleashed, because of all the different guitar tunings we used. When you listen to old R&B records, the women on them sang in a really fierce, kick-ass way. In general, though, women aren't really allowed to be kick-ass. It's like the famous distinction between art and craft: Art, and wildness, and pushing against the edges, is a male thing. Craft, and control, and polish, is for women. Culturally we don't allow women to be as free as they would like, because that is frightening. We either shun those women or deem them crazy. Female singers who push too much, and too hard, don't tend to last very long. They're jags, bolts, comets: Janis Joplin, Billie Holiday. But being that woman who pushes the boundaries means you also bring in less desirable aspects of yourself. At the end of the day, women are expected to hold up the world, not annihilate it. That's why Kathleen Hanna of Bikini Kill is so great. The term *girl power* was coined by the Riot Grrl movement that Kathleen spearheaded in the 1990s. *Girl power:* a phrase that would later be co-opted by the Spice Girls, a group put together by men, each Spice Girl branded with a different personality, polished and stylized to be made marketable as a faux female type. Coco was one of the few girls on the playground who had never heard of them, and that's its own form of girl power, saying no to female marketing!

I've never thought of myself as a singer with a good voice, or even as a musician. I'm able to put myself out there by feeling as though I'm jumping off a cliff. Neil Young once said that it's more about having an authentic voice than a good voice, though of course Neil has a great voice. From growing up listening to jazz, I picked up another, cooler aspect of the female voice—the idea of space, and in-between-ness, and the importance of phrasing. It's worth remembering that from the beginning, rock and roll was never based in musical training or technique, just as punk rock was never about being a good musician and No Wave was at its core about pure expression. Punk rock changed everything, including the whole idea of being a "rock star." It's strange to look back and listen to lyrics from 1960s bands and realize they felt unease when they began to gain fame that separated them from their "brothers and sisters" and from "the movement." I always loved "Out of My Mind," the Buffalo Springfield song, where Neil sang about rock star entitlement, that the only sound he could hear was the screams outside his limousine.

The rock star thing has always felt dishonest to me—stylized and gestural, even goofy. I've always felt uncomfortable giving people what they want or expect. Dan Graham once described Lydia Lunch onstage to me, how Lydia just stood there, refusing to move. "Lydia Lunch is a genius!" Dan said. "She is really frigid—see how she doesn't move her body at all? She doesn't want to give anything to the audience." Even though Lydia had a much scarier persona than I ever did, I could relate to that. Later I grew to really enjoy playing bass; it was a physical thing that connected to my love of dance, though when you're playing an instrument onstage, it's hard to feel that it can really move people. Eventually, when Jim O'Rourke joined the band, I was freed up to just sing, and move around more.

When Sonic Youth started out, I really made an effort to punk myself out, to lose any and all associations with my middle-class West L.A. appearance and femininity. When I first arrived in New York, Rhys Chatham would always say to me, "You know, Kim, you're *always* going to look middle-class." To be more punk, he was implying, you had to be somehow uglier, as if there was an authenticity to be found in looking like an underdog. What Rhys meant, I think, was that I was who I was.

There was a popular look at the time—the vintage dress, the makeup—that just wasn't me, nor was that the way people dressed in the art world. I didn't fit into the downtown scene, and I knew I was never going to be like Lydia Lunch. I was, and still am, more of the push-everything-else-under-and-let-it-all-out-in-the-music kind of girl. Otherwise I'd probably be a sociopath.

A lot has been written about Sonic Youth, so what follows are the songs, or the albums, or the times that I have the most to say about or remember the best. "Addicted to Love," for example, wasn't and isn't a song I liked, but the conceptual approach we took made the whole thing work. "The Sprawl" was fun to perform, and the music was always enveloping, whereas, for example, the lyrics of "Tunic" had a much broader meaning than I ever realized at the time. Here is what stands out for me.

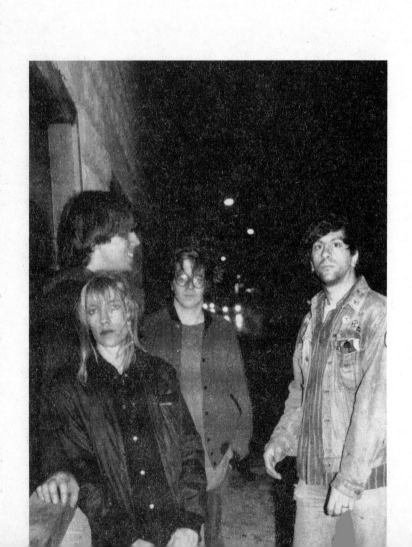

22

Confusion Is Sex: "Shaking Hell"

IN LATE 1982, the year we came out with our first full-length album, *Confusion Is Sex,* Dan Graham was researching the Shakers. This cultish religion that came out of the early days of America's religious-freedom-seeking escapists fascinated Dan, especially the practice of female members dancing themselves into a frenzied, almost orgasmic hysteria. The juxtaposition of this with what were otherwise very conservative beliefs and rituals was bizarre to him.

Dan wondered what rock-and-roll music and the Shaker sect had in common. Both were variations of ecstatic worship to his mind. Shakerism, he wrote, was akin to early American hardcore, with the shaven heads of the boys in the audience at punk rock concerts resembling the heads of some exotic monastic tribe. Dan was fascinated by Patti Smith and the intensity and sorcery of her performances, as was Thurston. Dan eventually made a documentary art film called *Rock My Religion,* and in it he included a live clip of Sonic Youth performing our song "Shaking Hell."

The lyrics—*"She finally discovered she's a . . . He told her so . . ."*—related to the idea of women as creations of film and advertising. I'd been reading the great feminist writer/filmmaker Julia Kristeva's essays about the "male gaze," as well as other books related to the idea of the always-passive woman and the always-active male protagonist.

On a more personal level, "Shaking Hell" mirrors my struggle with my own identity and the anger I felt at who I was. Every woman knows what I'm talking about when I say girls grow up with a desire to please, to cede their power to other people. At the same time everyone knows about the sometimes aggressive and manipulative ways men often exert power in the world, and how by using the word *empowered* to describe women, men are simply maintaining their own power and control. Years after I'd left L.A., I could still hear my crazy brother's voice in my ear, whispering, *I'm going to tell all your friends that you cried.*

Back then, and even now, I wonder: Am I "empowered"? If you have to hide your hypersensitivity, are you really a "strong woman"? Sometimes another voice enters my head, shooing these thoughts aside. This one tells me that the only really good performance is one where you make yourself vulnerable while pushing beyond your familiar comfort zone. I liken it to having an intense, hyper-real dream, where you step off a cliff but don't fall to your death.

Though it's hard to recall a time when she wasn't a part of the scene, I remember when Madonna made her entrance into the world of pop culture. Madonna was exploiting her own sexuality, willingly packaging and altering herself to please audiences. Me, I was a mutt, tucking my California style under East Coast plainness—"the librarian type hee, hee," as Mike Kelley would later describe my look back then.

With "Shaking Hell," I was trying to push my inner self out, with an edge that matched who I had become in New York. I bleached my hair unevenly, then dyed it magenta. In retrospect, it's ridiculous that anyone saw me as a fashion icon, since all I was trying to do was to dumb down my middle-class look by messing with my hair. Throughout the eighties I was invariably half-sure and half-confident about whatever it was I wore. I was going for a punky look, without really feeling I owned it. Later my look evolved into tomboy mixed with a slightly sexy Françoise Hardy cool—oversized indie rock T-shirts with boots, or corduroy shorts with seventies Jane Birkin–like tees on top, scoop-necked, flocked, with printed letters. My favorite one said GRACIAS. Still, I've always believed—still do—that the radical is far more interesting when it looks benign and ordinary on the outside.

The emotional intensity of the vocals in that song matched the music in a shamanistic way I don't think I've ever repeated. "Shaking Hell" was messy and bone-chilling to sing, especially when the music dropped to a low rumble during the *"Shake, shake, shake"* ending. It was as if the ground had dropped out from beneath me, and I was left floating, until my voice shot out and carried me. I wanted to take the audience with me, knowing, as I did, that the crowd wanted to believe in me, and us, as we created something that had never existed before.

We recorded *Confusion Is Sex* in the basement studio belonging to our friend Wharton Tiers. Wharton was the building superintendent, and whenever we recorded, he was professional enough to shut off the boiler. Years later, Julie Cafritz from Pussy Galore and I did an interview promoting an album from the side project we did together, Free Kitten. One of us made the mistake of mentioning Wharton and the boiler. We assumed no one would ever read the interview, but unfortunately one of the tenants did, and Wharton lost his job. I still feel bad about that.

Confusion Is Sex was recorded with an eight-track, or rather with four-tracks locked together. We did absolutely everything wrong while making that record, including mangling the tape during a crucial take of "Shaking Hell." In the end, we had to splice in the end of another tape to create the song.

The lyrics sprung from real life. "Making the Nature Scene" came from walking past the hookers lined up on Grand Street. In the dead cold of winter, they would flock there most nights, standing in a circle around a makeshift oilcan bonfire in leg warmers and stilettos. They were staples of the neighborhood landscape, standing tall like funky trees, leaning back, single hands on their hips, standing in a column "making the nature scene."

The gold sparkle of the ladies' leg warmers caught the light of passing cars, flashed in the dark spaces around nearby buildings. I'd been reading about the Italian architect and designer Aldo Rossi, who believed that cities never shake their histories, that they preserve the ghosts of their pasts through time. Rossi wanted to reclaim the small areas in between buildings to make the idea of a city human again, against the prevailing backdrop of large, looming, faintly fascistic architecture. In the early 1980s, the Lower East Side with its modest tenement and railroad apartments was still a small village. No one really cared that the hookers were there; they were part of the landscape. That is, until the new mayor decided to clean up his city and shoo them along.

After our first EP, we embarked on a mini-tour with the Swans. We played D.C., Virginia, Chapel Hill, and Raleigh, North Carolina. The Swans were a harsh, hard-to-listen-to band—they were all about plodding, minimal music, over which Mike Gira's nihilistically romantic vocals could perch—and Mike, whom I'd known slightly at Otis Art School, was a complete dictator in his band. A friend of ours who'd just got dumped by his girlfriend offered to drive us for free, so both Sonic Youth and the Swans squeezed into the back of an old van with an attached U-Haul. Mike, I remember, spent the entire ride fighting with his bandmate Sue Hanel. Mike was the leader of the Swans, after all, and having convinced himself he was uncompromising and hyperdisciplined in all things, he would scream and carry on at his bandmates if they didn't toe the line. Compared to the Swans, Sonic Youth was mild.

Here is a bit from a tour memoir I wrote about that period, entitled "Boys Are Smelly":

Chapel Hill: It was raining and sad as hell and the Swans played their set to jeering cowboys. Chapel Hill is one of the hippest places on earth to play, but in 1982 we were underground even for this place . . . In the van the Swans fought among themselves. Morale was very low and tempers were short. Our expectations were not as high as Mike's maybe, and we never fight among ourselves when we're traveling with another band that does; they do it for us.

Georgia: In Athens, Mike Gira jumped off the stage and pushed someone who was pogoing to their music, then he returned to the stage and apologized . . . Mike thought the guy was a poser who was making fun of him. In reality he was a nerd and Mike had never seen a nerd before. Thurston tried to discourage his sister, Susan, from coming to the show, because either he thought we were gonna suck or he thought he might have to protect her. He told her she'd be raped and murdered if she came, and at the time I thought it was just a ploy because she's so gullible, but now I realize he probably half believed it.

A few years later, from another tour, but the entries have the same feel:

Dallas: On our way to Dallas, we just melt, sleep, and nag our drummer Steve Shelley about driving too slow, and Thurston for driving too much like he plays guitar.

Boston: There was a point where I started getting sickened by the violence onstage. Thurston's fingers would swell up all purple and thick from banging his guitar. Usually I never know what's happening onstage, I would just see guitar-like objects whizzing through the air out of the corner of my eye. A couple of times Thurston pushed Lee into the audience, as the only way to end a song, but that was harmless fun.

Naugatuck, Connecticut: There's nothing like Naugatuck on a Saturday night . . . The club is next to a Chinese restaurant in a shopping plaza. River's Edge could have been filmed here.

I've never seen so many metalheads cruising the roads. They make perfect sense, though, when you look at the barren trees, the discount store, all this desolation and quietness—you want to crank up something really loud and ugly. I couldn't help wondering what the girls did while the boys were off playing with Satan. And I wondered if they were like me and craved the feeling of electricity and sound mixed together, swirling around my head and thru my legs. I always fantasized what it would be like to be right under the pinnacle of energy, beneath two guys who have crossed their guitars together, two thunderfoxes in the throes of self-love and combat, that powerful form of intimacy only achieved onstage in front of other people, known as male bonding.

We may have been in our infancy as a band, but our psychology was already beginning to form. The band gave us all new identities, thrilling but protected. None of us were alone anymore. Sometimes in a band it can feel as though you're together because you collectively suffer from a psychological disease none of you can name or acknowledge. Logic proceeds from a kind of group psychosis, but the force of the collective makes everything work. You're like a family who does what they do for ingrained, habitual reasons—except no one remembers why or what started the behavior. A band almost defines the word *dysfunction,* except that rather than explaining motivations or discussing anything, you play music, acting out your issues via adrenaline.

Greil Marcus, the music critic, wrote about our cover of Iggy and the Stooges' "I Wanna Be Your Dog" in his monthly *Artforum* column. His pieces were made up of small, and to Greil's mind meaningful, gestures that propelled the culture forward. Later Greil told an interviewer that *Confusion Is Sex* had gotten to him. It was a mess, he said, with some terrible singing, but he said he'd never heard anyone pull out her guts and throw them into the audience the way I had in "I Wanna Be Your Dog," and that Iggy Pop would be either ashamed or thrilled. "I Wanna Be Your Dog" was a song that had been covered so many times by so many people, but until then, Greil said, he'd never really known what it meant for one lover to say to another that she wanted to be his dog. "This woman knows stuff that I don't know," Greil wrote. In his opinion, Sonic Youth was a band that was taking big chances, really *pushing*. Greil was one of the earliest witnesses to understand what we were trying to do—maybe the only one.

It was the first time anyone had paid any real attention to us, and in *Artforum* no less. Thurston and I interpreted it as Greil's saying: "This small gesture is important and significant." Later, Greil and I got to be friends.

In fact, the lyrics for the song "Brother James" came after I read about the blues in Greil's book *Mystery Train*. "Brother James" appeared on an EP the band put out after *Confusion Is Sex* called *Kill Yr Idols,* a name we took from a Robert Christgau quote. Robert was the other big music critic of the time along with Greil, but he basically ignored us. Robert and the *Village Voice*, the downtown New York City weekly he wrote for, were never sympathetic to Sonic Youth or to the local rock scene in general, and the one night he came to one of our shows, someone in the audience tried to light him on fire. Playfully, though.

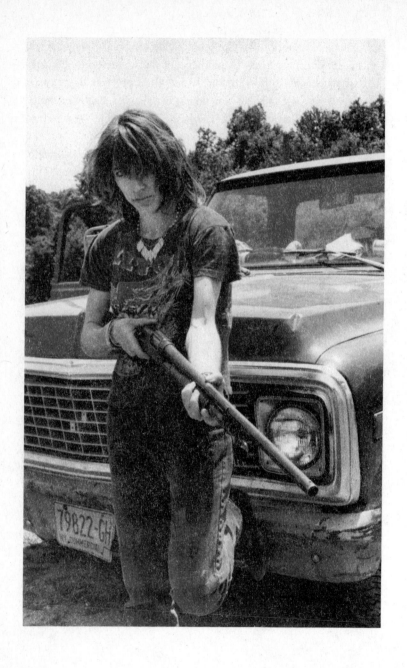

23

Bad Moon Rising: "Death Valley '69"

I WOULDN'T DESCRIBE Lydia Lunch as a friend, since friendship requires trust. I was a big fan of Teenage Jesus and the Jerks, and when Thurston and I got to know Lydia better, she was always trying to seduce Thurston. I always found her an interesting figure, and I liked her early music, but that doesn't mean I was a fan of everything she did. She was a little predatory, and she scared me somewhat. Still, Lydia was responsible for introducing Thurston and me to Paul Smith, who had previously managed a label for the English band Cabaret Voltaire. We sent Paul a tape—maybe they would like it enough to put out *Bad Moon Rising*. They weren't interested, but that's when Paul decided to find a backer via Rough Trade, a huge distribution company, who released the album on a new label Paul called Blast First.

Licensing advances meant a new beginning, one where I didn't have to work full-time and could focus instead on the new album. For the most part we were happy, though a little nervous, to lose our day jobs. Before writing the songs, Lee, Thurston, Bob Bert (our second drummer after Richard Edson), and I were passing around a book about the Velvet Underground. That book, for some unknown reason, brought everyone in the band together. We were now all in the same mood, which shows when you listen. We ended up calling the album *Bad Moon Rising*, after the Creedence Clearwater Revival song. We may have been preoccupied by the Velvets, but that's just the way we did things—borrowing something from a pop culture landscape and giving it a different meaning. Creedence Clearwater Revival was a faux–Southern country band in the same way we were a faux–Velvet Underground band. Plus, the title was badass.

Bad Moon Rising was the first record we ever recorded on twenty-four tracks. Every song flows into the next, with no gaps or spaces in between. When we played our music live, we were forced to create miniature segues onstage between songs. In those days, we had no guitar techs to help tune our instruments, and our twelve to fifteen guitars, each one tuned differently, constantly had to be retuned, or rechecked, or swapped out, which necessitated short breaks. Over time we developed an elaborate system for making those changes as seamless and fluid as possible.

We decided to re-create that illusion of seamlessness on *Bad Moon Rising*. At the time I was reading a book by the early postmodernist critic Leslie Fiedler called *Love and Death in the American Novel*. Naturally, Dan Graham turned me on to it, telling me how seminal a book it was for music critics like Lester Bangs, Robert Christgau, and Greil Marcus. Whether he was telling the truth or not, I really responded to the book.

Among other things, Fiedler talked about the homoerotic relationship between the early American settlers and the so-called savage male

American Indian. The title of the song "Brave Men Run (in My Family)" was taken from an Ed Ruscha painting that showed a tall ship. Ruscha's painting seemed to make ironic reference to the early heroics of American settlers. But as someone with gold rush traces in her own DNA, I could relate. From the few stories I'd heard, the women in my family were incomprehensibly strong. My great-grandmother who sold sewing patterns up and down the West Coast in the 1800s. My grandmother, traveling all over with a brood of five kids, finally landing in Kansas during the Great Depression. Stoic, enduring, no questions, no complaints.

When I sang "Brave Men Run (in My Family)," I was singing about those women. The song's phrase *"Into the setting sun"* refers to the westward pull, the American romance with death. And then there was "Death Valley '69."

When I was a girl growing up in Southern California, death, or the idea of it, kept pushing its way into my life, especially in 1969, when the 1960s hippie utopia merged with the Manson murders and bled into Altamont. So many people I ran into as a teenager had had brief encounters with the charismatic, wild-eyed little man who talked about "Revolution 9" and the desert and a future bliss of destruction. Peace and love had turned sordid, as the Stooges had written in their own sixties anthem: *"1969, okay, all across the USA."* "Make love not war" looked better on film than it did in real life, where cops killed college students and riots busted out in D.C., Chicago, and Baltimore. "Death Valley '69" has sometimes been misinterpreted as a pro-Manson song, especially by younger fans. Nothing is farther from the truth.

In 1985, when *Bad Moon* came out, hardcore groups were singing songs about Ronald Reagan. I wasn't interested in this and preferred to sing about the darkness shimmering beneath the shiny quilt of American pop culture.

I suppose you could say that Sonic Youth was always trying to defy people's expectations. We'd come out of a New York art context—though sideways—and merged with the rock scene. Just being a band from New York City who played *outside* of New York City messed with people's expectations. Audiences were expecting to come face-to-face with a bunch of squalid junkies attired in black.

Bad Moon Rising also kicked open the doors to England, which, for an unknown experimental rock band, was fairly unapproachable. After all, we weren't "gothy" like Lydia Lunch, and we had no "rock look" to speak of either. In that sense, by not caring about dressing up before we went onstage, we appeared more like the denizens of the American hardcore scene. Touring for the album, we played at the Institute of Contemporary Arts in London. Thurston had a cold, I remember, and was feverish. He did the show wearing his thick winter coat. Paul Smith had decorated the stage with carved jack-o'-lanterns with lit candles inside, creating a spooky, ghostly atmosphere, and as the band played harder, the stage got hotter and Thurston began peeling off his clothes. He even kicked one of the pumpkins off the stage. It was a classic punk rock move, one that affected the Brits so much that when one of the maintenance guys found a syringe backstage, he assumed it belonged to one of us. It didn't.

When *Bad Moon* hit, people frankly started looking at us differently, and college radio stations began playing our songs. The rock journalist Byron Coley interviewed us for *Forced Exposure,* and Sonic Youth made the cover of a popular indie-rock zine called *Matter.* In England, people had been loudly proclaiming the death of the guitar and the birth of the synthesizer, but Sonic Youth and other American guitar bands started to create a buzz. Most if not all of the other guitar bands were a lot more conventional than we were, but it seemed that together they, and we, were making an impact. The Australian band the Birthday Party had broken up and morphed into the Bad Seeds, and we were lucky enough to be asked to support them on a tour. Things were looking up but changing too.

Bob Bert, our drummer for this period, left the band and was replaced by Steve Shelley. Thurston and Lee had seen Steve play at CBGB with a Michigan hardcore band called the Crucifucks. Both of them believed Steve had something special that set him apart from other hardcore drummers. While Sonic Youth was on tour in the UK, Steve sublet our Eldridge Street apartment. When Bob left at the end of the tour, we asked Steve if he wanted to join the band and without hesitation he said, "Sure." Having struggled with different drummers over the course of our first two records, it felt like magic or destiny that Steve was right there in front of us. He was younger and didn't share in the band's collective New York history, but we had other musical influences and appreciations in common, the Birthday Party being one of them. Steve brought a power to Sonic Youth that we'd never had before.

Thurston had the idea of releasing "Death Valley '69" as a single, and contacted Stuart Swezey at Iridescence Records, who initiated a show we played in the middle of the Mojave Desert at a festival called the Gila Monster Jamboree. It was a dream bill, including Redd Kross, the Meat Puppets, and us, as well as Perry Farrell's first band, Psy Com. It was a magical night, one of my favorite shows ever. The venue, I remember, was kept a secret until the last minute. The moon was full and huge, the stage surrounded by a large pile of rocks that served as a kind of acoustic enhancement to the sounds coming off the amps. There was no stage, so we set up in the sand. The Meat Puppets sounded amazing, clear and mellifluous, and Redd Kross's set was just as good, their fur-and-glitter glam appearance making a surreal contrast to the desert's ritualistic campfire vibe. We just went for it. We had no monitors, only amps and a small P.A. system, which ultimately made our sound chaotic and hard to hear. Mike Kelley was there that night, dancing and drunk, having a great time. Someone shot the whole night on video, and if you know who you're looking for, you can make out Mike in the film. At one point during our set, I asked, "Does anyone have a beer? One beer for the band? Just one?" but since practically everyone in the crowd seemed to be on LSD or mushrooms, there was not a drop to be had in the desert.

The cover of "Death Valley '69" was a postcard of one of Gerhard Richter's paintings. It was Thurston's idea to use that postcard, of course. I would have been too shy to ask our friend if we could use his work. It didn't matter—the result was beautiful, a dark sinking sunset, perfect for the song and for the pure feeling of being out in the desert in California.

In 1984, Thurston and I got married. Frankly, I was afraid I wouldn't be able to commit to a long-term relationship. When I moved into 84 Eldridge, Dan kept teasing me about what a hippie I was, and even though I wasn't, his words had haunted me. By marrying Thurston, I was committing to something permanent, instead of always attempting to balance art with music, music with art, one or the other, back and forth. For someone so young Thurston was much more attracted to domesticity than I was. His faith made me believe our marriage could work.

Looking back, it's hard to believe how young we were. I was thirty-one, Thurston twenty-six. We were two creative people, and creative people usually delay becoming responsible adults unless there's a child involved. "I approach adulthood sideways," a film-director friend told me once. "I'm responsible to my legacy of work and I'm also responsible to my family, but it's hard." He added, "No one wants to lose the innocence they have for creativity." I held on as tight as I could to that innocence, but so did Thurston.

24

Evol:
"Shadow of a Doubt"

THE WAY THE BAND composed songs was pretty much always the same. Thurston or Lee would usually sing the poppy, more melodic things from riffs one of them wrote; I sang the weirder, more abstract things that came out of all of us playing together and rearranging until everything jelled. My voice has always had a fairly limited range, and when you're writing a melody, you tend to write it for your own voice. Lee, on the other hand, usually brought in songs that were complete and ready to go, then we layered dissonance over.

Over the years, Thurston and I always agreed on aesthetic things. We agreed about record covers pretty much all the time. For the most part we also agreed about mixes. If and when they took place, our fights mostly centered around how he treated or spoke to me. In the band's early days, our first drummer, Richard Edson, was the first to notice the dynamic between us. He would stand up for me, saying things like, "Hey, man, there's no call to talk to her like that."

Lee never said a word. Whenever Thurston spoke to me sharply or bluntly, it seemed to make him uncomfortable, and it was probably hard for Lee and Steve to figure out the boundaries of where Thurston and I started as a couple and stopped as bandmates. I was allergic to making scenes and did everything possible to maintain an identity as an individual within the band. I had no interest in being just the female half of a couple. When we were starting out, I was very sensitive, a hangover from my relationship with Keller, and let Thurston take the lead in most things. In the months leading up to our split, it was gratifying to me when Thurston, listening to some old live recording of ours, remarked, "Wow, you were playing some amazing things."

Gratifying but also strange to hear, as in our early days playing live, I had no technical ability to speak of, no knowledge of conventional chording. At the same time, I was always confident in my ability to contribute something good to our sound in at least an unconventional or minimalist way—a musicality, a sense of rhythm. All the No Wave bands, the jazz I'd listened to growing up, and the improv Keller and I had done back in our childhood living room came back to me onstage, blurring with the rock-and-roll riff or theater Thurston always wanted to convey. From the beginning, music for me was visceral. I *loved* playing music. When it was going well, it was an almost ecstatic experience. What could be better than sharing that feeling of transcendence with a man I was so close to in all other areas of my life, someone who was having the same experience? It was a feeling impossible to communicate with someone outside of the two of us. I wanted deliverance, the loss of myself, the capacity to be *inside* that music. It was the same power and sensation you feel when a wave takes you up and pushes you someplace else.

Thurston and I first met Raymond Pettibon in the early eighties during a trip to L.A., where I was visiting my parents. Someone told us about a house party in Hermosa Beach, where Black Flag was playing, so we drove down to South Bay, pulling up in front of a typical single-level house. The neighborhood was languid, slightly funky, as if it had tried and failed to become a beach resort, morphing instead into a shabby suburban neighborhood a walk away from the ocean. The house was small, the music ferocious, Henry Rollins in the kitchen, in full force, dressed in those signature small black shorts that I believe were technically an old-style nylon bathing suit. Slick with sweat, he was writhing around bumping into cabinets and people, at one point coming up to me and singing straight into my face.

Coming from the New York downtown scene, where people had no houses, or garages, and thus, no house parties, this was a completely new scene for us. The Black Flag show was one of the best gigs I'd seen before or since—scary, surreal, intimate. As the sound crashed and bounced off the refrigerator counter and shelves, and Henry Rollins twerked years before twerking existed, the performance fused hardcore punk with suburban sunlit banality, high theatre with the everyday, erasing any and all boundaries between band and audience.

At one point Thurston and I went out into the glare of the backyard, where Mike Watt from the Minutemen introduced us to Raymond Pettibon. To us, Raymond was already a semimythical figure, as a couple of years back we had become keenly interested in his zines. Raymond was shy, casually disheveled, altogether normal-looking. Still, it felt unbelievable to be hanging out with Mike and Raymond, and other musicians in bands whose records we owned. The L.A. scene!

At that point, in the mid-eighties, Ray had no relationship to the art world, and had never had a gallery show. At the time he was known exclusively for his SST covers. Later that same year, I wrote an article for *Artforum* about Raymond's work, as well as Mike Kelley's and Tony Oursler's—how the three of them eschewed the conceptual mantle of seventies formalism and mixed high and low culture. Soon afterwards,

Raymond began showing at the Ace Gallery in L.A. Like a flower, he slowly opened up, the only thing he needed was just a little attention.

That day sticks out so much in my mind not just because it was the first time I met Raymond, but because seeing Henry Rollins inspired the song "Halloween."

Even after *Bad Moon,* I never felt like I had a place in the New York music scene. Artists I had no trouble conversing with, but I had no idea how to talk to musicians. I felt confused about how I "should" look, and I felt frumpy and nerdy a lot of the time. I also had no confidence, really. I don't think artists ever feel like what they do is enough, and even though I was now part of a musical couple, I wasn't doing as much as I thought I should be doing individually—my art career was kind of on hold—and without confidence, it doesn't matter what you're wearing. I once interviewed Raymond Pettibon, who spoke about having to dumb himself down whenever he talked to musicians. Not that musicians are unintelligent, he said— they just don't intellectualize in the same way artists do. Criticize something in front of musicians, and they'll take it personally. Criticize artists, and they're more likely to take it intellectually. It's just different, that's all.

We weren't remotely a goth band, but *Evol* was our faux-goth record, the one that contains "Expressway to Yr. Skull," Sonic Youth's first socalled long song. *Evol* was also the first record we put out on the indie record label SST. SST, who put out records by Black Flag, the Minutemen, Hüsker Dü, and the Meat Puppets, was ideal for us.

The name *Evol* came from an art video that my friend Tony Oursler made, while the cover was a film still created by filmmaker Richard Kern. Richard's faux-horror films were dark, funny, and voyeuristic, typically shot from a height, with tongue-in-cheek gore.

The song "Shadow of a Doubt" came from an Alfred Hitchcock film. What I'm reading at the time tends to influence and inform what I'm working on—whether it's a novel or a Hitchcock bio. I tend to write lyrics with a sense of space around them, one-liners almost, short sentences containing pauses that build tension along with the music, as if

I'm awaiting some big drama or crash to occur, though it never does—the song just ends. I was always a big fan of early songs by the Shangri-Las, with their whispered, almost spoken-word approach leading up to a violent climax, such as in "Leader of the Pack" or "I Can Never Go Home Anymore."

In "Shadow of a Doubt," I was trying to describe the connection you feel when your eyes meet another person's. You project all kinds of things on those eyes, feel them seeing into and past you, sometimes feel the sex behind them too. The song imagines what would happen if you acted on that feeling, with things devolving into a scene from a pulpy film noir novel, and nothing you did could stop the inevitable.

A young filmmaker named Kevin Kerslake made a video for "Shadow of a Doubt," the first one we ever did that had the look and feel of something that could play on MTV. We had made videos before, notably for "Death Valley '69." For that song, in fact, there were two different videos, one more arty, one more hard-core. In the hard-core video for "Death Valley '69," I can remember lying on the ground, with blood everywhere, our fake guts spilling from our stomachs, while off camera Lee's first wife, Amanda, was having actual labor contractions. A vivid contrast between fake death and incoming life. In the video I also got to wield a shotgun. Girls with guns, girls in control, girls as revolutionaries, girls acting out—why is that such a perennial turn-on to people?

Evol also had a cover of Kim Fowley's "Bubblegum," as well as songs like "Star Power" and of course "Expressway to Yr. Skull," which contained what to my mind were Thurston's best lyrics: *"We're gonna kill the California girls,"* meaning, we're from New York and we're not pop or rock and we're coming to get you . . . we're coming to California. We did "Expressway" in one take, and I remember sitting in the dark studio with Thurston, Lee, and Steve listening back to it. It was absolutely thrilling.

Those were the moments I felt closest to Thurston—when I felt that together, he and I had created something special, music that would go out into the world and take on its own life. No matter what happened to that music, I was convinced it was good and would last forever. (When I listen to *Evol* today, I'm amazed by the amount of reverb on it. I had so little perspective back then . . . on everything.)

When Sonic Youth toured England, journalists took to asking me a single question over and over: "What's it like to be a girl in a band?" I'd never really thought about that, to be honest. The mostly male English music press was cowardly and nonconfrontational in person. They would then go home and write cruel, ageist, sexist things. I'd always assumed it was because they were terrified of women; the whole country had a queen complex, after all. I might have been projecting my own discomfort at acting out a prewritten role onto these writers, but I refused to play the game. I didn't want to dress like Siouxsie Sioux or Lydia Lunch, or to act out the role of an imaginary female, someone who had more to do with them than with me. That just wasn't who I was.

For that reason, I found the British band the Raincoats both cool and inspirational. They were an all-girl post-punk band, playing noncommercial music—rhythmic and off-kilter. They came across as ordinary people playing extraordinary music. They didn't use typical instrumentation, either. After their drummer Palmolive left, the experimental rock drummer Charlie Hayward joined them, adding to a sound that included the violin and a bunch of exotic secondhand instruments from Africa and Bali, like the balafon, the kalimba, and the gamelan. Here were women playing and singing against every stereotype there was, but doing it subtly and musically, gently and mystically, without the traditional aggression of rock and punk and without flying a freak flag. I'd spent my entire life never doing what was easy, never doing what was expected. I had no idea what image I projected onstage or off, but I was willing to let myself be unknown forever. Self-consciousness was the beginning of creative death to me. I felt at ease only when I'd recorded something I felt good about, or was in the middle of a gig and the sound swirling from the stage was so amazing that time stopped and I could feel the audience in the dark breathing as a single unit. That is all a fantasy, yes, but everyone needs to pretend. As J Mascis of Dinosaur Jr. liked to say when asked about being in a band, "It's not fun. It's not about having fun."

25

Sister:
"Schizophrenia"

IN 1987, THURSTON and I were both reading Philip K. Dick, whose writing has more in common with philosophy than science fiction, and whose descriptions of schizophrenia were better than those of any medical journal. Philip Dick had a twin sister who died shortly after she was born and whose memory plagued him his whole life—which is maybe how and why our new album ended up being called *Sister*. We never decided this, of course; everything between us always had an air of undiscussed ambiguity about it.

In high school, one of my English teachers told our class that the entire world was "schizophrenic." He rambled on about semantics and about the power of words, and even in the acid-soaked days of the late 1960s, I was never sure what he meant. I desperately wanted to be the smart one in the class and push the teacher, but being suffocated by social anxiety and self-consciousness, I never was.

As always, it started with Keller. The outsized rebel, the attention taker, at times so funny and charming, before the disease engulfed his head. If Keller was the problem child, the fire threatening always to burn our family to the ground, what did that make me? The one who never made waves. The one who, if she was good enough, could make our family normal.

"Pacific Coast Highway" from *Sister* is a twisted love story about hitchhiking up to Malibu and getting picked up by a sociopath. *"Come on get in the car . . . Let's go for a ride somewhere . . . I won't hurt you . . . As much as you hurt me."* It was a direct pull from the fears of my teenage years when I was focused on the lore surrounding Charlie Manson, who mirrored the darkness and swirl lying beneath West L.A.'s Disneygreen lawns and movie-perfect foliage.

Thurston and I had been married for three years and together for seven, and by now he knew me so well it was as though the two of us were joined in both our bodies and brains. Oddly enough, he was the one who wrote the lyrics to "Schizophrenia," somehow making the words sound as though they were mine. Even though the song wasn't explicitly about Keller, the Philip K. Dick references throughout *Sister* always made me feel they were.

I loved making *Sister,* and Sear Sound in midtown Manhattan—the oldest recording studio in New York—was the perfect place to record it. Following *Evol,* we wanted a rawer, more immediate sound, and Sear, with its huge collection of vintage analog tube equipment, including a great two-inch sixteen-track, was the fulfillment of our sound fantasies. Still, we ended up in a deteriorating studio that backed up onto the old Paramount Hotel, and the lousy acoustics of the room were good for the guitars but muffled the drums, which disappointed Steve to no end.

Walter Sear ran the studio and was a classical tuba player who, with

Robert Moog, developed the Moog synthesizer. As well as recording music, Walter and his partner Roberta were also in the B-movie business. Hanging from Sear Sound's walls were great B horror movie posters, and you could snack there all day long on sugary doughnuts, bagels, cream cheese, lox, and day-old popcorn, though despite the snacks it wasn't a movie theater, just a great old-school recording studio. Walter and Roberta were old-timey, chain-smoking New Yorkers. During our recording session, Walter was also casting a movie, and every day the band would pass by a line of hopeful actors and actresses. At night, when the studio emptied out, we sat around flipping through their headshots. Walter and Roberta lived a way of life that will soon be wiped out entirely from the Disney version of New York's theater district. First-generation bohemians were a dying breed even then.

Sister's cover was a loose collage of images that each band member individually chose. In the downtown art world, appropriation was commonplace, which is why we felt this was an acceptable approach. By collecting those images, we believed we were creating something new out of them. Among them was a Richard Avedon photo of a prepubescent girl and an image of Disney's Magic Kingdom. When Avedon threatened to sue us, followed by Disney's legal department, we responded by subsequently blacking out the offending images, a reminder forever that we'd been censored by people who had more money to spend on lawyers than we did.

26

Ciccone Youth:
"Addicted to Love"

CICCONE YOUTH was a side project, consisting of Steve, Lee, Thurston, and me. The four of us decided to do a record where we simply went into the studio and made it there, the way hip-hop is made: start with a beat or a loop, then build on it. Ciccone Youth is so different from any Sonic Youth music, we thought it was a good idea to confuse people, so we created this separate identity.

A year earlier, we had done a Madonna Ciccone "cover" called "Into the Groovey," as a twelve-inch, with Mike Watt doing another cover, "Burnin' Up," on the B-side. Madonna was cool in the eighties—her dance pop was minimal and fresh—and we were all fans. She was slightly fleshy in the beginning, and her main talents were pluck, willpower, and moving her body around. Her voice wasn't strong, and she wasn't an obvious diva, but she had a knack for knowing how to entertain, singing, *"Like a virgin / Touched for the very first time,"* with a heart-shaped pout and beckoning eyes perfect for MTV. Reagan, orange cheeked, was in office; Nancy, his wife, wore red; and Madonna rocked white like no one else. Her "Like a Virgin" video was shot in Italy, a combination of honeymoon ideal and Catholic bastion, with her riding down a Venice canal in a gondola. In the unsteady boat Madonna gazed up at the camera, turning us all into her lover.

It's hard thinking back on her now and seeing what critics called her "shocking sexuality." They rushed to embrace her sexualized image-branding as self-empowerment as well as marketing sophistication, and therefore feminist. To me, she seemed joyful, celebrating her own body. Most fun of all was her plucky attitude. She didn't have a perfect body. She was a little soft, but sexy-soft, not overweight but not as sculpted or as hard as she would later become. She was realistic about her body type, and she flaunted it, and you could feel how happy she was inhabiting that body. I admired what she was doing, though I was also skeptical about where it would all eventually lead. In retrospect Madonna was riding a cultural wave that has evolved into a landscape where porn is everywhere, where women are openly using their sexuality to sell their art in ways that before the 1980s would have been a male's idea of marketing. Porn, of course, is also a male fantasy of the world. When a woman does what a man used to do, I can't help but wonder if it leads us back in a circle.

Today we have someone like Lana Del Rey, who doesn't even know what feminism is, who believes it means women can do whatever they want, which, in her world, tilts toward self-destruction, whether it's sleeping with gross older men or being a transient biker queen. Equal pay and equal rights would be nice. Naturally, it's just a persona. Does she truly believe it's beautiful when young musicians go out on a hot flame of drugs and depression, or is it just her persona?

With Ciccone Youth, we wanted to go into the studio and work with drum machines, without any towering expectations. More than anything, we were interested in playing in the style of 1970s German prog rock, like Neu! and Can. I got frustrated sitting around the studio while the guys took turns manning the mixing board, so I took off, deciding to make a couple of songs outside the studio. One, "Two Cool Rock Chicks Listening to Neu," was created by Suzanne Sasic and me at 84 Eldridge. We simply recorded ourselves listening to Neu! while we talked about J Mascis's guitar playing. Later I took it to the studio, and J agreed to play a lead over a very minimal drum machine.

The other song we did was my cover of "Addicted to Love." There used to be a sort of karaoke booth on Saint Mark's, where anyone could go in and record themselves. I chose "Addicted to Love" because I liked Robert Palmer's video, with its background cast of zombie models identically dressed and holding guitars. I took the tape with the canned version of the song back to the studio, and we sped up the vocal to make it sound higher in pitch. Later I brought the cassette mix to Macy's, where they had a video version of the karaoke sound booth. You could customize a background while two cameras filmed you. For my backdrop I picked jungle fighters, and I wore my Black Flag earrings. The entire bill came to $19.99, and in a slick, commercial MTV world, it felt gratifying and empowering to pay for the whole thing with a credit card.

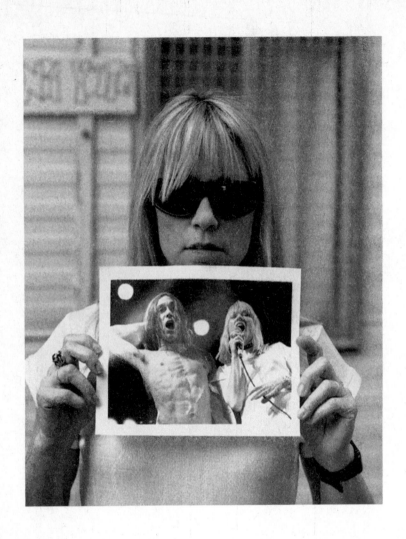

27

Daydream Nation: "The Sprawl"

EVERY TIME WE created a new record, the band ended up rehearsing it in an entirely new practice space. The best place we ever rehearsed was a place on Sixth Street and Avenue B that belonged to Mike Gira of the Swans—a storefront shell that Mike had cut in half, with his living quarters on one side and a rehearsal space on the other. The place was windowless, the entrance double bolted, a fortress against the racket of street gunfire at night. Inside it was dead sounding, with carpet-covered walls, making dissonance a nonissue and contributing to the end impression that each band member had brought in a vocabulary of sounds that melded together to create a unity—in other words, a song.

Parts of *Daydream* still sound that way to me today. We were on a tight deadline, I remember, and Thurston, Steve, Lee, and I wrote most of the album in an old building on Mott Street in Little Italy. I recall a long narrow corridor, sectioned off with equipment belonging to others bands, in rooms that looked like ships' dungeons. By now, we had changed labels and were on Blast First in the U.S. through a subsidiary of Capitol Records called Mute/Enigma, which is to say almost, but not quite, a major label. The last songs on the album we actually wrote in the Blast First office, just upstairs.

With *Daydream,* we had slightly more money for recording, which we did in a studio owned by Philip Glass, on Greene Street in Soho. At the time, Public Enemy and their producer, Hank Shocklee, were working there on the other board. Our engineer, Nick Sansano, had almost no experience working with electric guitars or rock music, but this bothered no one, and Nick seemed to understand precisely what we were after. When I recently ran into Nick, he told me how much he remembered the vibe of innocence and idealism in those sessions, as well as his visceral reaction to the music. "It's hard to believe so much time has gone by," he told me, "because some of those memories live as if it were yesterday." He said his students at NYU, where he teaches, ask him about *Daydream* all the time—"and I mean *all the time.*"

Daydream Nation came out in late 1988 as a double LP, at the end of Reagan's second term, and we were completely surprised when it became number one in the *Village Voice* Pazz and Jop poll that year. The record got a lot of attention. As always, critical appeal never completely translated into record sales but it ensured that our band never disappeared from view. Before *Daydream* came out, we did a shoot with Michael Lavine, and I remember walking around New York with the rest of the band in the hot, spongy summer. Michael had a panoramic camera, and in the photos he took I can still feel the dank, dirty moisture of the urban August.

"Do you want to look cool, or do you want to look attractive?" Michael asked me, as if the two were mutually exclusive. The silver paint; glitter-dabbed, faded cutoff jeans; and crop top with the sheer jeweled panel marked a turning point for me and my look. I decided I didn't want to just look cool, or just look rock and roll; I wanted to look more *girl*. Looking back, I was trying to make more of a definite statement about what my look was and how I wanted to present myself. Tomboy, but more ambiguous than tomboy, too. The increased media attention, and seeing more photos of myself, and of Sonic Youth as a band, had made me more self-conscious.

"Looking cool" has many different meanings and interpretations for people. For a girl, cool has a lot to do with androgyny, and after all I played with boys, and also played with other boy bands. The hardcore scene was extremely male, and in the post-punk American hardcore scene you didn't see many girls onstage. Kira Roessler, the bass player for Black Flag, was one of them. She was one of the most startling and great things I'd seen in a long time. For the band's second live album, *Who's Got the 10½?*, Kira wore a bra and garter belt with stockings onstage. It was such a contrast to Henry Rollins in his nylon workout shorts and sweaty, shirt-less, tattooed torso, his growling, torturedly aggressive, hypermale vocals. She must have been playing off the Madonna thing, and it worked, too.

Until that point, Sonic Youth still toured mostly outside the U.S., and *Daydream Nation* brought us for the first time to Australia, Japan, and the Soviet Union. On a previous tour I remember reading the Denis Johnson book *Fiskadoro,* a haze-filled dream world of a novel about the survivors of nuclear fallout attempting to rebuild their lives and society. In my head, *Fiskadoro* mingled with old 1960s movie themes of young women growing up in small towns, wanting to leave their hometowns behind and be somewhere, anywhere, and someone, anyone, else. Maybe they'd glimpsed a highway billboard that advertised clothes, a car, a golden future, a possibility. Maybe, thanks to the machine of consumerism, they felt they were missing out on something they hadn't even known existed.

When I wrote the lyrics for "The Sprawl," a song from *Daydream,* I took on a character, a voice within a song. The whole time I was writing it, I was thinking back on what it felt like being a teenager in Southern California, paralyzed by the still, unending sprawl of L.A., feeling all alone on the sidewalk, the pavement's plainness so dull and ugly it almost made me nauseous, the sun and good weather so assembly-line unchanging it made my whole body tense. The nutmeg headband of smog floating above my hometown reminded me of *Fiskadoro,* as if L.A. were already surviving its own nuclear fallout. *"I grew up in a shotgun house / Sliding down the hill / Out front were the big machines / Still and rusty now, I guess / Out back was the river . . . And that big sign on the road—that's where it all started."*

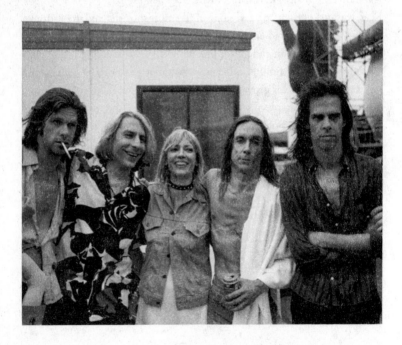

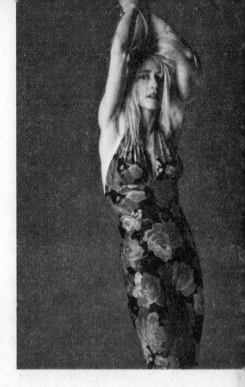

28

Goo and
Neil Young

IN 1990, SONIC YOUTH had been together for ten years, and we'd finally signed to a major label. We weren't happy with the job Blast First and Capitol did with *Daydream,* so we decided to look at major labels. At the time, we had no manager, so our lawyer, Richard Grabel, put the word out. We had seen other independent bands sign with majors—the Replacements, Hüsker Dü—and crash and burn, so we were cautious. But we felt confident that our band had been together long enough to ensure that if for some reason the major deal didn't work out, we'd survive, and that anyone who signed us knew who and what they were getting—a not-especially-commercial band with strong critical cred who could just maybe bring something to a label aside from top-ten hits. We were also frankly curious to see how more production money would affect our unconventional sound.

Soon the criticism started. We had sold out. How could Sonic Youth sign with a label as big and corporate as Geffen? It wasn't as if we hadn't heard all the stories about David Geffen himself, up to and including the fight he'd had with Neil Young after the release of Neil's records, *Trans*, and *Everybody's Rockin'*. Geffen had sued Neil for violating his contract by releasing albums that were "musically uncharacteristic of Young's previous recordings" or something to that effect. The suit was settled, finally, with Geffen apologizing. Right after we signed, Geffen sold the company, eventually founding DreamWorks with Jeffrey Katzenberg and Steven Spielberg. It was the beginning of real corporate ownership for Geffen Records.

The record advance we received from Geffen meant it was time to think about putting down some roots. Thurston and I bought a bigger place, on Lafayette Street, across from the Puck Building. It was the middle of the recession, so we got a great deal. It was time, too: our Eldridge Street landlord had sold the building, and a Chinese restaurant was taking over the ground floor.

In 1991, grunge was hitting the mainstream, thanks to Sub Pop Records and Nirvana. The *New York Times* published a famous interview with Megan Jasper, then a secretary at the Seattle record label Sub Pop, about the phenomenon and culture of the Seattle sound. The article said that the designer Marc Jacobs, who was working for Perry Ellis at the time, had been hailed by *Women's Wear Daily* as "the guru of grunge" when Marc exhibited models with carefully unwashed-looking hair and untied combat boots. Megan gave the *Times* the new lexicon of grunge. Old ripped jeans, she said, were "wack slacks." Sweaters were "fuzz." Hanging out was "swingin' on the flippity-flop." And if you were drunk, you were a "big bag of bloatation."

Megan made the whole thing up, much to the embarrassment of the *New York Times* and to the delight of folks in the scene out in Seattle.

But if anyone had any doubts about the power of music over fashion, Kate Moss was as much a poster child for grunge as any Nirvana performance, and musically pigmented fashion was sprouting up all over the place. But the East Coast never bought into the grunge aesthetic. In New York, there were stores like Patricia Field's on Eighth Street in the East Village that sold glitter, platforms, feathers, and silver leather hot pants. All the local trannies shopped there. I recently came across a photo of myself from that era, taken by Laura Levine for *Detour* magazine. In the photo, I am wearing one of Patricia Field's floral unitards, one I bought because it reminded me of my mother in the 1950s. Not that my mother ever wore florals, but the unitard had a vibrancy about it that reminded me of how beautiful my mother looked when she and my dad were leaving the house at night to go to a party. Like a lot of clothes Patricia Field sold, it was more club-trendy than fashion-forward. I always found it ironic that Pat Fields later became the costume designer for *Sex and the City*, importing a transvestite camp sensibility to middle America via Carrie Bradshaw.

Gary Gersh, our A&R guy at Geffen, was disappointed when we chose a black-and-white Raymond Pettibon drawing for the cover of *Goo*. I'm sure he was hoping for a glamorous picture of the band, something very of the moment, with me front and center. Raymond's drawings had been slapped on record covers for many bands on the SST label, especially Black Flag's. We loved Ray's zines and drawings and in the mideighties I had written about his work in *Artforum;* the black-and-white cover was based on the couple in Terrence Malick's film *Badlands,* while the inside was colorful, a riot of faux-glam goofiness.

In the early nineties I was slowly embracing a new idea: that if you wore sexier clothes, you could sell dissonant music more easily. I started creating a look for myself that had a campy late-sixties and early-seventies vibe. At a store in Cleveland, I found flared pants with green and white stars and stripes, and I wore them when we opened for Neil Young that year on his "Ragged Glory" tour during the Gulf War. Neil always hung the American flag from the stage. Still, I was always much more a visual person than a fashionable one, and my look was intended to be slightly humorous. I always liked the way Debbie Harry had a twist of humor about her, even when she was looking sexy and glam. It fit the genius of her guise as the female front person, the "Blondie" cartoon character, a doll who could dress up in different looks and styles.

The Neil Young tour was set up through Gold Mountain, but I also think Neil had some knowledge of Sonic Youth, even though the other opening acts were bands from his booking agent's or manager's roster. Opening for Neil was an amazing, eye-opening experience. We were all big longtime fans of his, and it felt like our first real brush with the mainstream. Of course, this prompted every music journalist to ask us, "So what's it like to finally be in the mainstream?" In reply I can say that Neil Young tour proved that Sonic Youth actually wasn't *in* the mainstream, and that if we were, the mainstream hated us!

Neil always drew big crowds, including legions of hippies loyal to his music. Those same crowds were incredibly put off by us, to the degree that if fans sitting among them appreciated or applauded one of our songs, they were aggressively shouted down. The Cow Palace in San Francisco is one of the only arena venues with an open floor, allowing the audience to surge forward during the opening act. Usually during what felt like an excruciatingly long twenty-minute set, we played to empty seats in front. Another band, Social Distortion, went onstage before us, and they had the favor of Neil's stage manager, Tim, since their tattoos, cut-off leather vests, and greasy styled hair screamed "rock," whereas Tim looked upon us as foreign pond scum. Our music disturbed him, and he was clearly uncomfortable that a woman was in the band. He kept referring to us as "kids" or "punks" and always seemed to be waiting for us to act the part, but we never gave him the satisfaction. I'll never forget the first show we played in Minneapolis. The band was in the catering room, in line, waiting our turn to eat, when Tim came up behind us and said, "Move along—you're holding everything up. What do you think you're doing anyway?" We literally felt like we were in a high school cafeteria, getting picked on by a bully. Throughout the tour, we were almost never allowed a sound check, so there were many nights when every guitar Thurston picked up was out of tune, since Keith, a friend who became our first roadie, had no experience with our tunings and unconventional stringing. Sometimes onstage Thurston got so frustrated he smashed his guitar.

But Neil's guitar guy, Larry, was amazing, and by the next day, Thurston's guitar would always be put back together. Since the bass is the only instrument with a normal tuning, I escaped the guitar drama, praying instead that I'd never break a string and that during the show Thurston's guitar wouldn't fly up and hit me. I lived in fear he would fall and hurt himself climbing up on an amp, and sometimes it distracted me from playing, wondering if he was going to have a good or a bad show. Duh, so I'm codependent, because when I look back on that tour, I realize I simply wanted everything to *work* to the best of our ability, but maybe that's rock, too.

The tour with Neil Young was grueling: the dead of winter, a frozen ocean of endless arena locker rooms. At one point we brought in a record player and a lamp, to make things more homey in our dressing room areas, which helped. And there was always the hope that Neil would burst in on his way to the stage, which did happen a couple of times. But the person who hung out with us the most was Neil's longtime guitarist, Frank Sampedro, better known as Poncho. Poncho was Neil's ears, and pretty much everything we said in his presence found its way back to Neil. Here's an example. Our friend Suzanne had become our lighting person, and Poncho overheard us commenting that we both thought Neil could use a haircut. One day during the tour, Poncho came up to Suzanne and asked if she was up for giving Neil a trim.

There are two particular things I remember about Poncho. The first is how much he liked "the ladies," which meant every time someone in Neil's crew or band had a birthday, strippers would materialize by the side of the stage. The second is that after every show, Poncho cooked dinner for Neil on his bus. One night I told him I'd do it—Poncho could pick when. Neil's longtime bus driver, who was always friendly to us, offered to fetch the ingredients for the chicken dish I planned on making. Unfortunately he forgot and ended up making an emergency trip to KFC to score a batch of uncooked chicken wings. I was nervous they would make Neil sick, but luckily they didn't.

That night, Thurston and I went onto Neil's bus to cook and hang out. Thurston was in his element: Neil and he talked about punk rock, which Thurston could talk about for days on end. Neil was lovely. He sat there tuning the sound of a cow mooing for one of his electric train cars. "Do you think it sounds too high?" he said. "How about this? Is that better?" and then he took the screwdriver and tweaked it. Neil was really into our song "Expressway to Yr. Skull"—he later said he thought it was the best guitar song ever written—and mentioned he went under the stage now and again to stretch out during that song's long ending. This may sound lame, and like a total understatement, but Neil was always incredibly supportive of us.

That night he also showed us his unreleased film from his European comeback tour, "Muddy Tracks," which he had shot himself with a camera he took everywhere. He called the camera "Auto," which I found adorable. During the shows, Neil set it atop his amp. In the bus, he sat it in the windshield as they drove from gig to gig, capturing the look and feel of the road at night. As you might expect, the audio was noisy but great. Thurston told Neil he should release a seven-inch that sounded just like that, a whirring industrial sound, like feedback in the wind. In response, Neil ended up recording an entire album of live feedback called *Arc*.

I thought back to Bruce Berry, the Crosby, Stills, Nash & Young roadie who OD'd, and how he'd been the inspiration for Neil's song "Tonight's the Night" and its eponymous LP. It blew my mind to realize how small the world was. Icons I never imagined I'd meet were now a part of my life. When Social Distortion left the tour, Thurston and I gave Neil cassette tapes of both Nirvana and Dinosaur Jr. I don't know if Neil ever listened to them, but six months later, Nirvana's album *Nevermind* broke big. True to the way big corporate rock operated, another band from Neil's booking agency, Drivin' N' Cryin', joined the tour instead.

Sonic Youth may not have won over any fans while touring with Neil, but our profile rose. Suddenly magazines like *Spin* were approaching me to do photo shoots, and later that year Neil asked us to perform at his Bridge School benefit concert. Neil and his wife, Pegi Young, started the Bridge School benefit in the mid-1980s to help found and fund the Bridge School in Hillsborough, California, which helps children with communication problems and physical disabilities. Neil has two sons, Zeke and Ben, who both have cerebral palsy. It's an acoustic-only charity event, and Sonic Youth had never played acoustically before. I'd brought along a guitar to smash, as I had a strange feeling that night that things were doomed to fail.

During sound check, we could hear our guitars, but when we came out to play, we heard nothing. For us, a band that relies on the interplay of the guitars, it was the worst possible situation, plus, we were playing for a mainstream rock audience. We got only halfway through a cover version of "Personality Crisis" before I yelled, "Fuck!" into the microphone and smashed the acoustic guitar standing nearby. Willie Nelson then came out to perform a medley of his songs, followed by Don Henley, accompanied by a full electric band. I felt terrible that I'd yelled out "Fuck!" especially when we walked offstage and I saw a row of kids in their wheelchairs sitting at the back of the stage. I had forgotten they were there. Later, Ben, Neil's son, came up to me in his wheelchair. "Everyone has a bad day sometimes," he said to me.

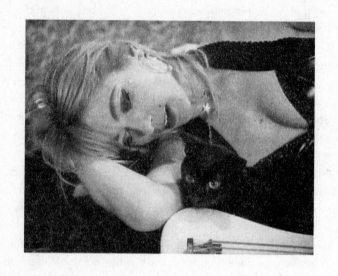

29

Goo: "Tunic (Song for Karen)" and "Kool Thing"

ONE OF THE SONGS off *Goo* was "Tunic (Song for Karen)." Karen Carpenter had interested me for a long time. The Carpenters were such a sun-drenched American dream, such a feel-good family success story like the Beach Boys, but with the same roiling darkness going on underneath. Obviously Karen Carpenter had a strange relationship with her brother, Richard, a great producer but also a tyrannical control freak. The only autonomy Karen felt she had in her life she exerted over her own body. She was an extreme version of what a lot of women suffer from—a lack of control over things other than their bodies, which turns the female body into a tool for power—good, bad, or ugly.

It began, as it always does with women, with a single remark: one night someone told Karen that she looked "hip-py" onstage. In the end I think she wanted to make herself disappear, and did that by unleashing destruction on herself. I always found Karen's voice incredibly sexy and soulful. She made every word and syllable her own, and if you listen to those lyrics, you go, *Wow*. But at the same time, was there any band ever more white-bread than the Carpenters? I didn't always appreciate their music. When they first had radio hits they were considered ultra-conservative, so "establishment" that their melodies could have been used in bank commercials. They were almost the definition of easy listening. But twenty years later, in another context, their music sounded beautiful to me, though it might have been concurrent with the release of Todd Haynes's bootleg video about Karen's life called, simply, *Superstar*, and starring Barbie and Ken.

I could make up a lot of reasons why the song was called "Tunic." The most obvious is that Karen was so thin from starving herself that her clothes hung on her bones like flowing biblical robes. She couldn't make peace with her own body's curves. She would never get the love she craved from her mother, who favored her brother, or from her brother himself. Their approval meant everything. How was she not the quintessential woman in our culture, compulsively pleasing others in order to achieve some degree of perfection and power that's forever just around the corner, out of reach? It was easier for her to disappear, to free herself finally from that body, to find a perfection in dying.

Tony Oursler shot a video for us of "Tunic," and Thurston had scored a reel of Carpenters videos, which were actually pretty funny. In the middle of the dreamy part of the song, we inserted snippets of video, but because we were on a major label, we weren't allowed to do that without permission. So to get around it, we blurred the Carpenters parts of that video.

I wrote this open letter to Karen once, for a magazine, I can't remember which one.

Dear Karen,

Thru the years of The Carpenters TV specials I saw you change from the Innocent Oreo-cookie-and-milk-eyed girl next door to hollowed eyes and a lank body adrift on a candy-colored stage set. You and Richard, by the end, looked drugged—there's so little energy. The words come out of yr mouth but yr eyes say other things, "Help me, please, I'm lost in my own passive resistance, something went wrong. I wanted to make myself disappear from their control. My parents, Richard, the writers who call me 'hip-py, fat.' Since I was, like most girls, brought up to be polite and considerate, I figured no one would notice anything wrong—as long as, outwardly, I continued to do what was expected of me. Maybe they could control all the outward aspects of my life, but my body is all in my control. I can make myself smaller. I can disappear. I can starve myself to death and they won't know it. My voice will never give me away. They're not my words. No one will guess my pain. But I will make the words my own because I have to express myself somehow. Pain is not perfect so there is no place in Richard's life for it. I have to be perfect too. I must be thin so I'm perfect. Was I a teenager once? I forget. Now I look middle-aged, with a bad perm and country-western clothes."

I must ask you, Karen, who were your role models? Was it yr mother? What kind of books did you like to read? Did anyone ever ask you that question—what's it like being a girl in music? What were yr dreams? Did you have any female friends or was it just you and Richard, mom and dad, A&M? Did you ever go running along the sand, feeling the ocean rush up between yr legs? Who is Karen Carpenter, really, besides the sad girl with the extraordinarily beautiful, soulful voice?

your fan—love, kim

———

"Kool Thing" was a complex song, influenced by everybody from Jane Fonda to Raymond Pettibon to Bootsy Collins and Funkadelic to an interview I'd done once with LL Cool J. A few years earlier, Raymond had shot a film about the Weather Underground, called *The Whole World Is Watching: Weatherman '69*, which, like most of Raymond's drawings, was full of dark humor and satire. Thurston and I both appeared in the film, reading Raymond's brilliant script off cue cards. I played Bernadine Dohrn, and in Raymond's script, I, or rather Bernadine, was drawn to leftist politics because I had a thing for male Black Panthers. I also loved LL Cool J's first record, *Radio,* which was produced by Rick Rubin, and when I interviewed him for *Spin* magazine, I asked him if he'd had anything to do with the samples and what kind of rock music he liked. I couldn't hide my disappointment when he said, "Bon Jovi." Then again, it makes sense that big, fat power chords would be ideal for sampling.

The band recorded "Kool Thing" at Greene Street. Chuck D from Public Enemy was also working there that week, waiting sometimes for Flavor Flav to arrive at the studio. You'd always know he'd come when you heard his big oversized shoes slapping down the stairs. We asked Chuck D if he would contribute to the call-and-response middle section of "Kool Thing," and he agreed. Having Chuck D work with us was amazing, as both Thurston and I felt he "got us" a little bit.

"Kool Thing" was also the first big-budget video Sonic Youth ever filmed. We chose Tamra Davis to direct, because we had all liked her "Funky Cold Medina" video for Tone Lôc. That video had a clean, fresh, minimal approach, with none of the excess of most major-label videos. In a funny, small-world link, I had met Tamra through her sister Melodie, whom I'd crossed paths with years earlier when I first moved to New York. When she introduced us, Melodie said, "This is my sister Tamra—maybe she'll make a video for you someday." It was one of those remarks you smile at and never think about again, but here was Tamra, now living with Mike D from the Beastie Boys, back in our lives.

I told Tamra that I somehow wanted to reference one of my favorite videos ever—LL Cool J's video for "Going Back to Cali." Released around the time of the East Coast–versus–West Coast rap wars, "Going Back to Cali" was a perfect song and video, with its Russ Meyer–like camera angles and jagged cuts, and the humorous way it made fun of the 1960s archetypal Southern California sexy white-girl aesthetic. The video was shot in stark black and white, so you really get a sense of the glare of the sun and the whiteness of the women's bodies, in contrast to the color of LL Cool J's skin, all against the backdrop of L.A.'s intense body-consciousness. By refusing to buy into that sensibility, LL comes off as a hero. I'm a sucker for any movie or TV show about L.A.

Tamra was a fantastic collaborator. She filmed us against a silver foil backdrop, a nod to Warhol Factory–era East Coast–ness. The video opened with Sonic Youth playing in a silver room. There were quicksilver shots of leather, black cats, lips, and juxtapositions of white skin and black skin, of the black struggle and the female struggle. The fashion is pretty 1960s-era, and the video has no clear story or message, really, but despite its style it was still a little controversial.

I suppose African-Americans could watch "Kool Thing" and say, "This is the way white people see us—as objects." But we were careful to make sure that everyone looked good and was photographed well. It disturbed me that many critics didn't understand that I was not talking to Chuck D—who was playing himself—but instead to an unseen third party. If the song made people uneasy, or if it caused them to question things, well, good, even if they got it wrong. I deliberately wanted there to be some ambiguity about who exactly in the song was saying, "*I don't want to.*" Was it the woman? Or was it the guy saying, "I don't want anything to do with you, white bitch!"

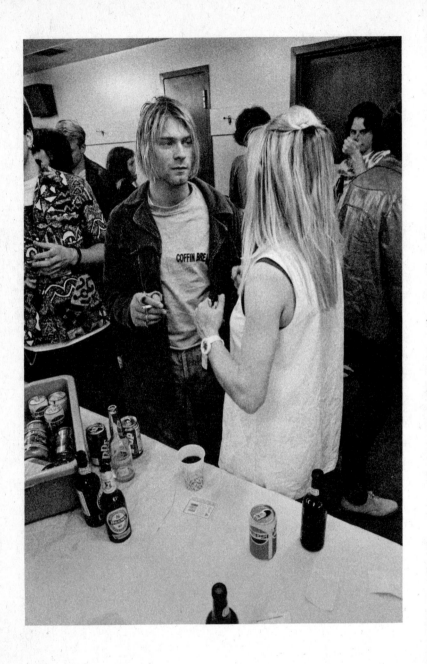

30

THE FIRST TIME Thurston and I ever saw Nirvana was at the famous music venue Maxwell's, in Hoboken, New Jersey. Bruce Pavitt, who founded the record label Sub Pop, told me that if I liked Mudhoney, which I did, then, I'd "love Nirvana." He added, "You have to see them live. Kurt Cobain is like Jesus. People love him. He practically walks on the audience."

Bruce had started Sub Pop as a cassette-subscription service before moving on to seven-inch singles, including Nirvana's, which was called "Love Buzz." Sonic Youth had done a "split single" with Mudhoney, covering their "Touch Me I'm Sick" while Mudhoney covered our song

"Hallowe'en." Thurston and I had both heard "Love Buzz," and our friend Suzanne had done the artwork for it. Nirvana was already popular in Seattle and we were curious to see what they were all about.

Nirvana was a great live band, and Thurston and I, like everybody else in the world, immediately responded to the mixture of good melodies and dissonance. Nirvana seemed part-hardcore, part-Stooges, but with a cheesy chorus-pedal effect that was more New Wave than punk. No one else could use that chorus pedal—which gives the shimmer effect you hear on the guitar in the intro to "Come as You Are," for example—and still be punk rock. As a performer, Kurt Cobain was both incredibly charismatic and extremely conflicted. One minute he would be playing a pretty melody, and the next he'd be trashing all the equipment. Personally, I like when things fall apart—that's real entertainment, deconstructed.

Maxwell's could be sleepy during the week, and there weren't a lot of people in attendance the night we showed up—maybe ten to fifteen. Aside from Kurt, Nirvana had a second guitar player, and I knew from Bruce that Kurt wasn't that happy with him. You could tell the band wasn't having the best gig, but it was also obvious something interesting was going on. The next night, we went to see them again at the Pyramid Club in the East Village. The club was practically full. I was surprised to run into Iggy Pop, but I guess he wanted to see what all the hype was about, too. Kurt ended up trashing the drums and almost managed to knock an amp down the spiral stairs on the stage leading to the dressing room below. Thurston and I both agreed it was an amazing show. Iggy, I remember, wasn't quite as impressed. We later went backstage. Kurt told us that he'd just fired his guitar player and his drummer. Standing in front of me, Kurt seemed small, close to my height, though he was actually five foot nine and I'm only five foot five. He had big, watery eyes, slightly hunted looking. I'm not sure why, but I felt an immediate kinship with him, one of those mutual I-can-tell-you-are-a-super-sensitive-and-emotional-person-too sorts of connections. Thurston didn't have the same thing going with Kurt; he'd be the first to say Kurt and I had some sort of good, inexplicable connection. We weren't close the way he was to Kathleen Hanna of Bikini Kill, or Tobi Vail, who was his girlfriend, or any of his male friends that he grew up with. I didn't know Kurt all that well—two tours' worth—but our friendship was unusual.

Onstage it was amazing to see how much emotional power came from the depths of his body—a gravelly stream of vocal sound. It wasn't screaming, or shrieking, or even punk vitriol, although that's what it sounded like the most. There were also quiet parts, low, moan-ish, when you'd half believe Kurt's voice was hoarse, and then he'd throw himself on the drum set, which in his anger and frustration he seemed to want to annihilate. He seemed always to be working against himself.

In contrast to Kurt, who was so physically small, Krist, Nirvana's bass player, was enormous. He was also seemingly unfazed by whatever played out onstage—Krist who I'll always remember hurling his bass up into the air and never once getting clobbered (except at the MTV Video Music Awards) or damaging his instrument. Kurt, who played left-handed, wrecked so many guitars that he ended up forced to play a lot of regular right-hand ones. But his destructiveness was different from when Pete Townshend or Jimi Hendrix smashed his guitar. Kurt was vulnerable where they weren't, mixed in with an edge of enormous explosiveness and a desire to say and connect more with the audience beyond music.

When Nirvana toured with us in 1991 before *Nevermind* broke, no one in Europe knew who they were. They were often the first band onstage at festivals, playing amazing shows filmed by Dave Markey, the filmmaker who came along with us to document the tour that later became the film *1991: The Year Punk Broke*. The movie had a lot of humorous moments of over-the-top self-indulgence—it was basically a spoof of rockumentaries. Kurt was always funny and fun to be around, and seemed to soak up any kind of personal attention. I felt very big-sisterly, almost maternal, whenever the two of us were together, and it shows in that film.

Later, soon after Kurt and Courtney got together and had their baby, Frances Bean, we were playing in Seattle, and the two of them came to see us. After the show, Kurt cornered me in the dressing room. "I don't know what to do," he said. "Courtney thinks Frances likes me more than her." Someone took a photo of us right at that moment. My back is turned to the camera, and I remember that conversation vividly, so telling in so many ways, the first being that Kurt had no one he felt comfortable asking for advice; the second being that yes, Courtney was utterly self-absorbed; and finally, that Kurt probably did spend more time with Frances than Courtney did.

Looking back, I can't imagine what life was like in the chaos of their drug-fueled life, and it's hard for me to remember that they were together for only a couple of years. It takes so little time to forge a life, or in this case, a brand.

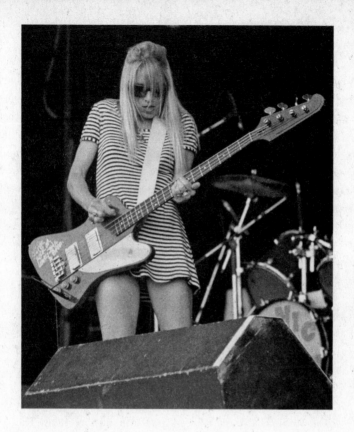

31

BEFORE THE INTERNET was born and if you weren't a mainstream band, it was nearly impossible to get your music heard on the radio. Sure, there was public radio and lots of little college radio stations, but it was mostly a winners' game. Touring was the only way to get a label to market your music. It may sound simple and obvious, but unless you were making commercial music, outlets like radio were beyond your control. Your band lived and died by the road.

In the nineties, people liked to talk about how American bands were so much better live than English bands. Why? Because the U.S. was and is a huge fucking country with no single focused media outlet—forcing

American bands to tour constantly. England, by contrast, was a little island with three weekly music papers covering majors, indies, and faux-indies backed by major labels. The U.S. had *Rolling Stone,* a biweekly that even back then sold copies by plastering sexy female entertainers on the cover and whose big progressive moment was to release a "Women in Rock" issue highlighting pop singers like Madonna. If I ever appeared in *Rolling Stone,* it was to answer questions like "What do you think of women in rock, like Madonna?"

Because I'd written about art in the 1980s, the *Village Voice* asked me to do a tour diary. I called it "Boys Are Smelly."

Before picking up a bass I was just another girl with a fantasy. What would it be like to be right under the pinnacle of energy, beneath two guys crossing their guitars, two thunderfoxes in the throes of self-love and male bonding? How sick, but what desire could be more ordinary? How many grannies once wanted to rub their faces in Elvis's crotch, and how many boys want to be whipped by Steve Albini's guitar?

In the middle of the stage, where I stand as a bass player of Sonic Youth, the music comes at me from all directions. The most heightened state of being female is watching people watch you. Manipulating that stage, without breaking the spell of performing, is what makes someone like Madonna all the more brilliant. Simple pop structures sustain her image, allowing her real self to remain a mystery—is she really that sexy? Loud dissonance and blurred melody create their own ambiguity—are we really that violent?—a context that allows me to be anonymous. For many purposes, being obsessed with boys playing guitars, being as ordinary as possible, being a girl bass player is ideal, because the swirl of Sonic Youth music makes me forget about being a girl. I like being in a weak position and making it strong.

After that, I started doing an occasional rock review for *Spin* magazine, at the time a hipper, more college-oriented alternative to *Rolling Stone*. No doubt it came about courtesy of our PR person, even though Bob Guccione Jr., the publisher and son of the owner, hated Sonic Youth. Aside from articles being written about the band, it was a sidelong way for us to get our name out there.

Riot Grrl, the underground feminist punk rock movement that got under way in the early nineties, maintained a media blackout, and for good reason, too. Bikini Kill and other female bands didn't want to be co-opted, exploited, and turned into products they couldn't control by a corporate, white male world. Later on, Courtney Love would take up the role that the press was always fishing for—a punk princess, thrilling and dark, refusing to play by the rules. No one ever questions the disorder behind her tarantula L.A. glamour—sociopathy, narcissism—because it's rock and roll, good entertainment! "Doll Parts"—great lyrics! Having survived a childhood with Keller, I have a low tolerance for manipulative, egomaniacal behavior, and usually have to remind myself that the person might be mentally ill. That isn't to say you don't get sucked in, at least at first, which is how I came to produce Hole's first album.

Joe Cole took Thurston and me to see Hole play in L.A. Joe was an author and a roadie for Black Flag and Rollins Band. He, along with Dave Markey, was one of the people Thurston and I always hung out with when we visited my parents in California. I can't really tell you what Hole's music was like—*messy* is the best description—but Courtney surely had charisma.

Joe, who wrote a book called *Planet Joe* and appeared in a few Raymond Pettibon films, was later murdered. He and Henry Rollins were sharing a house in Venice, which in the early nineties was still a ghetto, with one street gentrified and the next a war zone. One night, as they were getting home, they were ambushed by robbers, and after telling them the truth, that they only had fifty dollars between the two of them, one shot Joe point-blank in the head. Henry managed somehow to escape by running out the back door of their house. When Henry called to tell me about Joe, I burst into tears. I didn't get over it for a couple of years, to be honest. The senseless, random act of violence against someone so full of life and innocence was mind-blowing, and I hated Los Angeles for a long time after that. I wrote the song "JC" about Joe, while Thurston wrote "100%." It was hard to sing without tearing up.

32

Dirty: "Swimsuit Issue"

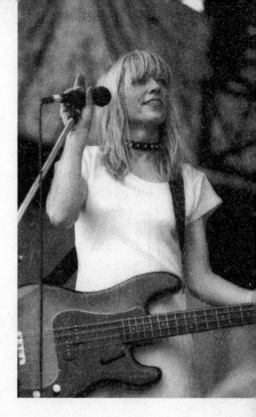

WHEN OUR ALBUM *Dirty* came out, the band made a video for "100%" with Tamra Davis directing again. It was intended to be a celebration of Joe. Thurston had seen a skateboard video that a young director named Spike Jonze had shot, where skaters drive the old car they're riding in over a cliff, and decided to ask Spike to shoot the skate material. Tamra then showed Spike how to edit for a music video, and, after that, Spike's career really took off. Jason Lee made an appearance in the video as the skater, and I also met Mark Gonzales, the skater-artist, who showed up at the shoot and opened his car trunk to show us painting after painting on brown paper bags. "Take whatever you want," he said, but despite his generosity I took only one.

Later during that same shoot, Keanu Reeves showed up. He was good friends with the producer and had let me use his bass rig. Thurston and I had seen Keanu's band play the night before at the Roxy in Hollywood. The audience seemed to be mostly made up of hookers with fake breasts and stilettos angled exclusively on Keanu, who spent most of the show with his back to the audience. Until then I didn't know that so many hookers hung out at the Roxy. Keanu was incredibly sweet, and I had a huge crush on him.

In the video for "100%" I wore a bootleg Rolling Stones shirt that said "Eat Me." As a result, MTV, which showed any number of videos of naked women grinding away, was reluctant to run ours. They felt my shirt sent a bad message to viewers.

After the band signed with Geffen, a story came out about an executive there who had sexually harassed his secretary. That was the inspiration for "Swimsuit Issue." I found it strange that Geffen, like a lot of companies, had a "Secretary's Day," but secretaries never seemed to get promoted to anything above that level. The song was meant to spotlight that hypocrisy.

> *I'm just here for dictation*
> *I don't wanna be a sensation*
> *Bein' on 60 Minutes*
> *Was it worth your fifteen minutes?*
> *Don't touch my breast*
> *I'm just workin' at my desk*
> *Don't put me to the test*
> *I'm just doin' my best.*
> *Shopping at Maxfields*
> *Power for you to wield*
> *Dreams of going to the Grammys*
> *Till you poked me with your whammy*
> *You spinned the disc*
> *Now you're moving your wrist*

I'm just from Encino
Why are you so mean-o?
I'm just here for dictation
And not your summer vacation
You really like to schmooze
Well now you're on the news
I'm from Sherman Oaks
Just a wheel with spokes
But I ain't giving you head
In a sunset bungalow
Hhh, hhh . . . Roshuma, Judith, Paulina, Cathy, Vendela, Naomi,
Ashley, Angie, Stacey, Gail . . .

For the "Dirty" promo we participated in an MTV-sponsored event, inviting people to submit videos anonymously. Our friend Phil Morrison's was the best—it showed a parade of shirtless guys smoking cigars in a living room, slinking toward the camera—but when MTV found out it was his, and, worse, that he was a friend, they wouldn't crown him the winner.

We also did a big-budget video for "Sugar Kane," directed by Nick Egan and involving a lot of people who would later make big names for themselves. It was Chloë Sevigny's film debut, for one thing. At the time she was working as an intern at *Sassy,* Jane Pratt's magazine, and my friend Daisy asked Andrea Linett, who would later go on to cofound *Lucky* magazine, if Andrea knew anyone who could play the part of a girl disrobing during a catwalk fashion show. Nick, it turned out, knew Marc Jacobs—Marc had just released his "grunge" collection for Perry Ellis—and Marc agreed to let us use his showroom and his clothes, and also helped score models and fashion-world people to appear in the video. It was pure coincidence that it was Marc's "grunge" collection—I don't think we even realized it at the time.

Nick shot a lot of the "Sugar Kane" video on Super 8, and in the end, rather than keeping it normal-scale, we perhaps made the mistake of reducing it so the finished video on-screen looked like Super 8, which made it less commercial and airplay-friendly. Still, that was the beginning of Thurston's and my friendship with Marc as well as Chloe.

In the early nineties, before social and online media, people still read newspapers and magazines and watched MTV, and the word on the street mattered more than anything. In 1990 my old friend Mike Kelley had a series called *Arenas*, where he would set down crocheted blankets on the floor, populated by used, thrift-store stuffed animals or dolls. Mike called them "Gifts of Guilt," referring to the fact that the many hours it takes to crochet something makes the person receiving it feel the heaviest possible obligation to cherish it, and they're stricken with guilt if they get rid of it. For the cover of *Dirty*, we used one of Mike's images, which he'd titled *Ahh . . . Youth!* Inside the leaflet was the rest of the photo series taken from that time. They were a perfect symbol of American culture, where newness replaces the old, messy, fragrant, real, humanized form of anything, lest we ever be reminded of dying.

33

SOON AFTER THURSTON and I met Courtney at her L.A. gig, Courtney wrote me a letter—people wrote letters then—asking if I would produce her band Hole's first album.

At first I said no. I could tell she was either a borderline personality or had some other kind of crazy, contagious energy, and I try to avoid that kind of drama in my life. I didn't have much experience as a producer, either, having only done Julie Cafritz's band STP's record, alongside Don Fleming, who was best known for working with the Scottish alternative band Teenage Fanclub on their breakout record *Bandwagonesque*. But then I changed my mind, reasoning that she had something interesting going on and, well, it can be hard to say no to things.

Hole had a very small budget, and the record had to be finished in a week. Luckily Don agreed to coproduce with me. Hole consisted of Eric Erlandson on guitar, Caroline Rue on drums, Jill Emery on bass, and Courtney on vocals.

From the beginning, I had a feeling that Courtney, who was cunning, smart, and ambitious, asked me along only because she wanted my name associated with the record. Courtney was the kind of person who spent a lot of time growing up staring in the mirror practicing her look for the camera. Some people are just born that way, and in the studio I felt she was performing for us. But Courtney put her all into her singing, and when she felt the band wasn't up to her level, she would do something extreme to motivate them, like throw a glass bottle or shatter something against the drum set—all for the good of the record.

Hole recorded everything in four days, and we mixed it over the next three. Eric Erlandson was a really good guitar player, serving as the dissonant backbone of the band. If it weren't for his playing, the record would have been nothing. I'm sure Courtney was after a more polished sound for her entrée into the music world, but the end result was raw. She had a great punk rock voice, and the song titles and lyrics were pure provocation: "Pretty on the Inside" and "Teenage Whore." Her early career as a stripper gave her great material to work with, and she had an instinct for commanding attention. She was always sweet to Don and me because we were going to take her somewhere new and better, she hoped, but she yelled and screamed at everybody in her band.

If Courtney wanted something from you, she would use 100 percent of her charm and persuasion to get it. Back then Courtney had a ragged scar across her nose, as if her roommate tried to give her an impromptu nose job. In an otherwise charismatic face, it was hard not to notice. Years later, at Lollapalooza she described to me all the plastic surgery she planned to get. She said, "You probably didn't know this, but I had a nose job once." I think by then she'd had a couple.

At one point during the recording, Courtney told me she thought Kurt Cobain was hot, which made me cringe inside and hope the two of them would never meet. We all said to ourselves, "Uh-oh, train wreck coming." She also asked us for advice about her "secret affair" with Billy Corgan from Smashing Pumpkins. I thought, *Ewww*, at even the mention of Billy Corgan, whom nobody liked because he was such a crybaby, and Smashing Pumpkins took themselves way too seriously and were in no way punk rock. (It was a debate as old as time, who was "punk rock" and who was "alternative.") Sure, everybody took their music seriously, but there was something grating about Billy Corgan and Smashing Pumpkins—were they too pretentious? too image-conscious and acting?—that rubbed people the wrong way.

That Courtney was attracted to Billy came as a surprise, as she was clearly so punk rock. But she was also ambitious and manipulative, as Don and I learned well during the recording process. Courtney could be honest and real, too—you just never knew which direction she would go—but knowing she could turn on me at any moment, I always kept her at arm's length.

Over the years, Courtney has said plenty of awful things in the press about me, and about Thurston, too, though he was practically the only person nice to Courtney after she punched Kathleen Hanna in the face on the first night of Lollapalooza in 1995. This happened as Kathleen stood on the side of the stage, watching our set, minding her own business. Courtney and Kathleen had never met before. Thurston wasn't attracted to Courtney, but in hindsight I see that he's drawn to that level of darkness.

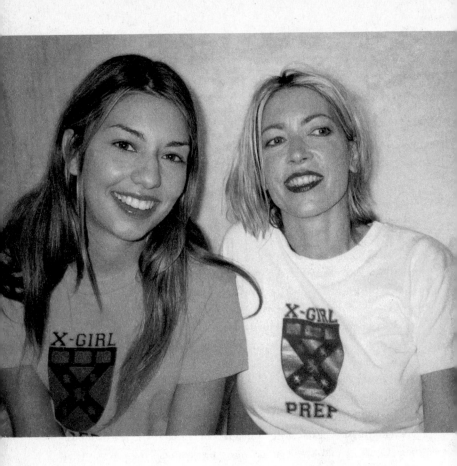

34

IN 1993, Julie Cafritz's sister, Daisy, and I decided to launch a clothing line called X-Girl. In those days, not much was going on fashion-wise in lower New York. Downtown street-wear—a combination of vintage, punk, and oversized skatewear—was evolving in (and from) stores like A.P.C., Daryl K, Betsey Johnson, Urban Outfitters, and Liquid Sky, the rave store where Chloë Sevigny worked for a while. There was the big flea market on Twenty-Third Street in Chelsea and of course Canal Jean on Broadway, where today you can find a huge Uniqlo. Aside from Patricia Field on Eighth Street, the original shopping hub for hipsters was the East Village, with its scattered vintage stores.

At a time when oversized, shaggy-looking, grunge-inspired skate-wear was a prevailing trend, Daisy and I were forever on the hunt for a closer-fitting, cleaner, more casual look—seventies-style Levi's boot-cuts and scoop-neck seventies T's, clothes vaguely inspired by Brian Jones or Anita Pallenberg circa *Exile on Main Street,* or Anna Karina as she appeared in the Godard film *Pierrot le fou.* Through the Beastie Boys' Mike D, we were friendly with the brothers who ran the boys-only line X-Large Streetwear, and one of them asked Daisy, who was working at their East Village store at the time, if she was interested in doing a girls' line. Daisy in turn asked if I would collaborate with her.

Instead of oversized skate-wear, Daisy and I wanted to design fitted pieces in shapes that would flatter all body types. Someone later described it as "preppy-tennis meets skater-cool-girl." Fit—that became our core struggle as we sent samples back and forth from New York to L.A. The backbone of our label was the name itself, X-Girl, and Mike Mills's amazing graphic designs. From her own teen years growing up in Washington, D.C., Daisy contributed a preppy sensibility, whereas I guess I brought the rock, though Jean-Luc Godard and Françoise Hardy were our common muses. As much as she's a stylist, Daisy is also a keen social anthropologist, and X-Girl began as a fun, informal project, with neither of us really having any idea what we were doing. We had a small budget, and no real control over production, and our clothes came out either too big or too small in the beginning.

I was four months pregnant when the first shipment arrived. The clothes were tiny. But somehow I managed to wiggle into a skirt and T-shirt for our "Bull in the Heather" video. Originally, I wanted to bring in the Knicks City Dancers to spoof traditional MTV choreography, but Kathleen Hanna made a cameo instead. Bikini Kill and other Riot Grrl bands were still enforcing their media blackout, and asking Kathleen to appear in our video came from my perverse desire to have her infiltrate the mainstream. That way, people could see her also as the playful, mischievous, charismatic girl she is—a woman who controlled the action by dancing around us as we stood stationary in a rock stance, playing the song. It was courageous of Kathleen to appear in a mainstream MTV video and risk criticism from the huge community she'd created.

For X-Girl's first line, Spike Jonze and his then girlfriend and later wife Sofia Coppola had the idea to mount an X-Girl guerilla-style fashion show on the street during Fashion Week. At six months pregnant, I wasn't paying attention to much of anything. Spike and Sofia found the models and the site and produced the entire event. Marc Jacobs was having his first show since leaving Perry Ellis, and the X-Girl show took place in Soho directly after Marc's, with a lot of people who'd come to see Marc's show staying to see ours.

A couple of days before that, I was in Daisy's loft on Crosby Street for a meeting. I was lying on Daisy's bed when the phone rang. Daisy handed me the phone: it was Thurston. He told me he had bad news. My first thought was that he was going to tell me that Mark Arm, the lead singer for Mudhoney, had OD'd. Mark wasn't a regular user, but he'd OD'd more than once, and I was so prepared for Thurston to say the name *Mark* that I didn't process what he was saying—that Kurt had shot himself, that Kurt was dead. Of course I was totally shocked, but I wasn't entirely surprised.

There had been an incident in Rome, where Kurt had OD'd, but the details were never clear. Obviously, though, Kurt was headed down an even darker path, and after he hooked up with Courtney, it was only a matter of time before he completely self-destructed. But I was shattered and feeling as if I were moving slow-motion inside some strange dream. My first impulse was to go out into a clean, normal world and do regular, everyday things. I remember walking over to the Pat Hearn Gallery, where my good friend Jutta Koether was installing a show. Along with some other artists, Jutta had asked me to contribute to her installation—a show within a show. Telling Jutta what had just happened, saying the words aloud, felt bizarre. The words fell far short in conveying the feeling of loss that everyone, not just me, was feeling.

The night after Kurt's death, during a candlelight memorial service for the public, a recording of Courtney reading aloud Kurt's suicide note was played. As the vigil continued, Courtney appeared in person and started handing out some of Kurt's clothes to fans. It was as if she were stepping out into her destiny—a platform of celebrity and infamy. A week after Kurt died, Hole released their major-label debut, *Live Through This*, which elevated Courtney to a new kind of perverse stardom. The timing couldn't have been better.

The public mourning had already begun, and I found it traumatic. The tasteless T-shirts with Kurt's face lining the sidewalks of New York, Nirvana's songs blaring from every radio station. As I write this, it has been twenty years since Kurt died. Coco will turn twenty this summer. Nineteen ninety-four, the year my daughter was born and the year Kurt died, was quite possibly the happiest year of my life, but it was also bittersweet, the most extreme year in my life for joy and for sadness.

It's funny how often I think about Kurt. He was always so susceptible to kindness, with his vulnerable, passive side. One element of his self-destructiveness was choosing Courtney in order to alienate himself from everyone around him, at the same time fame was alienating him from whatever community he had.

I'll always remember, too, his smallness, his thinness, the frail appearance, like an old man, with those big, illuminated, innocent, childish, saucer-sized eyes like ringed planets. Onstage, though, he was fearless as well as something even scarier. There's a point where fearlessness twists into self-annihilation, and he was too familiar with that space. Most people who saw Nirvana live had never before witnessed that degree of self-harm in someone, as he hurled himself into the drum set as if in some privately negotiated death dance.

A few years ago, Frances came to see us play at the Hollywood Bowl, and afterward she came backstage. She seemed very sweet. We gave her some old photos of herself and her dad when she was little. I will forever wonder about her, how she's doing.

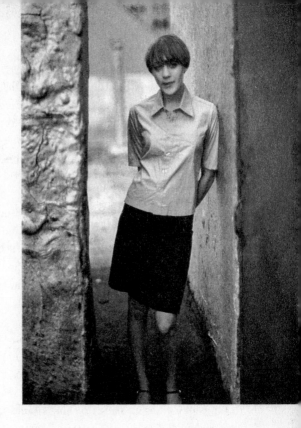

35

X-GIRL'S SIDEWALK GUERILLA fashion show was a success in that it came off at all. A video documentary of that day exists online, which people still occasionally refer to today. In it you can see Francis Ford Coppola, who knows me only in relation to X-Girl and who is naturally proud of his daughter, Sofia, and the show she's just put on.

Throughout my pregnancy, I did one X-Girl–oriented photo shoot after another. Lean over a tire, on my back. Stand, seven months pregnant, on a rickety, rotting picnic table holding an umbrella. (I refused.) When I started Free Kitten, my band with Julie Cafritz, Mark Ibold, and Yoshimi, I remember having an amnio and taking the rest of the day off. When I was eight and a half months pregnant, Sonic Youth appeared on *Late Night with David Letterman*. The machine never stopped, even though what I really wanted to do was lie down all the time, in part because I had a fibroid tumor that grew with the baby.

When Coco was born I took only a little time off. There were always small things happening, and even though artists are never truly on vacation, they can enjoy free time without the pressure to "enjoy themselves." They aren't escaping exactly, just shifting focus. And then it was on to the next thing, in this case a fashion event in Tokyo.

Someone had asked us to put on an X-Girl show right before a Beastie Boys concert. Daisy didn't want to go, so Sofia Coppola volunteered. Coco was five months old at the time, and Thurston came along with us. We arrived in Tokyo tired and jet-lagged, but despite that, Sofia and I went out onto the street to recruit girls for the show. My friend Yoshimi also helped in the effort, and the Beastie Boys' Adam Yauch knew an American girl who modeled in Tokyo who helped round up a few of her friends. I remember cruising around a local department store with Adam and Coco. Adam was very sweet, and I was surprised he wanted to hang out with us instead of rushing around shopping like everybody else. He bought Coco a little hat with bunny ears, and Spike took a photo of Coco wearing it.

Via the front desk of our hotel, I somehow managed to find a babysitter, an older woman who didn't speak a word of English. We all drove an hour outside of Tokyo to the concert hall. As Sofia and I dressed the models, I remember the Japanese woman gazing down at Coco, who'd fallen asleep, never once taking her eyes off her. At one point she even started picking threads off the back of my shirt. It made me long to bring this woman home with me and let her take care of the entire family.

Somehow we pulled off the event, but when I look at photos of Sofia and me from that weekend, I can't believe I don't have dark circles under my eyes. I was exhausted from the jet lag, still breast-feeding, and had a baby who didn't sleep through the night. We had press responsibilities, too, where everyone asked variations of the same questions: "How did X-Girl start? What does the name mean? What's it like to be a mom in rock?"

Instead of a live presentation, for our next season of clothes, Daisy and I decided to make a faux-Godard-ian film filled with tongue-in-cheek Marxist references we could present to fashion magazine editors. Chloë Sevigny, Rita Ackermann, and Daisy's friend Pumpkin Wentzel played the main characters. Phil Morrison and his writing partner wrote and directed it. Phil did an amazing job delivering everything we wanted and more. The film was fantastic and still holds up today in its YouTube incarnation. We even had an X-Girl store on Lafayette Street across from Liquid Sky, where Chloë still worked, convenient to Daisy's loft on Crosby Street and our apartment. It was also inconvenient, because if X-Girl production was late, or something else was screwed up, we felt embarrassed to walk down the street.

Daisy dealt with the day-to-day stuff of the business, and we hired someone to manage the store and sketch our ideas. It was more a burden for Daisy, and in time, both of us felt X-Girl had run its course. We sold the company to a Japanese firm and made some money in the process. Afterward, we could walk along Lafayette Street with our heads held high again.

We assumed that as a relic of its time X-Girl would die out, but it hasn't, and the brand still exists in Japan. It's weird when you sell a name, or a brand, and it no longer has anything to do with the original or with you. In a way X-Girl gave me far more notoriety than Sonic Youth ever did.

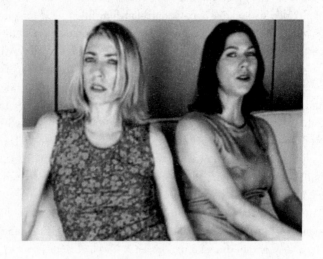

36

Washing Machine:
"Little Trouble Girl"

COCO HAYLEY GORDON MOORE, born July 1, 1994. Yes, she changed our lives, and no one is more important to me. But the band played on.

When Coco was two months old, Thurston and I flew to L.A. to shoot a video for our cover of the Carpenters song "Superstar," shot by Lance Accord—who brought in a gold microphone that, to my mind, made the whole video—with Dave Markey directing. I loved Thurston's singing, and the whole production looked gorgeous. ("Superstar" has some of the best lyrics ever.) I was still feeling heavy with extra baby weight and managed somehow to fit into a giant red velvet prom dress. Traveling to California with a two-month-old baby was another "new mom" thing to have to worry about; dripping breast milk during a video shoot is not very rock!

Then, in the spring of 1995, when Coco was ten months old, we all flew to Memphis to work on our new record.

Feeling we had too much baggage now as a band, we wanted to change the name Sonic Youth to Washing Machine. People always like to discover something new, and we'd been around awhile, plus *Washing Machine* seemed like a good "indie rock" name. Our record company naturally thought we were insane, so instead we used it for the title of the new album. We had T-shirts printed before the record was done. Two adorable thirteen-year-old boys wearing them came to one of our shows with their dad, and I took a picture of them, believing it would make a great album cover. Unfortunately, when the time came, we didn't know their names, or where to reach them, so for legal reasons we had to cut off their heads!

Memphis, I remember, was warm and green, and we took countless trips for barbecue sandwiches from Payne's, a sagging, shuttered building with two ancient Jaguars parked out front. On Easter Sunday we went to Al Green's church and on another night to a juke joint in the middle of a cornfield, where they made moonshine, and the walls were hung with amazing black-velvet paintings of Michael Jackson and other popular African American celebrities and heroes. Maurice Menares accompanied us to help take care of Coco, and I still have a great picture of Coco perched on the studio recording console. One afternoon Maurice and I took Coco to the Memphis Zoo. It was without a doubt the most depressing zoo I'd ever been to in my life. There was next to no foliage or, for that matter, animals, which for the animals at least was probably a good thing. Coco probably doesn't remember, but she's visited more zoos and aquariums around the world than any other kid, though her favorite places have always been hotels.

Having Coco made me think of the Shangri-Las again, with their overdramatic songs with morbid scenarios and unhealthy relationships.

"Little Trouble Girl" was my ultimate homage to the Shangri-Las' half singing, half speaking style.

At the time I was reading a book called *Mother Daughter Revolution,* about first-wave seventies feminism. It's about how feminism fails to address the relationship between mothers and daughters because of its emphasis on escaping the house. I didn't finish it—who has the time or the energy to read when you're a new mom?—but I remember how the book talked about the pressure to please and be perfect that every woman falls into and then projects onto her daughter. Nothing is ever good enough. No woman can ever outrun what she has to do. No one can be all things—a mother, a good partner, a lover, as well as a competitor in the workplace. "Little Trouble Girl" is about wanting to be seen for who you really are, being able to express those parts of yourself that aren't "good girl" but that are just as real and true.

> *If you want me to*
> *I will be the one*
> *That is always good*
> *And you'll love me too*
> *But you'll never know*
> *What I feel inside*
> *That I'm really bad*
> *Little trouble girl*

I asked Kim Deal of the Pixies to sing the melodic part. Why? Because I couldn't! Her voice was perfect.

The video, directed by Mark Romanek and shot by Harris Savides, was the first time the band went with someone else's idea without coming up with it ourselves. Later, I got to work with Harris Savides on *Last Days,* the film Gus Van Sant made about Kurt. Harris was an incredibly sweet, talented man who sadly enough died a few years ago. Shooting the "Little Trouble Girl" video was the first time I'd ever been away from Coco, and I remember panicking when the video shoot went late, making me miss the red-eye back to New York, where Thurston was taking care of her.

At the same time, I loved hanging out with Kim Deal, and when I rewatch the video, my favorite part is seeing the two of us together singing and looking hot. Maybe everything always looks better twenty years later. When Kim showed up in Memphis to record the song, she had the engineer play it back into the big room, and she sang without any headphones. Then and now Kim's voice has an incredibly cakelike quality—like the sound when you say *cake*, a lightness, its body thinned out—that's so classic pop.

Washing Machine is one of my favorite-sounding records, and "Washing Machine" and "The Diamond Sea" were fun songs to record. The latter we performed in one take, and later, when Sonic Youth went on tour first with R.E.M., then with the Lollapalooza festival, Spike created a video shot from various live performances of that song.

When we started the R.E.M. tour, Coco had just learned to walk, and it was during a visit to Kansas that Thurston, Michael Stipe, and I drove out to visit William Burroughs. I remember William began asking Michael about Kurt—"What about the boy?" he said. "So sad . . ." Michael, slightly embarrassed, deferred to Thurston and me since we had more of a history with Kurt and Nirvana.

For Lollapalooza, the band traveled on a bus with a port-a-crib strapped down in the back, where Coco fell asleep to the giant roar of the engine. She was a great bus sleeper. The first night took us to the Gorge, in Washington State. That night we were unofficially co-headlining with Hole and a bunch of our friends were in the lineup, too: Pavement, Beck, Jesus Lizard, Cypress Hill, Elastica, Mike Watt, Superchunk, and Yo La Tengo. That was the night Courtney came up to Kathleen Hanna and punched her in the face. It set the tone for the rest of the tour, with Courtney being someone to avoid and ignore, even more than ever before.

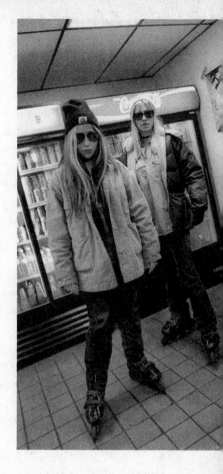

37

Free Kitten

JULIE CAFRITZ IS one of the funniest people I know, under-acknowledged as an indie rock "girl" guitar player and singer-goddess. When Julie and I first met years earlier, her band Pussy Galore had just moved to New York and was looking for a drummer. I introduced her to Bob Bert, who had just quit Sonic Youth and seemed perfect for them. Julie and her bandmate Jon Spencer were slightly scary, I remember, all black clothes with tons of 'tude. But Thurston and I both loved their EP *SugarShit Sharp,* as well as their radical non-PC reputation as Washington, D.C., people who dissed the straight-edge subculture of hardcore punk that asked its adherents not to drink, smoke, do drugs, engage in promiscuous sex, or even drink coffee. It wasn't some Puritan thing. Straight-edge was asking adherents to take control of their lives, not be blind consumers, and not be tricked into thinking that drinking and drugs were cool since in fact they were the tools of a previous generation. Julie turned out to be surprisingly approachable, and the two of us became friends.

It wasn't, as some people believed, that we started Free Kitten as a joke band designed to make fun of the CBGB improv scene of experimental, free noise and jazz, where people played abstract music for very long stretches of time. In spite of some great stuff, like John Zorn, and the jazz street saxophonist Charles Gayle playing alongside Thurston and other musicians from the East Village scene, we felt that men didn't always know when to stop. We were more inspired by the American alt-rock band Royal Trux, a two-piece band. At that time, Royal Trux—comprised of Neil Hagerty and Jennifer Herrema—were performing a bunch of gigs around New York, and every show was completely different. Royal Trux was rock swagger perfected, with minimum effort, and even though they were completely on drugs the whole time, the effect was both amazing and mysterious. Not to mention that Free Kitten was also an excuse for Julie and me to hang out and do something together.

When we released our first EP, no one seemed to get us. The reviews could be boiled down to "Really—is this all they can muster? They're pretending to be bad musicians?" Eventually Mark Ibold and Yoshimi joined Free Kitten. Both are amazing players, and Julie and I both liked them. We never really knew what Mark was doing and left it up to him to figure out what to play, and we would fly Yoshimi over, make up the songs in the studio, and then overdub the vocals before mixing the songs. Julie and I would have to relearn the songs before going out on tour.

Coco was seven months old when we did our first two-week tour in England. Again, thanks to the jet lag and the breast-feeding, it wasn't easy, but Thurston came along to take care of Coco. He wouldn't have missed it anyway. He was always a very big supporter of whatever I did in and out of the band, and I loved that about him—his generosity. Creatively, I never felt any sense of competition with him. He was protective, too. Once the band was playing a gig in Switzerland, and some guy bit my ass while I was onstage, and Thurston was so pissed off he threw a bottle at the guy. Afterward, I remember someone told me, "If you were Ivy from the Cramps, you would have dug your spiked heel into that guy's head."

I can't even tell you today what the Free Kitten records sounded like. Our only goal was to make them and put them out without getting too self-conscious about what it was we were making. Mostly I wanted Julie to have a musical outlet and to write songs again. Having said that, being in two bands when you're a new mom is a lot of work. Naturally Sonic Youth was the priority, and Yoshimi had her hands full with her own band, Boredoms. Mark was still playing with Pavement, so Julie and I did what we could, keeping Free Kitten fun while hoping it would stand on its own and be taken seriously, too. It's always hard doing something outside a familiar context. *What are you doing exactly?* everyone wanted to know. *Is it a supergroup, a side project, an inside joke?*

In 1993, Free Kitten played Lollapalooza on the tiny side stage. It was hot and dusty, and we could hear Rage Against the Machine thundering away at the same time on the big stage. As part of our antirock stance, Julie and I wore matching housewife-y shifts and Pro Keds and sweated it out in the ninety-plus-degree heat.

In high school, Coco started her own band, Big Nils. On the rare occasion I hear a Free Kitten song somewhere, usually I don't recognize it. I think, "Hey, who is this—Coco?" and then I realize . . . *Oh yeah, right*. It's the strangest feeling, rediscovering your own self and, if enough time has gone by, listening to it without hating it. It is sort of like looking at old photos of yourself and realizing you looked pretty good after all. Recently I came across a photo that my old friend Felipe took the first time he and I visited New York on a break from college in Toronto. I'm on the subway with a backdrop of graffiti; my hair is dark; my coat, once my mom's, is frumpy; and I look dazed. Reading Rachel Kushner's novel *The Flamethrowers,* I could relate to the sensation of being young in New York, living on the outside of the art world, and that photo sums up that uncertainty, and that time, exactly. I love it.

38

BY THE LATE 1990s, the underground experimental music scene had mushroomed, thanks in part to the Internet. After Nirvana, mainstream music nosedived back to its default level of blandness, with "grunge" just another way of marketing big, boring rock music. Still, the underground was alive, growing. Music was getting interesting again, thanks to noise bands like Wolf Eyes and Lightning Bolt, and more women showing up in what had once been an all-male record-collector scene. When Sonic Youth played Detroit, a trio named Universal Indians opened for us, and a girl in the band strummed her guitar with a big rock—one of the sexiest moves I've ever seen in music.

Sonic Youth took some of the money we made from Lollapalooza and got our own studio down on Murray Street. Around that time, we began releasing our music on our own label, Sonic Youth Records, or SYR. Our goal was to release less commercial, more experimental music that we wouldn't have to promote. I was listening to a lot of Brigitte Fontaine, the French chanteuse from the sixties and seventies, and at one point, we ended up recording on her new record with her partner Areski Belkacem. The Sonic Youth song "Contre Le Sexisme" is inspired by her. That was the beginning of Jim O'Rourke's musical involvement with Sonic Youth. Jim played on our *Goodbye 20th Century* record, which my old childhood friend Willie Winant spearheaded, leading us through the scores, which can be pretty abstract.

As we were recording *A Thousand Leaves,* my father died, having contracted pneumonia in a nursing home. I still feel sad whenever he comes into my mind. Even though he could be one of the "distant dads," as a lot of men of his generation were, he was always kind and understanding, a very gentle soul. I wasn't with him when he died, a big regret of mine. By the time I made it to L.A., he was gone. Even today, I feel protective of him. It is my guilt-driven impulse, as well as my pattern with men, starting with Keller, ending with Thurston.

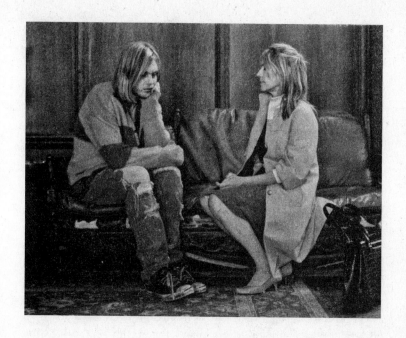

39

A FRIEND OF MINE once described Cannes as a giant gift shop, but because it's in France, along a beautiful blue ocean, it's better than that, the peak of fabulousness, the place where the red carpet was invented. Walking up the stairs to the Palais—as if it's the highest achievement anyone could ever attain—is as good as they say.

In 2005 Thurston and I were in Cannes for the screening of *Last Days*, Gus Van Sant's film based on the mysterious end of Kurt's life. In the ten years since Kurt had died, neither Thurston nor I had ever done an interview about him. Now, suddenly, in the two days leading up to the screening, we were doing a lot of them, in between cocktail parties and dinners. Thurston joined the film as a consultant to make sure Gus got the music parts right and also to debrief the movie's star, Michael Pitt.

It had come as a surprise when Gus called and asked me to play a part in the movie. The role was a small cameo—I played an empathetic record company executive, if such a person exists—but it's also the only time the Michael Pitt character interacts with anyone in the film. Before we shot it, Gus discussed the scene with me and asked me what I would say. I based the character on Rosemary Carroll, who was Courtney's lawyer and also the wife of Danny Goldberg, the head of the management company that represented us both. Rosemary is an eccentric, unconventional woman who at one point early in her life was married to the poet Jim Carroll.

We ran through the improvised dialogue several times, shooting it more than once. At the end of each take, Gus would toss out slight suggestions like, "Make it shorter." Michael Pitt bore an amazing resemblance to Kurt, though when I stood facing him I was taken aback by his height, remembering Kurt's smallness, the fragility contrasting with the explosiveness.

I did the film because I trusted that Gus would make something interesting, and he did. Overall it was a painless, positive experience that spoiled me for other film experiences, since after all, I've worked only with the best—Gus, Olivier Assayas, and Todd Haynes! Haha! Acting is something I always thought I might have a natural ability for doing. It connects to some odd three-dimensional sense I've always had, a spatial confidence of knowing where things are at all times, of being able to move around a stage without looking, always knowing where the audience is, or in this case, the camera. When I write lyrics sometimes I've pretended to be someone else, a character, tried to put myself in her head or situation, while drawing from some real-life emotion I've experienced, as I did in "The Sprawl" and "Pacific Coast Highway." I've always gotten inspiration from the movies, whether for lyrics or fashion ideas, and I could watch films for hours. As an actor I don't think I could ever be great, but maybe I bring something different, strange, new.

When we arrived at the stairs to the Palais, a song kicked in from a seven-inch that Thurston and I did together under the band name Mirror/Dash—a lo-fi, intimate, melancholy song—and it blew my mind that they would play it at such a public and glorified event as the Cannes film festival.

Going up the stairs involves an intricate choreography that gets repeated over and over with each film that makes it to the Palais. Guards flanked the sides of the stairs, holding—I'm not kidding—*guns*. The cast members linked arms, all in a row. Asia Argento, Gus, Michael, Michael's girlfriend Jamie, and I took a few steps together. We paused. We took a few more steps, paused again. I assume this was to add even more ceremony and ritual to the pomp, the constellation of flashbulbs. Oddly enough, the experience was calming, especially as the sun was setting into dusk. Honestly, it was one of the highlights of my career.

At the same time, during an era where I'd grown used to averting my eyes to the most grossly commercial aspects of Kurt's legacy—bootlegs, sidewalk drawings, T-shirts, posters, magazine covers—here I was in a film that took poetic license with Kurt's last days. Some people, I knew, would hate the film, mostly those ardent fans who wanted a more literal, less abstract, or sordid interpretation. I had never wanted to exploit whatever friendship or kinship Kurt and I had, and even in his death I wanted to protect him, which is why I feel weird even writing what I have in this book. But as I wrote earlier, I think about Kurt quite often. As with many people who die violently, and too young, there is never any resolution or closure. Kurt still moves along inside me, and outside, too, with his music.

40

Murray Street . . . and Beyond

BY NOW OUR official studio was Murray Street, and Jim O'Rourke was officially playing with us and helping us engineer and mix our records. On *Murray Street,* I'd switched over to playing guitar more than I ever had before. It was great having Jim play bass—he was a much more facile bass player than I was—and it automatically altered the songwriting process. It was probably more fun for Steve, too, drumming along with someone less minimal.

Everyone in New York has his or her own 9/11 story. At the time Jim was basically living at the Murray Street studio, which was only a couple of blocks from the Twin Towers. I was at our apartment on Lafayette

Street getting ready to go to Paris to perform with an improv quartet that I was part of at a party thrown by the Gap. We were supposed to fly out that night. Thurston was at our new house in Northampton with Coco. The night before, I'd attended a huge Marc Jacobs party on one of the piers off the West Side Highway following his Fashion Week show. Marc was launching his first perfume line, and thousands of white gardenias formed an archway into the party, which was pitch-black in contrast to the pier's sparkling lights. It had rained recently, and my high heels kept sinking into the soft gravelly ground. It couldn't have been a more decadent, over-the-top but still-beautiful fashion moment.

The next morning Daisy called and told me to turn on the TV because a plane had just flown into the World Trade Center. Daisy's husband, Rob, worked in a building across from the Towers but hadn't left for the office yet. I called Jim and told him to leave the studio, and then I called Thurston. Jim knew nothing but told me that dust was starting to gather through the open windows. It was difficult for me—for everybody—to make any sense of what was happening. I had no TV or radio, but the phone worked, at least at first. By the time the second plane hit, phone service was crackling away to nothing, and when I called Thurston a second time, I couldn't reach him, but I finally convinced Jim to come to our apartment. As Jim was leaving Murray Street, the second tower was collapsing and people were jumping out of windows. Lee, his wife, Leah, and their kids, who lived downtown, showed up at our apartment, too. Below us, literally right outside our door, Houston Street and Lafayette were barricaded, and police weren't letting anyone go south of Houston without ID and proof of residence.

It was a surreal, terrifying day. People—stranded models, people who'd come to town for Fashion Week—were wandering around Nolita and Soho in a daze. Jim arrived finally, completely traumatized. We all slept there that night.

The next morning, I remember walking down Bleecker Street to Daisy and Rob's apartment. The streets were empty. I got very emotional thinking about New York as I looked down to where the towers once were and saw a big nothing. It felt like the end. The five of us, Daisy, Rob, their two children, and I, wound our way up the island, not knowing what streets we could drive on and what streets would be barricaded. Both FDR Drive on the East Side and the West Side Highway were closed. That day, Daisy and Rob took their two kids to Northampton, and I hitched a ride with them. That was it for them and New York. Lee and his family drove out to Long Island. Jim caught a later ride to Northampton.

For the next week eight people from New York lived in our house. Jim stayed there for over a month. He was too shaken to go back. I was still shaken too—who wouldn't be? Every morning I got up early and turned on CNN just to make sure nothing else had happened, and I woke up in the middle of the night, too. This is still my sleep pattern. It took a while before the band was able to return to the studio and when we did, we had to get permission to pass through Chambers Street. Later I found out that most of the power downtown in the financial district ran directly underneath Murray Street, and the plane crashes had fried our mixing board. Murray Street itself had chain-link fencing on both sides of the sidewalk, and for months it was one big gaping hole, with the sidewalks and pavement regularly wetted down to dissolve the dust still permeating the air. *Is this to wash away the dust of all the people killed in the towers?* I kept thinking.

There was nothing else to do but return to work. Despite the circumstances under which we made it, the album *Murray Street* is still one of my favorite records, containing the nine-minute-long "Sympathy for the Strawberry." I remember what a challenge it was coming up with vocal ideas over large masses of abstract music. As a non-singer singer, it was probably easier for me than it would have been for a more conventional singer, but I gravitated to what I thought I could pull off, and more and more I went with emotionality. With his more natural approach to mixing, Jim didn't try to make me sound like a singer.

Sonic Nurse, the next record Sonic Youth put out, we did with Jim too. The song "Pattern Recognition" was based on a William Gibson book I'd read and liked. It wasn't one of his sci-fi titles but a thriller set in an extremely contemporary present about a woman who is a "cool hunter"—an amazing term, I thought, to describe a person hired by corporations to smoke out trends for brands. "Pattern Recognition" was one of my favorite songs to play live, a sexy song with a lot of moves that traveled to multiple places. I also loved singing "I Love You Golden Blue," though I was often on the verge of tears whenever I sang it. It's a song about someone who believes he can't show himself to the world. Believing he'll only destroy the people he cares about, he avoids all in-timacy. He's stuck. I couldn't help thinking that was true about a lot of boy-men I'd known in my life.

After Jim left the band and moved to Japan, we began working on our album *Rather Ripped,* the last of our so-called trilogy, with John Agnello. John brought a bigger, more concise sound to the band—not better, just different. After years of trying to mix as a group, it came as a relief to have first Jim and then John in our midst. By then Mark Ibold had started playing bass with us full-time. "Jams Run Free" off *Rather Ripped* was a much more natural song for my voice. Whirling around in the middle of the stage, with Mark on the bass, I was freed up, and it became my favorite song to sing live. I could swirl around so fast that everything blurred, the lights and the sounds colliding and smashing together. That's a point where you lose all sense of your body and feel carried completely by the music, a moment that makes all the drudgery, exhaustion, and boredom of touring worthwhile.

For our next record, Thurston chose the title *The Eternal.* Maybe he knew it would be our last record as a band. "Massage the History" was the only song I wrote about our relationship. It has the line "*I dreamed*" in it, maybe because I was dreaming of the first record we ever made. It was before I found out what the dark cloud following Thurston around consisted of, but I had already felt it.

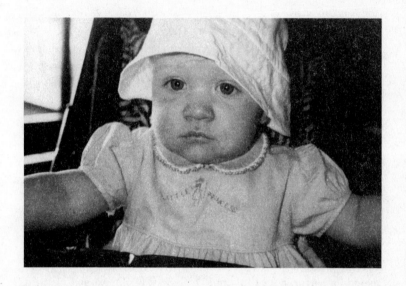

41

SOMETIME IN MY late thirties I'd begun looking at babies. Babies on the sidewalk, in strollers, on shoulders. The problem was, I could never figure out the best time to start a family. Thurston's and my life as a couple, and as a band, was all about writing, recording, doing press, endlessly touring. Still, once the idea came into my head it was hard to push back.

As always, Thurston's self-assuredness and outward confidence helped convince me we could carry the parenting thing off. He didn't talk much about having a child, but he didn't discuss much of anything at length—the music connected us, taking the place of words, and we ended up in agreement about most things.

But after Coco was born, I realized we had never talked about what kind of parents or partners we wanted to be. I'd simply assumed Thurston was supportive of feminist issues, like equal participation in child care, equal responsibilities around the house, and so forth.

Like most new moms, I found that no matter how just and shared you expect the experience to be, or how equal the man thinks parenting should be, it isn't. It can't be. Most child-raising falls on women's shoulders. Some things, like the laundry, are just easier to do yourself than to have to explain in detail to someone else. Other things were biological. As a baby, whenever Coco cried I felt it immediately, physically, because my breasts began to leak. Thurston, and any man for that matter, would never feel that same kind of urgency, that desire to make the crying stop not only to comfort your baby but for your own body's sake. This doesn't make men bad parents, though it can make women feel alone in what they'd hoped would be an equal division of labor. This is a dynamic that carried over to other parts of our relationship.

Being pregnant made me nervous. In my third trimester, I remember going to a party where I ran into Peter Buck of R.E.M. and his then wife Stephanie. They'd just had twin babies, Zelda and Zoe, and I was frightened when Stephanie asked me if I wanted to hold one. I also had a series of anxiety dreams. In one, Coco was a baby who talked and went out to lunch without me. In another, right after Kurt killed himself, someone left Frances Bean in my charge. (In real life, whenever Courtney had visited New York, her nanny Jackie brought Frances over to play with Coco. I have photos of Frances curled up in our disgusting cat bed. Crawling babies seem to gravitate to the places you least want them to go.)

Thurston immediately took to fatherhood. He was a natural, in fact. I'd read my share of parenting and baby books, but he was much more experienced around kids, having done a lot of babysitting when he was younger. He was never awkward holding Coco or getting down on the floor and playing with her.

At the same time, it was hard to tell him anything I was feeling without his getting offended, since he took everything so personally. I wish he had sometimes said, "Tell me what I can do to help out," but he never did. That's no slam; it's just the way it was. But it made me feel like I was the only one in control, the only one looking out for us as a family, the lighthouse keeper. I wasn't always comfortable in that role, but I had little choice. I had to do what was right for our family.

Having a baby also created a huge identity crisis inside of me. It didn't help that during press interviews, journalists always said, "What's it like to be a rock-and-roll mom?" just as over the last decades they couldn't help asking, "What's it like to be a girl in a band?" I'm sure Thurston got the same question, but at least on the surface it didn't appear to bother him as much. Like a lot of guys, he was the "cool, fun dad," which was great for Coco in many ways. In the end he was probably a better dad than he was a partner, as more and more he'd begun pulling away from me, wanting to do everything his way. Looking back, I think it was probably because he didn't want to be with me anymore.

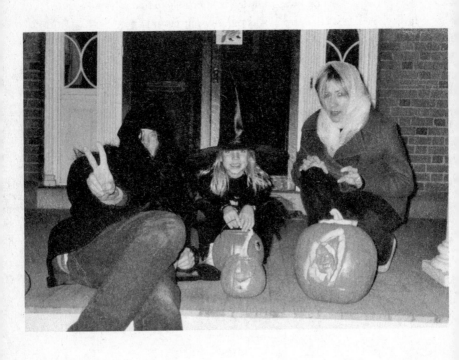

42

IT WASN'T THAT our apartment on Lafayette was all that cramped, more that it was simply time for a change. Anyone who leaves New York knows that when the city isn't working for them the way it used to, the only question is where to go. Portland, Oregon. Raleigh-Durham, North Carolina. We considered both those places, and we also scoped out Brooklyn—Carroll Gardens and Cobble Hill—but outer-borough prices were more than we wanted to pay, and I didn't want to live any farther out in the New York suburbs.

I was thinking ahead, too. I didn't want to raise Coco on Lafayette

Street. Not on the fringes of Soho, not with giraffe-packs of skinny models on every sidewalk within the Soho pedestrian mall of high-end consumerism. The New York nanny culture also bugged me, both parents working all day to be able to afford to pay a stranger to take care of a child they never got to see. The expense and the inconvenience, and later down the line, schools and tests and applications and micromanaging your child in a city where no kid can walk around unaccompanied, where there are no yards and no real neighbors to speak of—all of these were factors in our decision to go.

Northampton, Massachusetts, was a longtime secondary market for us. It was a student town. Smith was there, and close by were Amherst, UMass Amherst, Hampshire, Mount Holyoke. Williams was an hour away, too. It was filled with lots of New York City transplants, so it didn't feel like a traditional suburb or a commuter town. Northampton is also one of the most liberal small cities in America. The main drag was a spiky blur of coffee shops, tattoo parlors, vegetarian restaurants, yoga studios, and therapists' offices. Underlying the decision to move there was the hope that maybe Thurston, Coco, and I could become more family centered, more unified, less scattered. Helping to smooth things were the good friends we had in the area, like Byron Coley and his family, and J Mascis, who lived in Amherst.

But moving from the city to the country still felt exotic. A Realtor showed us a few properties, mostly farmhouses with rectangular unlit rooms and ceilings that grazed your scalp. Thurston had grown up in an extremely old house with ceilings so low he couldn't stand all the way up in his own bedroom. When we found a big rangy brick house with three floors and a backyard for sale close to the Smith College campus, we jumped on it, or rather Thurston did. He approached things with a kid-like overconfidence, unlike me, who stood back and questioned things more. In the end, using the money I'd gotten from the sale of X-Girl, we bought the house. We held on to the Lafayette Street apartment, but we were now New Englanders.

Before we'd even moved in, a local newspaper, the *Gazette,* ran a front-page story about Thurston's and my moving to Northampton, which bugged me, because now everybody in town knew where we lived. One night, I remember, someone dropped a demo tape on our front porch. Another night two Smith students who lived in senior housing across the street from us left a note taped to our screen door asking if Julie Cafritz and I would deejay at a Smith College radio show. Julie and her husband, Bob, had moved to the area a few years after we did. Julie and I ended up doing it, and we had fun, too.

Compared to New York, everything felt more affordable in Massachusetts, and the house gave us a whole new feeling of space and freedom. The basement was ideal for playing, and also provided storage for Thurston's huge LP collection. Over time it would fill up with books, cassettes, and VHS tapes, plus assorted Sonic Youth archival material and merchandise, all sharing the stage with family furniture I'd inherited from my parents, as well as other souvenirs, including clay figurines I'd made when I was a teenager.

Over time I grew to like living in Northampton. It was New York–centric rather than Boston-centric—people read the *New York Times,* not the *Boston Globe*—even though New York was a three-hour drive south and Boston less than ninety miles to the east. It was also rural and beautiful, a small town with the sophistication of a bigger city. The last thing in the world I ever wanted was to live in suburbia, but with its students, academia, hippies, farmers, New York transplants, and old Yankees, Northampton was something else entirely. A few years after Thurston and I moved, I ran into Lawrence Weiner, the artist, at an exhibition in New York. "Are you still living in Massachusetts?" he asked. "Then why are you here? Don't you need a passport to leave?" Lawrence's fantasy of Northampton, and of all of New England, was that the Puritans were still running the show. I laughed.

Whatever fantasy I had about living in Northampton couldn't make me overcome the fear any ex–New Yorker would feel of being surrounded by blandness and conformity. But no place gives you everything. I'm equally mistrustful of the energy bursts New York gives you, which fragment and exhaust you. Living there gives you a phony sense of self-importance and confidence. If you're at all anxious, the city acts out your anxiety for you, leaving you feeling strangely peaceful.

43

THAT FIRST NEW ENGLAND winter was hard. Snowstorms, then more snowstorms, with long icicles dripping from the gutters like swords or freeze-frames of lightning, and the responsibility of taking care of things we'd never had to think about before, like shoveling the back stairs or the walkway. Sometimes when I drove along Route 9 into Amherst in January or February, everything looked so gray and ugly, especially the shut-down vegetable stands and of course the mall, filled with suburban big-box stores like Home Depot, Chipotle, Target, Walmart, just like in every suburb in America.

We'd wanted a change, something different, and now we had it. But when I look back, maybe we'd moved in an attempt to get away not from New York but from an unspoken tension that had been growing in our marriage since Coco was born. The game Thurston and I seemed to be playing, without saying a single word, was, *Who's the adult here?*

Coco had started kindergarten at the local lab school affiliated with Smith College, less a true lab school than a small private school with a few progressive ideas. It was only a block from our house, an easy stroll in the mornings and afternoons, and it reminded me of the UCLA Lab School I'd attended at that age, the one with the beautiful campus and the gully.

Other family matters were taking up space, too. On the next-to-last day of a tour we were doing with Pearl Jam in 2000, the same year Al Gore lost the presidential election to Bush, my mother was involved in a serious car accident. Her caretaker was driving her on various errands when she made a left turn at the wrong time. Heroic measures were taken to revive her. My old L.A. friend Margie, who was almost an older sister to me, called to give me the news a few minutes before we went onstage in Washington, D.C. Ian MacKaye, the iconic performer from Minor Threat and Fugazi, was there. He said to me, "There's tour reality, and then there's reality." Thurston and I got on a plane to L.A. I was sobbing the whole plane ride.

My mom had suffered a severe head injury and was in a Los Angeles ICU for more than a month. Thurston could stay only a few days, and then he had to fly back east to take care of Coco, whom we'd left with her babysitter. I was still in Los Angeles when Coco went to her first day of first grade. Thurston took a sweet photograph of the two of them on their way to school, and my heart broke not to be there, to feel split in half between the joy of seeing Coco starting first grade and keeping vigil over my mom. But I also felt lucky and secure that Thurston was a good dad who could give our daughter everything she needed even if I couldn't physically be there.

My mom remained in the hospital for another two months. She ended up with a feeding tube, unable to communicate during the last three years of her life. But she was lucid, knew who everyone around her was, and her personality was intact. Sometimes I wondered if she was look-ing at me with bitterness or reproach about her condition—had it been the right decision to consent to heroic efforts to save her? Hard to say, and I'll never know.

Eventually, my mom returned home with a cast of caregivers. I flew back and forth every two months to see her and check on her progress, and when I couldn't be there, Margie was there, filling me in on her prog-ress. I could never have survived that period without Margie. My mother had worked so hard in her later years to make sure she never ended up in a wheelchair—she did yoga, played golf, and walked every day—so it was crushing for me to see her like this. Plus, it was painful to me that she'd lived her entire life in Los Angeles without having a major car accident, only to be brought down by someone else, a caretaker, at the wheel.

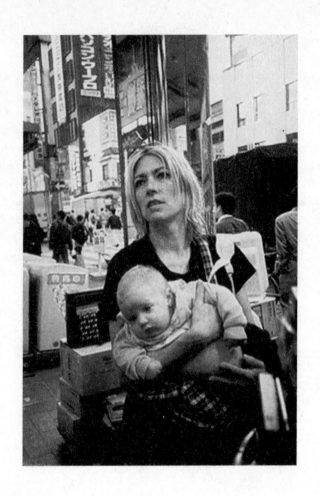

44

IT WAS ONE THING to leave New York, still another to get used to a new town, a new house, a new daily rhythm. In the morning, either Thurston or I would drop Coco off at school and mill around with the other parents. Many, as I said, were city transplants, sophisticated and smart, but none came from our rock-and-roll world. That world was one I'd never identified with myself much anyway. No matter how local the two of us felt, or how engaged we were in the town, our lives were different from other people's. No one else was going out on tour, then coming back home to figure out what was next.

One morning after dropping Coco off at school, I stood around chatting with one of the dads. He was sharp and funny, a scientist. "I'm going to go to the gym," he said to me. "What do you have going on for the day?"

"I have to go home and interview Yoko Ono over the phone," I said. The words came out before I could edit them.

"Wow," he said, "you lead a pretty glamorous life, don't you?" I didn't, though. Interviewing Yoko Ono was just another thing I ended up doing that fell into my lap, in its own way stressful.

The hardest part of being a mother in a band had to do with logistics. For the most part, Sonic Youth toured around Coco's school and holiday schedules. Until she was about ten, Coco always came along with us. After this, she would stay home and spend the few weeks we were gone with a babysitter. At one point, Thurston's niece Katie started accompanying us on tour to help take care of Coco. Coco adored her, and Katie got to see a little bit of the world. During the nontour weeks, Thurston, I, or both of us had to go to New York for rehearsals, recording, interviews, and photo shoots, and all that schlepping wasn't easy on a child. Depending on her mood that day, Coco was either the most flexible or the least flexible child on earth. When we needed her to get up early and board a plane, she was great, especially for a kid who could be hard to rouse in the mornings. But if you walked into a hotel room, and for some reason it wasn't right, even though she hated it she would stubbornly refuse to leave.

Even with Katie along to help, touring with a child was nerve-wracking. Packing, unpacking, rushing to catch planes, boarding a van to the hotel and then to sound check. In airports, Beanie Babies call out every fifty feet. Disciplining a child in public is no picnic, especially when a few eyes are on you. Accidentally forgetting a treasured stuffed animal can create hours and even days of anguish. Once when Coco was eighteen months old, we were touring Southeast Asia with the Beastie Boys. Coco had a Zoe stuffed animal—Zoe is Elmo's sister. As we were barreling across endless streams of traffic in Jakarta, we dropped Zoe, and she got run over. By some miracle, a taxi driver stopped his car, picked Zoe up, and returned her to us, streaked with mud marks. That same trip, we left Zoe behind in Auckland, and our amazing tour manager, Peter, shipped her to the next gig we were playing in Wellington.

Then there were the dressing rooms and bathrooms. Every female musician who has ever toured has a mental history ingrained of what the tour was like, based on the dressing rooms backstage and the dingy bathrooms. CBGB is a good early example. The bathrooms had no doors or toilet seats. The sinks were broken, and graffiti plastered the walls and the mirrors. Most rock clubs don't have bathrooms backstage for the musicians. You have to pass through the hot, sweaty club before you go on, in order to change or pee, trying always to keep your clothes or feet from touching the floor. Usually you have to wait in line for one of the two available stalls, which a lot of the time are stuffed with toilet paper and can't be flushed. Festivals have their own version of bad bathrooms, a row of disgusting porta-potties. This is how I know I'm old, because today I have a very real intolerance for crappy, ugly, badly lit dressing rooms and dilapidated toilets. At a certain age, your brain just says, *No*.

It always felt good to come home. We had our group of unconventional friends in Northampton. Byron Coley and his wife, Lili Dwight, had two kids, one Coco's age. There was J Mascis and his girlfriend and later wife, Luisa, who'd become one of my closest friends. Julie Cafritz was also there, with her then husband Bob Lawton, Sonic Youth's longtime booking agent. Julie moved to Northampton a year or two after we did, and a day after 9/11, Julie's sister and my X-Girl business partner Daisy and her family drove to Northampton and never left. Daisy wouldn't return to New York for years, even for a visit.

For me, it was hard, working on art projects, running the house, raising a daughter, and having a full-time music career. I've never had any domestic talents or hobbies. I'm a good cook and could fill the house with art supplies, but that was pretty much the extent of my homemaking side. Coco once repeated to me something a friend's mother had said to her, that the reason I couldn't do anything—by which I assumed she meant domestic things like crafts, sewing, or baking—was because I was a musician. It hurt my feelings that her friend's mother, who I liked, would say that. Maybe Coco had misinterpreted it, or maybe I had, or maybe neither of us had. Truth was, I never wanted to be a housewife. I never wanted to be anything other than who I was.

Thurston had more going on around Northampton than I did, including performing. There was and is a fairly healthy experimental music scene around Northampton—"the Happy Valley," as the locals called it. Thurston and Byron Coley had also embarked on a bunch of record and book projects. They put out a book about the No Wave scene and started their own record label, Ecstatic Yod. Me, I didn't mind being less busy. I was in Northampton for Coco's sake, even if that meant that with travel, artwork, and other responsibilities, I couldn't be around some of the time.

Byron's daughter, Addie, and Coco grew up together, and in third grade, the two of them began attending another local school, the Center School, a progressive place a half hour to the north. As Coco entered middle school, she started getting much more self-conscious about having Thurston and me as parents. She was wary of anyone—teachers, other students—who expressed any interest in us or told her they liked our music. She worried about leaving her core group of friends and going into high school with the shadow of her parents hanging over her. "You don't know what it's like to be your daughter," Coco said more than once, and it was true, we didn't, mostly because I never thought of Sonic Youth as being that well-known.

Still, references to the band came up here and there. Someone would mention the *Simpsons* episode Thurston and I had appeared in, or I'd run into a parent at the local grocery store who would tell me how impressed he was that "Kool Thing" had ended up on the latest Guitar Hero. The Jason Bateman character in the movie *Juno* mentioned us, and we also showed up on episodes of *Gossip Girl* and *Gilmore Girls*.

At home, because we had extra rooms to fill, we'd created a mock extended family of sorts. First there was Keith, who worked as an unofficial caretaker before we moved in and who lived on our big third floor while we remodeled the house. Keith was an interior designer,

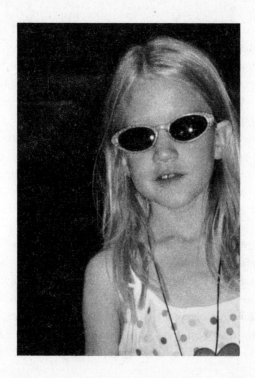

incredibly helpful in finding local workers and an architect. During the summers when we went on tour, he looked after the place for us. There was Thurston's other niece, Louise, who moved to Northampton to attend high school and to live with us when Coco was around eight. Louise wanted to escape the confines of Bethel, Connecticut, where her mother had moved the rest of the family to be closer to Thurston's mother. Louise turned out to be a great companion for Coco, but no matter how self-sufficient she was, it was another person to nurture, and take care of, and worry about, if only at a distance.

After Keith left, two musician friends, Christina Carter and Andrew Macgregor, moved into the third floor. Andrew was helping Byron out at a record store he had opened and needed a cheap place to live. Christina, who recorded beautiful music in her bedroom, lived off her music by touring. Andrew and Christina kept their own hours and were lovely to have in the house. One summer when Thurston and I were on tour, Andrew took our dog, Merzbow, to an experimental music festival he was performing at, where people were camping out. When Andrew recorded his set, you could hear Merzbow barking in the background.

Keith, Andrew, and Christina kicked off our tradition of always having someone living on our third floor. It was helpful when Thurston or I had to go to New York, and though none of our tenants had much experience around children, they were responsible people, and I have to think they liked being around a kid, too.

It was always hard leaving. We usually left to tour right as the weather was turning nice, meaning we had to miss the entire summer. When June came around, we'd have a week or two off, but then we'd be gone until just before Labor Day, when Coco's school started. I never felt like I got anything close to a vacation, maybe because I never did.

Still, we tried to make overseas travel as fun for Coco as we could, and later, when she was in middle school, she would invite a friend along for part of the tour. I think she was happy to show her friends once and for all how unglamorous the whole rock star life really was.

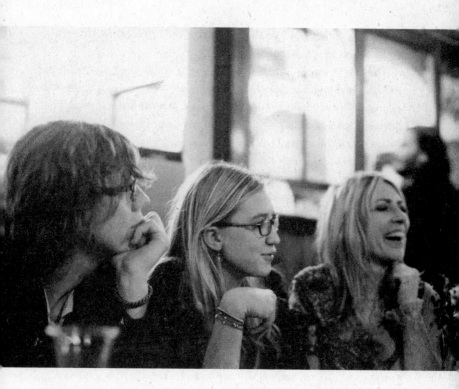

45

GOING DOWN THE stairs, the basement smelled musty, its darkness broken up only by a single lightbulb hanging on a long cord in the middle of the room. An old carpet covered part of the cement floor. Toward the back of the room, a small bass amp and a guitar amp were set up, along with a small drum kit and a single mike on a stand directly underneath the swinging bulb.

Teenagers drifted down into the room. Three girls and a young boy made their way over to the instruments. A petite girl with purplish-red hair cut into a long, curly Mohawk picked up the guitar, while another girl, tall and big-boned, plugged in the bass. The drummer was skinny and unassuming as he took his seat behind the drum kit, looking like a shorn kitten, sleepy and oblivious.

The singer was tall, with shoulder-length blond hair cut bluntly, as though she'd taken scissors to it herself. She wore tight gray jeans and a circa-1980s Mudhoney T-shirt that read, TOUCH ME I'M SICK. The drummer clicked off the song, and the girl leaned into the mic to belt out the words *"Wake up, wake up, wake up . . . ,"* moving the mic stand slightly side to side, not with a lot of movement, just enough to show she was self-assured and not trying too hard.

The voice was familiar, reminiscent of my own. The singer's moves, too, were like mine, but more confident. She wasn't giving away much, but enough to show that if she wanted to, she could.

A small mosh pit formed around the group, two teenage boys with Mohawks dancing around in front, though the singer towered over them. At one point, she leaned over to a friend of mine, who was filming the whole thing, and whispered, "I hate those two boys, they're so annoying."

The girl was my sixteen-year-old daughter, and I wasn't actually there in person but instead watched the video at home in my living room because Coco didn't want Thurston or me seeing her play. The lightbulb swung overhead, casting weird shadows across the screen before blaring white into the lens. It sent chills of pure joy up and down my spine.

Since I became a mother, journalists always threw out the question "What's it like being a rock musician who's also a mom?" It's a question I could never answer to my, or anyone else's, satisfaction without giving one of those "Like any woman balancing a family and a job . . ." answers—the most boring one I could think of, which only seems appropriate.

Maybe for me this moment was like seeing your child graduate from high school. I couldn't put it into words. It wasn't something I dreamed about or hoped would happen, or ever thought Coco had any interest in doing. The fact that she was so good blew my mind, and the fact that her band, which began as a laugh, a bunch of friends hanging out and having fun, came together almost magically was just so rock.

A few weeks later, Thurston and I went to their show and hid out in back. They were opening for a band called Yuck, a band supposedly influenced by Dinosaur Jr., Teenage Fanclub, and Sonic Youth. Through the club sound system, Coco's band sounded amazing. The guitar player seemed perched to jump off, or onto, something, creating genuine tension. Her playing was linear, like Pavement's, and the bass player sounded like early Public Image. Their sound was curling, all splattering dissonance, the drummer swingy and energetic. I would have killed to play with him myself. Again, the singer, my daughter, was fearless in her non-singer punk style that haunted me like a song I couldn't recall.

The next morning over breakfast, I asked her if she and the other members of her band had spent time with Yuck. Sure, she said—they hung out and talked a little. I couldn't help asking if they knew who her parents were. "No way," she said. How cool is that?

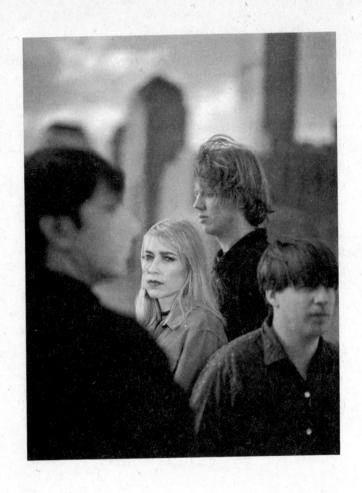

46

EVEN WHEN YOU'RE in the public eye, you never understand how you come across to other people. For some reason, Thurston and I seemed to intersect with a generation of late baby boomers who'd lived in cities, had kids in an attempt to create rock-and-roll babies, and didn't want to age the same way their own parents had. They had music in common with their children. Even if they were in their forties or fifties, they still had a banked fire in them, a raised finger, a sneer, hidden under years of living. As time went on, it seemed, Thurston and I had come to symbolize that feeling for many.

Within the band, though, it was business as usual. For as far back as I could remember I'd been careful not to come across as the female half of a "power couple." I also went out of my way never to bicker with Thurston in front of Lee and Steve. My whole life I've accommodated other people's feelings—ironic, given how often the press likes to remark on my strong-seeming persona. Unless it was something burningly important, I held my tongue for the greater good—the music—though maybe it went deeper than that.

On the other hand, Lee and I regularly butted heads, usually during mixing. Lee would go off on tangents, insisting on hearing the mix in various different ways before returning to the original version we'd already agreed on. Sometimes Lee had a good idea, and his tangents were worth it. I grew to realize that his love of different versions was just his way of working. Ultimately I felt that Lee and I could work out our issues and that we'd eventually reach some agreement—we were both just very stubborn people.

When Thurston didn't like something, he would just turn off. He would sulk, placing the rest of us under his cloud, not wanting to talk about things, unable to take confrontation of any kind. At those times I became an ambassador, a diplomat. In 2011, Sonic Youth provided a soundtrack for a French film, *Simon Werner a disparu,* directed by Fabrice Gobert, and I remember vividly that Thurston didn't want to be there, though at the time I didn't realize he was already involved with another woman. Sonic Youth shared all publishing rights, and I think over time Thurston grew to resent that. Bands are the ultimate dysfunctional family. If Steve was bothered by something Lee did, he usually told Thurston first. I'm pretty sure I must have been a source of annoyance to Steve, as I would usually say what was on my mind during mixing, especially about the drums, since they heavily affected the sound of the whole record. But then, so did Lee.

As we became more experienced, the band dynamic got easier, and we found people to work with who could deal with us. After I became a mother, I stepped back a lot, recognizing I couldn't be involved in every decision involving the band, that I lacked the energy, and in some cases even the interest. I trusted Thurston to make good decisions. In response, he would always present the available options to me and for the most part I concurred with him. I was just more selective about what I cared about.

It was complex, since Steve and Lee were in New York, and for the most part, Thurston and I were in Northampton. After 2000, the studio in the city became more and more theirs. I was busy trying to balance and schedule our lives. If Thurston and I were rehearsing in New York, for example, that meant it made more sense to fly out of New York on tour, rather than flying out of the nearest airport in Massachusetts. If we were heading out for a short series of dates, that meant I would have to enlist a babysitter or caregiver to watch over Coco while we were gone.

Thurston didn't have that same amount of forethought. Most people saw him as an exuberant, seemingly joyous person who lived entirely in the present. Privately, I knew that he was more calculated, because his lyrics were always well crafted, with rock allusions, and he put a lot of thought into his rock-and-roll strategy. Dan Graham once saw us play the song "Confusion Is Sex" at CBGB and said later, after watching Thurston self-consciously trying to make a "rock moment" happen, "You're supposed to scream and *then* fall down on the stage, not fall down onstage and *then* scream." I would never have attempted something like that—it just wasn't me, and Thurston was the true rock-and-roller, the punkologist, the guy who idolized Richard Hell with his music, his poetry, and his self-adoration.

After we moved and Thurston got older, he got better at saying no to offers once in a while. If he hadn't, he would have shot off back to New York every couple of days. To be fair, I don't think he really wanted to live in a small Massachusetts town. That's probably why he kept so busy, so as not to think about it. Maybe it reminded him of his own childhood in Bethel, Connecticut—his old yearning to escape and be free. Small-town silence almost obliges you to have inner resources, which the racket of New York doesn't. New York is all about distraction and what's next. The city has seasons, but they're muted, and the transition of summer to fall to winter has more to do with changing temperatures than it does with the leaves turning, or the trees getting bare, or the grass going from brown to green, or getting older. With its dopamine running wild all over the streets, New York was probably good for Thurston's nerves, acting them out for him. Whenever he would return from the city, he would be in a great mood. He would come into the kitchen and wrap me up with his long arms, a big kid.

Toward the end, though, he stopped doing even that. He seemed lost in his own weather pattern, his own season. After a couple of days back from New York, the lack of distraction would get to him. He'd be on his phone, fingers racing, chasing after the things he felt he was missing out on. When he came into a room, he spoke in a big captain's voice, commanding attention. It was as if he were talking over his own mood, pressing it down, distancing other people from what was really going on. He'd lost that youthful glow. He wasn't happy, I knew, which made me feel lonely, and somehow at fault.

It's hard to figure out when it all started. I was aware of his unhappiness, but I made excuses, too. I had my own doubts about our relationship, but I pushed them under, reasoning that every long-term relationship has its pitfalls, nothing is perfect, no one can have everything. In many ways, Thurston's and my musical, creative life was ideal, despite the fact that I wasn't being true to myself if I didn't follow through with my artwork. When we moved out of New York, my life as a visual artist became almost my biggest concern and preoccupation. I saved up whatever time I spent away from Coco and home and the band for doing art. In 2003, I had a show at the Participant Inc. gallery in New York. That was also the year that I met "her" for the first time, when she came into the gallery in the middle of the installation.

47

"Cotton Crown"

Love has come to stay in all the way
It's gonna stay forever and every day
It feels like a wish coming true
It feels like an angel dreaming of you
Feels like heaven forgiving and getting
Feels like we're fading and celebrating
You got a carnal spirit spraying
I'm gonna laugh it up
You got a cotton crown
Gonna keep it underground

You're gonna take control of the chemistry

And you're gonna manifest the mystery

You got a magic wheel in your memory

I'm wasted in time and I'm looking everywhere

I don't care where

I don't care where

Angels are dreaming of you

Angels are dreaming of you

Angels are dreaming of you

Angels are dreaming of you

New York City is forever kitty

I'm wasted in time and you're never ready

Fading fading celebrating

I got your cotton crown

I got your cotton crown

I got your cotton crown

I got your cotton crown

I got your cotton crown

I got your

48

OUR MARRIAGE COMBUSTED when I inadvertently discovered a bunch of texts between Thurston and the other woman. The shock of it was overwhelming, and the only reason I didn't have a complete breakdown was because of Coco. I would have done anything in the world to shield her from having to deal with what was going on between her parents. Not only is it horrible to find out that you're not the most adored person in your father's life, betrayal also changes the way you see men, and right as you're entering the world as a so-called adult, too.

And so it all started, in slow motion, a pattern of lies, ultimatums, and phony promises, followed by e-mails and texts that almost felt designed to be stumbled on so as to force me to make a decision that he, Thurston, was too much of a coward to face. I was furious. It wasn't just the responsibility he was refusing to take; it was the person he had turned me into: his mother. I could either put up with the humiliation, or I could end things.

We tried to save it. We were both in therapy and seeing a marriage counselor too. But it was like dealing with an addict who was unraveling, who couldn't stop himself. He and I still slept in the same bed—it was a big bed—but in the mornings, we would get dressed and go downstairs and do our own thing. I'd make breakfast for myself and Thurston would disappear into his office on the first floor or into the basement, where his vinyl collection lived. During the day, whenever I saw him, he'd be texting away madly on his iPhone, as if searching for something.

Before Thurston, she, the woman, was romantically involved with a former close associate of Sonic Youth I'll call Tom. All of us had seen this very shy, anti-technology, anti-domesticity guy transform into a man clutching a cell phone, which he started calling his "walkie-talkie," whose private number only she knew, and how Tom began talking about moving in with her, and about marriage, and having children, and how the second he came offstage he already had his phone to his ear as if she had become a part of his body.

It had ended badly, theatrically, crazily, like some tabloid story. No one could really understand how Thurston, who had always had a good nose for the user, the groupie, the nutcase, or the hanger-on, had let himself get pulled under by her, too. She was a current that dragged you underwater and you were miles from home before you even realized it.

Someone told me later the woman would have been happy seducing anyone in the band. In fact, I was the first one she pursued. Two years earlier, she had walked into the Participant Inc. gallery, where I was setting up a show, and introduced herself as an editor at a well-known publishing house. Then she zeroed in: "I'm leaving town tomorrow," she said, "but would you be at all interested in doing a book?"

It turned out she needed someone—me—to edit a book about mix tapes she was publishing. "Thanks, but I'm not all that interested right now," I said. I didn't think Thurston would be interested, either. He wasn't the coffee-table-book type, which is what the project sounded like. When I asked Richard Kern about her, he told me that he was keeping his distance, which made me laugh, because if a filmmaker whose work involves a lot of aesthetic exploration of extreme sex, violence, and perversion wants to keep his distance, chances are she's something else.

But when I told Thurston about the mix-tape project, and brought up the sexual predator part, he *was* interested. Two years after Tom had moved across the country to escape her, Thurston and the woman—who was then involved with someone else, and also had a baby daughter—started up a small book-publishing company, Ecstatic Peace Library, the goal being to publish limited-edition art, design, photography, and poetry books. They set up an office in our Lafayette Street apartment, which was empty most of the time by then.

Later I found out she had pretty much set up house there, cooking meals and leaving plates and pans to dry by the side of the sink, and even lining up all of Coco's old childhood dolls across the bed on the nights her daughter slept in my own daughter's old bedroom.

The few books Ecstatic Peace Library published were mostly to her taste, which surprised me. The first was by one of her photographer friends, James Hamilton, who worked at the *Village Voice* in the seventies. She had an idea for a Yoko Ono book that would turn into a kite. It seemed like a book meant for the MoMA gift store.

During this time I suspected nothing, even though everyone who met or encountered her had the exact same toxic, dark reaction, the same feeling of "What was *that*?" as if someone, or something, was trying to take them over. She would say the strangest things to me as she grabbed my arm and steered me toward a cab. "I want to be your personal assistant," and "What can I get you? Do you need any stockings?" Vanishing, she would come back fifteen minutes later with half a dozen pairs.

Her solicitousness was all the more strange since she knew how much I disliked her, especially when I saw what went down between her and Tom. "Why are you working with her?" I asked Thurston once. "She seems so crazy to me."

"Well, she's professional when we work together," Thurston said. He added, "I know how to deal with her."

49

MY FRIEND JULIE later told me that she had suspected for a long time Thurston and the woman were having an affair. "It was the cigarettes," she told me.

Thurston and I were spending a week on Martha's Vineyard at Julie and Daisy's rental house in Chilmark. Thurston kept going outside, or for long walks, and when he returned everyone could smell smoke on him. He'd always been a casual smoker, but recently he'd been on a tear, though he always made it a point never to smoke in front of Coco or me. It was always outside, away from the house, the stubbed-out, stepped-on butts on the lawn or the driveway the only evidence.

"Don't you think it's weird that Thurston keeps his smoking secret from you?" the woman said to me once. "That he wants to hide it?" She laughed. "What do you think *that's* all about?" She seemed to take a sadistic kind of pleasure in my not knowing the answer.

Thurston left the Vineyard early to attend a memorial service in New York for Tuli Kupferberg, a member of the Fugs, a band he and Byron Coley were planning on writing a book about. At least that was his official explanation. I missed out on the conversation my friends had that night as they sat around talking about Thurston and why he had left the island early. "I think he's having an affair with her," Julie said flat-out.

"Stop," someone said. "Just stop with that line of thinking."

Someone else said, "Let's try and be positive here."

"It's the cigarettes, I tell you," Julie said. "The cigarettes are always a giveaway. Mark my words." When the truth came out, Julie told me she always smoked the brand of cigarettes of whomever she happened to be going out with at the time, and that Thurston was smoking the same brand the woman smoked.

One morning I got up to go to yoga. Thurston was still asleep, and I looked down at his cell. It was then that I saw her texts about their wonderful weekend together, about how much she loved him, and his writing the same things back. It was like a nightmare you don't ever wake up from. At yoga class I was trembling, and when I came home I confronted him. At first he denied it but I told him I had seen the texts—just like in the movies, only this was painfully real.

Thurston claimed that he wanted to break it off. He claimed he wanted to come back to our family.

In time I found the e-mails and videos from her on Thurston's laptop, and the hundreds of text messages between the two of them proudly displayed on our monthly cell phone bill. When I confronted Thurston again, he denied it, then admitted it, then promised things were all over between them. It was a pattern that would happen over and over again. I wanted to believe him. I understood that the cigarettes were a mark of some secrecy between them, a ritual and a taboo that could only happen outside the home when no one else was around.

In October that same year, Thurston flew down to North Carolina for a second memorial service, this one for an old friend named Harold, who had been the best man at our wedding twenty-seven years earlier.

Thurston seemed nervous and I offered to go with him, since I knew how much he loved Harold and that it would probably be an emotional experience for him. I chalked his nerves up to the fact he and Harold had become somewhat estranged over the years. But a couple of weeks later, with my paranoia now ramped up, it came to light that Thurston and the woman had met up in North Carolina, and that he'd made two separate hotel reservations, one at some no-name hotel—to put me off the scent, maybe—and the other at a more expensive B & B.

I didn't find out about this until I was in New York and about to go to a publication party for Ecstatic Peace. By this point, Ecstatic Peace Library was all but dissolved, but the book she and Thurston had been working on was still being published. Arrangements had been made to make sure she didn't show up. I didn't want to go—it was traumatic to even be in the same room with James Hamilton, who knew about the affair—but I had to stake out the territory of what was left of my marriage.

That day, when I discovered the truth about the rendezvous, I can remember wandering around New York shaking, trying not to cry. I called my therapist back in Massachusetts, though I can't even remember what she said. The book party was just as painful as I feared it would be. The next day, Thurston was scheduled to fly out to L.A. to record an album produced by our friend Beck, and I was planning on driving home. When I confronted Thurston about his rendezvous in North Carolina, we ended up talking in the front seat of my car, as a friend was spending the night at our apartment and there was no privacy.

I don't remember what Thurston said, only that it convinced me to put off ending the marriage on the spot. It was just a stupid backslide, he told me, and it wouldn't happen again. I still wanted to believe him.

Over the previous months, I had told Thurston that as someone who had been betrayed by him, I felt I had every right to look at his laptop, especially if, as he kept saying, he had nothing to hide. It didn't take long to find an unsent e-mail to the woman tucked away in his desktop trash. The drug that was her had turned him into a serial liar, to the point where two of our very good friends had recently told me they were so put off by what one called Thurston's "darkness" that they didn't want to come by our house anymore.

50

I HAD ENCOURAGED Thurston to work on the solo album with Beck. Even though it wasn't his first solo release, my reasoning was that if Thurston had more of a solo presence as a musician, and if he could work outside his comfort zone, maybe he would feel less swallowed up by the band and be happier with his life.

He and Beck began recording in Malibu. In early January, Thurston and I flew out to L.A. for one of those sessions. During the plane ride, Thurston was extremely moody, in tears one moment and detached and distracted the next.

Two or three days later, he told me he had seen her again, that the two of them had hooked up after Christmas before he and I had flown to England to perform a New Year's gig. Before we left for that UK concert, I had come across an incredibly disturbing photo of her in Thurston's junk mail. The photo seemed staged, weirdly Cleopatra-like. The woman was posing in a very expensive-looking hotel room. She was wearing some kind of satin lingerie, with satin cuffs around her arms. She was saturated in light. Thurston assured me the photo had been taken a long time ago, but something about the way he was acting made me believe it had special significance to the two of them, and that if I ever found out the truth, I'd end our marriage then and there. Our entire London trip had been painful and strained.

When Thurston told me he had seen her again around Christmas, I left Beck's house and drove to the house of my manager, Michele, who's also a good friend, to tell her the whole story. Michele wasn't home, and as I was waiting for her to get back, Thurston showed up at her house. He was upset. I had told him he had blown whatever chances I'd given him and that things were now over between us. He sat there in a chair as I screamed at him to leave, but for whatever reason he wouldn't move. Finally Michele came home, and Thurston left, and then I flew back home the next day.

That night, my cell phone rang. It was Thurston, calling from Malibu. He had had a moment of clarity, he said: he did not want to lose me, or Coco, or our life together.

Thurston's solo record, called *Demolished Thoughts,* was like a collection of sophomoric, self-obsessed, mostly acoustic mini suicide notes. When I first encouraged him to record it, I hadn't given any thought to what the lyrics might be about, but hearing pieces of one or two songs, I realized I could never listen to it again. "I think the lyrics are probably about *both* of you," Julie said helpfully, but to me, the lyrics, and the songs, were, and always will be, about her.

"I don't even know what to do with this record," Thurston told me. "I just feel like walking into the woods and disappearing." Our management had let him know he could delay its release but instead, he simply refused to promote it, basically pretending the record, and all the songs on it, didn't exist. Like the cigarettes. Like her.

Later someone showed me a comment posted on the Sonic Youth website. "She looks like a hot little number," a fan wrote in. He must have seen a photo of the two of them on some website, or picked up on the gossip going around. He added, "Kim beware, men are pigs after all and more affairs happen at work than any other arena." Finally, the fan wrote, in a catchphrase he took from *The Dark Knight*, the second of director Christopher Nolan's three Batman movies, "Some men just want to watch the world burn."

A few months later, around Coco's seventeenth birthday, I found out Thurston had seen her again, at a concert he played in Europe, though he had promised his therapist that if she showed up again or contacted him, he would call his doctor and tell me, too. He did neither. I went back to checking his e-mail, where I found several short, porno-like videos that she had sent him. Thurston denied ever responding to them, but sometime after that I found an e-mail he'd drafted to her with a photo of him attached. Maybe he didn't send it because his vanity got the better of him, or maybe he wanted me to find it. I asked him to move out of the house.

The official announcement of our breakup was timed so we could sit down and tell Coco before the news hit the Internet and strangers started discussing our lives. The web is trouble enough, especially when you're in your senior year of high school and stressed out about college. Even though Thurston and I had separated in August, so far we hadn't made any public statements, but people were starting to speculate.

It didn't stop Coco from being angry with me for not telling her sooner. Kids believe everything is a family matter and that they should have an equal vote or some control over everything that goes on in their family's lives. And being a teenager makes everyone doubly self-conscious. We had already more than ruined her senior year of high school. As she had told us, we couldn't possibly know what it was like to have us for parents.

I did feel some compassion for Thurston, and I still do. I was sorry for the way he had lost his marriage, his band, his daughter, his family, our life together—and himself. But that is a lot different from forgiveness.

51

THE OTHER DAY, I was thinking about where music has gone, where it's been, how it's evolved. The 1960s were so beloved. More than any other decade, they embodied the idea that an individual could find an identity in a music movement. Not the same identity that comes from sexual awakening—that's more of a 1950s thing—but a group awakening, the kind involving hysterical teenage girls crying together, lighting and propelling one another, a blurred contagion of tears and desire. By the late 1960s, the chilled-out tripping hippie vibe had started to mesh with a desire for money, and with that, the music and the movement began to drift apart.

The crack of idealism between the performer and the audience signaled the end of the 1960s. Altamont, inner-city riots, Watts, Detroit, the Manson murders, the Isle of Wight Festival. There, the audience broke through the makeshift walls, walls that didn't used to exist. In the huge outdoor space came chants of "Rip-off!" Expecting free music, they wreaked havoc on the festival vibes and caused some performers to cancel, and others to fear for their safety. At one point, Joni Mitchell quit playing in the middle of a song and began crying. The audience wasn't really listening, and she must have realized in that moment that it—the sixties, that freedom—was over.

I once saw another documentary, made right after Woodstock, this one at a small festival called the Big Sur Folk Festival. The festival took place at Esalen, a hippie spa whose mission was to develop self-awareness through the body. This festival was a mix of rock, folk, and soul, with the audience on one side of a swimming pool and the performers on the other. Crosby, Stills, Nash & Young came on. During their set, a member of the audience got up and trespassed onto the band's side. He began ranting about the fur coats they were wearing, accusing them of being sellouts. There was an altercation, a scuffle, with Stills trying to calm the guy down and using the incident as both a lesson and an intro to the next song—how we can *all* fall into the trap of money. But what was he really saying? Whose side was he really on?

The 1970s was the first era that learned how to exploit youth culture, and it was the birthplace of corporate rock. It didn't last long. By 1977 the Clash had written a song with the lyrics *"No Elvis, Beatles, or the Rolling Stones"* and Iggy Pop and the Stooges had burst forward as the first punk rockers. But Iggy had been there all along, rumbling under the beatific skies of the 1960s—a disruption into what was supposed to be entertainment and positive vibes. Iggy walked out into the audience, broke glass, smeared himself with peanut butter. Was it a stage show? Was it rock music? Was it real life? Iggy gave audiences something they had never seen, and his estrangement from their expectations created something wild and new. "We're gonna have a real good time tonight," he said, almost forcing the idea down the audience's throats. I give Iggy credit for deconstructing the very idea of entertainment. What is a star? Is stardom a kind of suspended adulthood? Is it a place beyond good and evil? Is a star a person you need to believe in—a daredevil, a risk-taker, a person who goes close to the edge without falling?

There were others of course—the Velvet Underground, the Doors—who took risks in the 1960s, when no one knew where any of it was going. Before them were the Beats and before the Beats the avant-garde artists, the futurists, Fluxus, and before that, the blues, outsider music, a mourning for what's expected but will never happen, so why not dance and play and forget for a few moments that we're all alone anyway?

Cut now to Public Image Ltd. performing at the Ritz in 1981 in New York City. Sid Vicious was dead and the Sex Pistols were over. Public Image Ltd. had made an impact and their third album, *The Flowers of Romance,* had mystery, with its girl on the cover. The Ritz crowd anxiously awaited the band's appearance. The huge movie-scale screen where videos were projected before bands appeared was still down. The screen was a natural barrier, used to create and motivate the crowd's re-action. First up came a huge image of John Lydon's face, laughing. Then he began to sing. Projected onto the screen was a strange film of a dark alley and the girl from the cover of *The Flowers of Romance* getting out of a garbage can. The film stopped, but the screen stayed in place, and suddenly behind it, the shadows of the three band members appeared. The screen stayed still. Furious at seeing the ghostlike, ritualistic fig-ures of the group out of reach behind the screen, the audience became agitated; they couldn't see the band in the flesh. They started yelling. A few of them threw metal chairs. The band ran offstage and the audience proceeded to destroy the screen.

Public Image didn't go out there intending to cause a riot. They were simply trying something new. The audience's expectations were dashed. The band's pure audacity had drawn crowds to the Ritz in the first place, but then the audience couldn't accept what the band was offering. It was too much. And that experience, that feeling, will never appear on YouTube, will never be downloaded onto anyone's laptop or phone. Today you will never find a picture of it, because the Internet didn't exist, and no one was paying attention, or bothering to document what was taking place right before their eyes, with the exception of a zine started by a bunch of fifteen-year-old New York girls called *The Decline of Western Civilization.*

Elvis Presley, Eddie Cochran, Jimi Hendrix, Janis Joplin, Jim Morrison, Sid Vicious, Darby Crash, Ian Curtis, Michael Jackson, and others all died, after a fashion, because of our need for "heroics." Using their egos to sculpt their music—in some cases believing in their own media-created selves—they used their own images to destroy the standard of what had gone before while giving rise to new forms. The audience paid to watch. They also paid to watch the destruction of the artists' own lives—that illusory freedom becoming an actual freedom.

For that reason, the 1980s were similar to the 1960s. Now they're all part of the same pre-Internet era. Today, the nostalgia for pre-Internet life is pervasive. What was it like back then, wandering around in an eternally unknowing state, scrounging for bits of information? Is what we get out of a performance today any different now than it was then? No, it's the same thing: the need for transcendence, or maybe just a distraction—a day at the beach, a trip to the mountains—from humdrum life, boredom, pain, loneliness. Maybe that's all performance ever was, really. An unending kiss—*that's* all we ever wanted to feel when we paid money to hear someone play.

Did the 1990s ever exist? Mainstream American music today is just as conservative as it was back in the 1980s. Experimental music has become a genre. Late-night TV ads for music compilations mix and merge the eighties and nineties in a way that makes me nervous. For Sonic Youth, there was almost something hard-won and unself-conscious about fighting our way through the obstacles of drugs and greed, past clubs of overly burnished bodies and buffed teeth. Then, as the millennium neared, music became all about repentance and atonement for everybody's thoughtless and decadent climb to success.

Sometime last year I went to see the comedian Dave Chappelle performing at the Oddball Festival in Hartford. It was the first time someone, in this case Live Nation, had put together a traveling festival made up entirely of stand-up comics. Before Chappelle came on, Demetri Martin and Flight of the Conchords performed, and while each one had a bit of a hard time with the audience, who were coming in and out and talking loudly, they handled it with humorous aplomb.

Stand-up comedians hate nothing more than people talking during their sets. No one is more vulnerable than comedians. They aren't like actors doing a skit. They use their personalities. They like to control and squash the situation, to own the space, and if they lose an audience, they'll try to win them back.

When Dave Chappelle came out to loud, glorious, much-anticipated applause, it was a great moment, and I almost teared up. After about ten minutes, Chappelle started asking people to stop talking, to let him do his act. But no one listened. They just stepped up the banter, yelling things out to him. Chappelle then took out his pack of cigarettes and announced he was a patient man and would simply wait out the twenty-five minutes his contract called for.

He did just that. He hung in there. He even stayed longer than his time, continuing to talk to the audience, whose behavior by that point had gotten even messier. Then he said good night and walked offstage. The next night, in Pittsburgh, I heard he killed it.

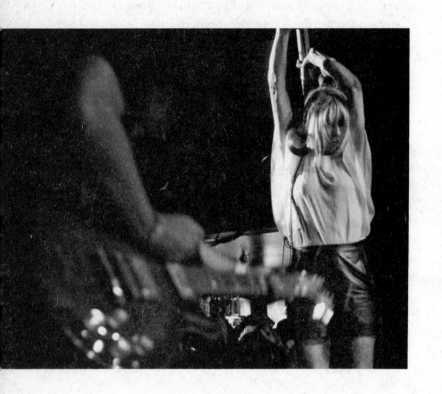

52

THE FIRST TIME Jutta Koether and I met, she was an editor and writer at *Spex* magazine. She was interviewing Thurston and me during our European tour for *Daydream Nation* and seemed confounded by the fact that Sonic Youth, known as a sort of punk rock band, would use the Gerhard Richter candle image for our album cover. In Germany, Gerhard was and is their biggest contemporary artist, but it felt to Jutta as though we'd made a banal, status-quo-oriented artistic decision. After weeks of doing interviews where for the most part journalists asked the same three or four questions, it was great having someone challenge us. To me, Gerhard's cover was an aesthetic Trojan horse decision—disguising subversion under a benign exterior, just as the Reagan eighties concealed torment and volatility.

Jutta and I became friends. A day after she'd moved to New York, I bumped into her as she was walking down St. Mark's Place, and the two of us started hanging out. She was practicing art but also doing music and art performances.

Over the years Jutta and I began what would become a series of collaborative installations and performances. The first was called *Club in the Shadow* at Kenny Schachter's gallery in the West Village, an unconventional space designed by Vito Acconci. The location was made funnier to me for being situated in an alleyway next to Richard Meier towers filled with multimillion-dollar Hudson River–facing condos owned by people like Calvin Klein and Martha Stewart.

We also did performances—one-act plays, we called them—where we combined text and improvisational noise music. Recently we collaborated on a show at PS1 in New York, for the last night of Mike Kelley's retrospective, and again at the Geffen Contemporary, where Mike's show was opening in L.A. In 2012 Mike was found dead in his home in South Pasadena, an apparent suicide. At PS1, we showed one of Mike's videos behind us in the big dome tent alongside the PS1 buildings. Early on in his career, Mike formed a band with Tony Oursler and others called the Poetics, whose songs boomed from a cassette player onstage, and Jutta and I improvised around them. The text we used came from an old interview Mike once did with me, and Jutta and I switched off being Mike and being me halfway through the performance. It was a pleasure to be able to riff off something Mike had done. It helped make his death seem less final, more a continuation of a dialogue with his work and his ideas, and his sense of humor. It's difficult to think of Mike so defeated and giving up, when for all his life, he never gave up, always wanted to succeed.

I started another band, too. From the beginning, Body/Head, the group I formed with the musician Bill Nace, was a strange concept.

Most people have a really hard time with the idea of improvisation, believing it must not be any good or that it doesn't mean anything. A year after my marriage, and the group, ended, Coco left to attend art school in the Midwest. There were still people living in our house, but it was time to do other things. Starting a new group seemed like an interesting thing to do.

Bill had played in a duo with Thurston, and the three of us had played together a few times. Later, Bill and I started playing in our basement as a duo, recording ourselves on cassettes. The second we came up with a name, we knew we were a band instead of some one-off. I wasn't necessarily trying to get away from Sonic Youth, and I sometimes used Sonic Youth guitar tuning, but as soon as you omit the drums, everything sounds different. I had no desire to do anything that sounded explicitly rock. I'd taken the rock musician thing as far as I could take it. It was more about creating what Bill and I wanted to hear—modern music, noisy, dynamic, emotive, and free. We gave Sonic Youth's label, Matador, the right of first refusal, not really thinking they would want to put it out. But they did, and it was a double LP.

One of our tracks, "Last Mistress," was influenced by Catherine Breillat's 2007 film, *Une vieille maîtresse*. Breillat had wanted to go to Paris to attend film school, but as a woman they wouldn't let her in. Thinking, *Well, Robbe-Grillet wrote a book that turned into a movie,* she wrote a book. I thought: *How does a girl who came out of a super-strict Catholic-school upbringing in the French provinces develop that level of sophistication? Maybe it was an avant-garde Catholic school.*

The best kind of music comes when you're being intuitive, unconscious of your body, in some ways losing your mind: the Body/Head dynamic. But what Bill and I did together didn't necessarily come across as improvisation. Since we played together so much, Body/Head's music was crafted, and inevitably we repeated certain elements in the course of performing. I still considered it music, though—eccentric noise/rock music, as opposed to, say, performance art, which is a term I loathe.

Whenever we performed, we showed a film behind us in slow motion, a collaboration with Richard Kern. It was music as film, as if the audience were observing a film soundtrack. It meant that the crowds we played to brought in fewer expectations. They knew, for instance, I wasn't all of a sudden going to burst out with a Sonic Youth song.

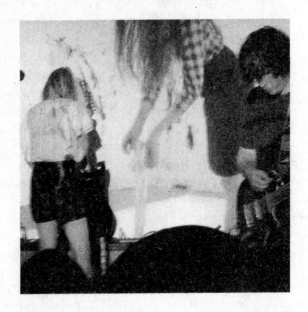

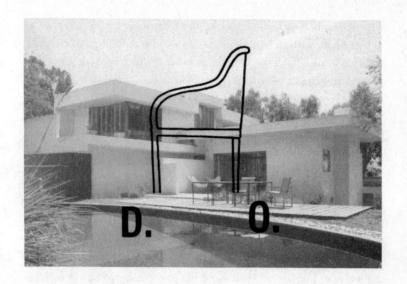

D. O.

53

COMING BACK FROM three weeks in California this past winter made me realize how heavy New York and Northampton now make me feel. In the East, the snow is gray and high and melting, and everyone looks pasty. The memories I have, and the house I still own, are both filled with stuff adorning a life I no longer live, feelings that I no longer have.

I would never have bought our house, or decorated it the way I did, if I weren't trying to create a home. I wanted to give Coco the most normal life possible—something close to the middle-class stability that Thurston and I both knew growing up. The Northampton house is boho and messy, filled with art and books. But I frankly never felt that a house as big as ours, with all its dark squeaking wood and professorial comfort, was to my taste. It was a compromise, far from the New York sensibility of modern juxtaposed with history, and the L.A. sensibility, that light, transitory, bungalow-like feel.

To get away from the ice and the snow, I spent part of this past winter on top of a hill in Echo Park. My Airbnb host and landlord lived next door, in a similar-looking, similar-feeling house. To live in an almost-unfurnished house was invigorating. I could see the Hollywood sign, all of downtown, and, if the day was clear, almost to the ocean. It was old L.A., no McMansions or wall-to-wall office buildings. Two thousand miles back East I had a huge, three-floor house filled with artifacts re-lating to a life that no longer felt relevant, but in the glorious L.A. light, I could turn that idea away. Maybe this was how Thurston felt, living, as he was, in London, a hipster boho life unencumbered by any respon-sibility. He had returned to the life he had back in New York when the two of us first met, although the woman is still with him, and Thurston hasn't really been single, not emotionally, not attentionally, for, as he told someone in a recent interview, six years.

The older I get, the smaller the world seems. Larry Gagosian came back into my life—this time sponsoring a show of my artwork at a house atop Laurel Canyon and Mulholland Drive. Who would have thought I would end up showing with Larry Gagosian?

Last fall, Mark Francis, a well-respected curator who works for Larry in London, put me in a group show with a lot of my favorite painters— Yves Klein, Lucio Fontana, Chris Wool. The show was named after a Wool painting entitled *The Show Is Over*. Afterward, Mark asked if I wanted to do a small exhibition in L.A., and I said yes. Originally I was hoping to do it at some small, anonymous ranch house—model-home communities have always fascinated me—but the Schindler house in Laurel Canyon turned out to be a perfect location and frame for a series of two dozen wreath paintings I'd been doing, an exhibition I called *Coming Soon*.

To me, wreaths were symbols of pure suburbia—a low form of decoration that could somehow be transformed into something else. I liked the idea of how a wreath, an everyday object, could be, or mean, nothing at all, an object onto which others project whatever they want. Mine were centered, lopsided, Yves Klein blue or multiple ocean blues, copper, silver, gold chrome. I wanted to reframe the idea of staging a house, the way you see on real-estate reality TV shows. The Schindler house had a great indoor/outdoor relationship with nature, a lordly quiet, the light creating drama with its proportions, making it ideal midcentury-modern "house porn." Nearby on Mulholland, real drama was happening: fire engines, helicopters, and traffic zooming up and down the canyon on a thruway in and out of West Hollywood to Studio City and beyond. Mulholland Drive has more filmic and real-life drama than any other road in L.A., as well as being the favored route of the Manson family for crosstown travel and creepy crawling exploits from their place near Calabasas to Hollywood.

I used the beautiful basement to make all the paintings. A thin layer of clear plastic was placed on the cement floor, plastic so transparent it looked as though I was painting directly on the floor. The wreaths were then layered on top of the canvas on the floor, spray-painted, then removed, the wreath becoming a masking, delineating blank, or negative space, where it had been placed on the surface. As part of the house installation, I flung a pair of leggings on the bedroom floor. Aaron, the Gagosian rep, was free to move them around if he wanted to. *Kim Gordon Design Office* is the way the show was credited, carrying on the name *Design Office* that I started back in the early eighties.

A few days after the show opened, Lisa Spellman asked me officially to join her 303 Gallery in New York, and I said yes to that too. But as much as I'm always trying to move away from performing, music keeps pulling me back in—because in the middle of everything else, I got another invitation to which I also said yes.

Early last spring I took the red-eye from L.A. to New York for several days of practice with Nirvana band members Dave Grohl and Krist

Novoselic. Nirvana was being inducted into the Rock and Roll Hall of Fame, the first year of their eligibility, and Dave and Krist decided to ask several women to sing with them, to represent Kurt's voice: Joan Jett, Annie Clark (otherwise known as St. Vincent), Lorde, and me. It was a bold, extremely un–Rock and Roll Hall of Fame gesture, but I was incredibly flattered they asked me and so happy to be with the surviving members of Nirvana, sharing a moment that was taking place almost twenty years to the day after Kurt died.

Dave and Krist had also invited all their old drummers and crew members, most of whom had also worked for us when Nirvana toured with Sonic Youth in the early nineties. The same management, the same record people—they were all at the Barclays Center that night, too. The only people missing the reunion, really, were the other members of Sonic Youth, Kathleen Hanna, and Tobi Vail. As for the Rock and Roll Hall of Fame itself, Kurt would have hated being a part of that, but I also think he would have been happy having four women sing his songs.

Onstage I was reminded that Kurt was the most intense performer I'd ever seen. During the show all I could think of was that I wanted to get that same kind of fearlessness across to the audience. I sang "Aneurysm," with its chorus, *"Beat me out of me,"* bringing in all my own rage and hurt from the last few years—a four-minute-long explosion of grief, where I could finally let myself feel the furious sadness of Kurt's death and everything else surrounding it. Later that night when we sang more songs at a small Brooklyn club and I looked down into the pit and saw both Carrie Brownstein and J Mascis, whom Kurt at one point had asked to join Nirvana, it was like I was home. It was a true nineties reunion for all of us who were there back then. After the Hall of Fame show, Michael Stipe, who had officially inducted Nirvana, came up to me and said, "Your singing was the most punk rock thing to ever happen, or that probably *will* ever happen, at this event." The best part of the night took place later, at a small metal club in Brooklyn, at an after-party, where we all performed more Nirvana songs along with J Mascis and John McCauley from Deer Tick.

Then I flew back to L.A. Back to art.

I can still feel in my mind the sensation of making out with someone parked on a hill in front of the Echo Park house. The guy and I had remet at a party through friends the night before. He was charming, and I was super attracted to him, too. Later he gave me a ride home, parking in the middle of my street, on a hill, the motor still running, emergency brake pulled tight. He was a player, I knew that full well, and our good-night kiss turned into a full-on grope. I had to pull away, since I was catching a flight in two hours. He looked shocked, as if to ask, *Gee—you don't want to fuck me right here in the car?* I know, it sounds like I'm someone else entirely now, and I guess I am.

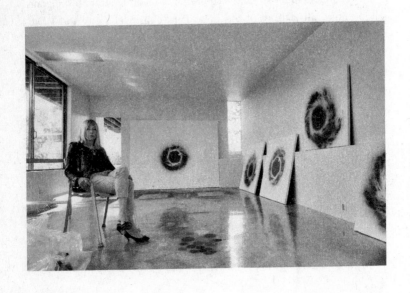

About the Author

KIM GORDON is an artist, musician, producer, fashion designer, writer, and actress. She is a founding member of the experimental post-punk band Sonic Youth. Following the breakup of Sonic Youth, Gordon formed the group Body/Head. A collection of her early critical art writing entitled *Is It My Body?* was released by Sternberg Press in January 2014. Recent art exhibitions include a show of paintings at the Gagosian Gallery in Los Angeles and a major survey show at White Columns in New York. Gordon currently shows with 303 Gallery in New York City. She lives in Northampton, Massachusetts; New York; and Los Angeles.

Credits